UNDERACHIEVEMENT SYNDROME

CAUSES AND CURES

Sylvia B. Rimm, Ph.D

Apple Publishing Company
W6050 Apple Road
Watertown, WI 53094

Library of Congress Cataloging in Publication Data

Rimm, Sylvia B.
Underachievement Syndrome: Causes and Cures

Bibliography: p. 313
Includes index
1. Education   2. Parenting   3. Counseling

Illustrations by Katherine Maas

© 1986 by Sylvia B. Rimm, Watertown, Wisconsin 53094
   Published by Apple Publishing Company
Educational Assessment Service, Inc.
W6050 Apple Road, Watertown, Wisconsin 53094
(414) 261-1118

Printed and bound in the United States of America.

Second Printing, August, 1986

Third Printing, March, 1987

Fourth Printing, March, 1988

Fifth Printing, January, 1989

Sixth Printing, April, 1990

Seventh Printing, October 1991

ISBN 0-937891-00-2

Library of Congress Catalogue Card No. 86-070536

to my family

Buck,
Ilonna, Joe, Miriam, Benjy,
David, Janet, Danny,
Eric, Allison,
and Sara

CONTENTS

PREFACE

To be healthy and happy, to be self-confident and to achieve: these are the initial hopes that each of us, as parents, feel as we first cuddle our neonate. Even as our helpless infant nestles in our arms we sense the fear, the challenge and the excitement of the heavy responsibility of parenting. We look back to our own family life and hope that we can continue what was good and that we can correct what was bad. We are aware that there is much that we don't know about parenting, but we resolve to learn so that we can become effective mothers and fathers.

Smiling faces, twinkling eyes, crisp clean apparel and shiny new shoes file into our classrooms each fall. As teachers we survey the eager expressions and wonder what this school year will bring. Will they learn and will they grow in self-confidence? Will these be good classes or will there be behavior management problems? Which children will be the stars and which ones the "pests?" Which students will be motivated to work up to their abilities?

The beginning of each new school year stirs within teachers the questions, the frustrations and the anticipation of guiding those students in their classrooms. Since teachers want to teach well and because they know that there are many children unwilling to learn, they wonder how they can motivate these nonlearners toward achievement.

It is for the parents who value achievement in their children and for the teachers who are challenged to motivate all students that *Underachievement Syndrome* is written. It is my purpose to assist them in guiding the many children and adolescents who want so much to be bright and important but who have not learned that the path to achievement and personal control includes commitment and perseverance. The trifocal model which was created at Family Achievement Clinic, S.C., targets children, their parents and their teachers in the cure of Underachievement Syndrome. Therapy conducted at the clinic is not theoretical but is practical and based on real life problems in our homes and schools. It makes the assumption that parents want to parent well and that teachers want to teach well. Yet despite those excellent intentions, we all accidentally perpetuate problems because of the confusion of children's behaviors or because conflicting life events pressure us into responding to children in ways that reinforce their nonproductive patterns. If some of the scenarios described make you feel uncomfortable or guilty, please remember that none of us are perfect parents or teachers. Please, keep reminding yourself of all the right and good things you've done as you search for the techniques to improve the problem areas.

The first section of the book describes the symptoms and causes of Underachievement Syndrome. The prototypical children and parenting situations may seem so familiar that you wonder if I've been in your homes and classrooms. The second part of the book documents the practical techniques which we use successfully with parents and teachers. There will be more and we continue to create or adopt additional ideas. Last, we ask you to continue our work by inventing your own methods. Our trifocal model furnishes a framework and Rimm's Laws of Achievement summarize the most important principles. Please use what we have learned and add your own experiences.

Underachievement Syndrome is epidemic. It enters every classroom and most homes. It is only with the help of many parents and teachers that we can impact on an illness which destroys family life, minimizes classroom efficiency and robs from children their motivation and their sense of personal control. Please use this book to cure Underachievement Syndrome in your home and in your classroom.

I wish to acknowledge my own family, first, for providing the basic, day-to-day, trial and error learning which helped make this book possible. I especially want to thank my husband, Buck, my partner in parenting from whom I have learned so much. Family appreciation extends to my own parents and my children, as well as my siblings, in-laws, nieces and nephews.

Parents and children clients and the Clinic provided the next most important source of information and experience. Therapy brings the psychologist very close to the personal lives of many and I have often felt so intensely commited that it has been almost as if many of these children were my own. Their parent's problems were my problems. I want to extend to those parents and children my appreciation for their confidence as I carefully, and I hope sensitively, used their lives to build a theory and a model in the expectation that I also could help others. My appreciation to the Clinic also goes to those therapists who have helped me to develop my clinic and my model, but especially to Frances Culbertson and Michael Cornale.

When I enter a school I always feel a special warmth that reminds me that good things are happening in this building. Schools and education are a real love for me, so I wish to acknowledge the many teachers and administrators who contributed to my love of learning, to my commitment to education, and to so many ideas and practical suggestions included in this book. I want to remind them of how important they are to our children and ask their continued help in building knowledge for reversing Underachievement Syndrome.

There are many people who assisted me in my writing of this book. A special thank you to Gary A. Davis who carefully and meticulously proofread the copy and made many extremely helpful suggestions. My thanks also go to Leroy Haley, Michael Cornale, Carol O'Brien, Lenny Ruder, David Friedberg, Judy Litwin, Welda Sved, and Claire Topp for their review of the pre-publication draft. My secretaries, Marian Carlson and Barbara Ruder, merit my deepest appreciation for their contributions to the typing and editing of the manuscript. Finally, a special word of acknowledgement to my computer whiz son, Eric, who, despite his marvelous erasure, did not succeed in preventing the book from being completed in a timely fashion.

PART I

CAUSES

1

Definition of the Syndrome

Our nation continually searches for better ways to educate our children. National studies and blue ribbon commissions routinely report depressing statistics about lack of basic skills, inadequate knowledge of science, inept critical thinking or problem solving abilities and even poor social skills. The villains censured individually or collectively are television, the economy, breakdown of the family, low teacher salaries, lack of racial integration, not enough class time, shortages of funds and poor discipline. Educational issues are doubly complicated by the use of such inside jargon as cultural deprivation, learning disabilities, tracking, test bias, Title I, Chapter I, bilingual education and mainstreaming the handicapped. The controversy continues endlessly, complicating the schooling process to the average person.

There is an essential error in our efforts to determine why American children do not learn as well as they should. Even if we add time to the school day, give fine new titles to federal funding, increase teacher salaries, reduce class size, label children as "LD" or "EMR" and change tests to reflect differences in cultural environments, we have not faced a central problem in our schools. Millions of children who are very capable of learning - children with average, above average and even gifted abilities, including those from middle class homes where education is supposed to be valued — are simply not performing up to their capabilities. These children suffer from Underachievement Syndrome. Their true capabilities are obvious to both their teachers and their parents. They may be very creative or verbally or mathematically precocious, yet despite their gifts they do not do well in school. Underachievers sit in every classroom and live in many families. They waste educational resources, try the patience of even the best teachers, manipulate their families toward chaos and destroy their own confidence and sense of control. It is time for families and schools to recognize this basic problem, and it is time to correct it.

What is Underachievement Syndrome? Why do they underachieve? There is no gene for underachievement — no neurological or biological explanation for inadequate school performance by capable children. Nor can we find in the educational institution one particular cause for their underachievement, for there are many other children with similar ability who achieve well in the same classrooms.

Underachievers begin as apparently bright and frequently very verbal preschoolers, but at some point their satisfactory school performance changes — for some gradually, for others suddenly and dramatically. The change in their achievement pattern can be easily seen by comparing their year to year achievement test scores. Percentile scores are stable while children are in an achieving mode, but they decline steadily when they enter the underachieving mode. There are other more apparent indicators, the most obvious one being the direct communication from teachers that these children are not working up to their ability.

What are the characteristics of children with Underachievement Syndrome? They tend to be disorganized. They forget homework, lose assignments and misplace books; they daydream, don't listen, look out the window or talk too much to other children. They have poor or no study skills. They consider themselves having studied if they've briefly read the material. Some are slow and perfectionistic and they may tell you that if they finish their work it will probably be wrong anyway. They dawdle. Others, the opposite extreme, will complete their assignments quickly but are much more concerned about being done first than about doing quality work. Their papers have so many careless errors that one wonders if they gave any thought to the assignment at all.

Some underachieving children are lonely and withdrawn. They don't seem to want any friends. They may cry, whine and complain or may be teased and tormented by their peers. Others are bossy and lose their tempers easily. They are aggressive and may start playground fights. If underachievers show any interest in school it is related to their social life or sports. They may select one subject or teacher they like, but by and large they don't like school.

Some never read books while others immerse themselves in reading. They especially like to read when they are supposed to be doing homework or some household chore. Television or computers may serve as alternative escapes, and conveniently, they rarely hear a parent calling when watching the tube or pecking the keys.

Some underachievers are literal and concrete in their thinking and apparently cannot solve abstract problems at all, while others display very creative and unusual thinking. The creative underachievers may have many ideas but seem unable to bring their ideas to closure. They rarely complete what they begin, and incomplete projects make little contribution to their education. Some creative underachievers immerse themselves so completely in their one chosen project that little else is attended to, and they fall behind in their other school responsibilities.

Underachievers are virtually all manipulative, some less obviously than others. They may overtly attempt to manipulate parent against parent, teacher against parent, parent against teacher, or friend against friend. Covertly they may manipulate parents to do their homework for them or teachers to give them more assistance or less challenging assignments.

What do underachievers say about their school problems? They have innumerable defenses. School is "boring" when they are young, "irrelevant" when they are older. The boredom or irrelevance is constant and tend to be unrelated to the actual assignments. The poor grades which they say don't matter are typically blamed on "terrible teachers." They think drama, sports, music or social life are more important than schoolwork. "Who wants to be a brain anyway?" they retort. They sometimes claim they don't have the ability to do better and that the tests must be wrong. They call achievement their parents' goal, not theirs, and blame their problems on unfair comparisons with sisters or brothers. They excuse themselves from making an effort by saying that they'd rather not do the work unless they can do it perfectly or that they are putting themselves under too much pressure and probably shouldn't expect so much of themselves.

Underlying the poor study habits, weak skills, the disorganization and defenses are feelings of absence of personal control over their educational success. Underachievers don't really believe that they can achieve their goals even if they work harder. They may readily acknowledge that their lack of effort is the cause of the problem. However, after exploring further they are likely to admit that they would need to make considerably more effort to achieve their high goals, and even then, they're not certain they could achieve them. Effort might make a small difference, but small differences are not enough and not worth the investment and risk. They set their goals too high and as a result they guarantee failure. They want to be millionaires, professional football or baseball players, rock stars, ballerinas and presidents, and they have magical ideas about the efforts to arrive at these unrealistic goals. They may say things like "If a person works hard enough they can achieve any goal they set," but they have not yet discovered what the word "work" actually means. They translate it as having a romantic and mystical air which is closer to fun and action than to the persevering effort that is required for achievement. They cannot build firm self-confidence since they have not learned a real sense of effort. It is from accepting and conquering challenge that one builds self-confidence. It is from actual achievement that one develops a strong self-concept. Underachievers have denied themselves the opportunity to build confidence since they have not experienced the relationship between process and outcome, between effort and achievement.

This is a competitive society and families and schools are competitive. Underachievers are highly competitive but that may not be obvious. They aspire to be winners and they are poor losers. If they don't believe they can win, they may quit before they begin or they may select only the school experiences where they are certain of victory. They are competitive, internally pressured children who have not learned to cope with defeat. It is not possible to be productive in our society or in our schools until one learns to deal with competition, and dealing with competition means coping with losing in a productive way. It is a fallacy for parents and teachers to believe that they can create home and school environments where children can always succeed. Children who learn to lose without being devastated and use failure experiences to grow will achieve in the classroom and in society.

Learning to compete effectively is central to achievement in our schools. Underachievers have not internalized this basic competitive message. Instead, they manipulate their families and school environments in fear of failure. They learn to avoid the competition unless they can win, and in the process they miss important skills. As their underachievement cycle continues they feel less and less capable. Their fear of failure increases. Their sense of efficacy decreases. They feel helpless and hopeless as the skills gap between where they are and where they should be widens menacingly. The cycle continues downward in an inertia which perpetuates the problem. Underachievement Syndrome adversely affects the child and sometimes the entire family. It feeds upon itself and grows until something or someone either deliberately or spontaneously intervenes to reverse the cycle.

In unplanned interventions, a teacher, a friend, a mentor or other important person may be the catalyst which helps the underachiever to begin to build confidence. In some cases, it is their support which is most critical; other times they serve as a model for the underachiever. Since within the personality pattern of underachievers, there typically is the potential for high achievement, they may take great leaps in the skills required for their new roles. Examples of "underachievers turned superachievers" are the unimpressive classmates one remembers from high school who return to tenth high school reunions with high-level college degrees and impressive careers. They are confident and successful and one wonders how someone who appeared to lack high ability could accomplish so much. They are often termed "late bloomers."

Unfortunately, only a small percentage of "late bloomers" emerge from their latent states to develop their talents. Our society includes many who continue their downward cycle to become high school dropouts. If they manage to remain in school until graduation they show only marginal achievement and have little interest in learning. They join the work force of underachievers and lead lives in which they drastically underuse their abilities to their own frustration and to society's loss.

Parents and teachers can help cure Underachievement Syndrome. They will be able to do this better if they learn to identify the causes of the underachievement patterns. They can accomplish even more if they work together. If you suspect you have an underachiever in your family or in your classroom, this book will help you to recognize and deal with your underachiever's problems. First, try to identify your type of underachiever. After that, look further for the family pattern that may have shaped the underachievement style. Finally, try those recommendations that will help you to reverse the underachievement cycle at home and at school. Realistically, it usually is easier to identify your underachiever and the family pattern than to change them. So plan for patience and perseverance. You may not be able to (or wish to) change every error you uncover, but even small improvements will be gratifying. A sense of achievement for your children and for underachievers in your classroom will build their self-confidence. Children who don't seem to care about school and grades can be motivated to learn and to achieve by parents and teachers who understand the underlying causes of their problems. They can master the skills which will enable them to cope with the competition in our society and therefore can be freed to experience the joy of self-motivated learning and accomplishment.

What Do Underachievers Look Like?

Underachievers come in many varieties, and although they are truly individual, they usually fit into prototypical categories. In real life the prototypes are not pure but may blend in any one child. However, the descriptions in this chapter will help you to determine if your child has Underachievement Syndrome.

If you're not sure your child is an underachiever, think of the last teacher conference. Consider your child as you see him or her at home. Compare your child with the children I describe. If your child reminds you of some of these descriptions, it is likely that he or she has Underachievement Syndrome.

Hyperactive Harry

Harry is disorganized, sloppy and has nonstop high energy. In school he's out of his seat continuously — touching, tapping, slapping other children. Schoolwork is not completed. Some may make it home; other papers mysteriously disappear into a messy school desk, messy locker or messy bedroom. He listens to his teacher sporadically and tunes out instructions, tunes out rules, and tunes out threats and warnings. He mysteriously but clearly hears praise and rewards, also messages that relate to food or recess time. His handwriting is illegible and math problems are sloppily incomplete. Inconsistency pervades. Grades vary between A's and F's and there are no obvious explanations for the variations.

At home Harry's room is chaos. Last week's underwear is tucked between the mattress and the box spring, and bread crusts from last month, yesterday and yesteryear are crunched up among his books, toys and papers on the shelves. His behavior is equally chaotic. Sometimes he disappears down the street without a word and reappears hours later with apologies to mom who is frantic with fear. She blends scolding with loving as she puts her arm around him with affection but furiously threatens to "ground" him for a month. Life settles down for an hour or so and he's gone again, only to return to the same ceremonial scolding and hugging. At meals he converts a normal chair into a one-legged rocker and never leaves a meal without at least four separate sets of reprimands. His activity pattern at home is continuous — continuous change, continuous mess, continuous noise and continuous turmoil.

"Wifey, dear, it seems so quiet today. Where's Harry?"

"Yes, my darling, it is so nice and quiet. Harry's at grandmas."

"Ah, yes!"

Passive Paul

Paul slouches at his desk. He yawns, daydreams, meanders through math. His assignments are rarely complete and never completed well. He raises his hand to ask questions, but not to answer them. When called upon he gives nonresponses, such as "I don't know" or "I'm not sure" or "I don't understand" or "I forgot." He is a likable, pleasant, "good kid" who just doesn't get his work done but never seems to worry about it.

"I'm doing much better now, mom," he says with confidence.

"Yes, I have all my homework done," he bends the truth reassuringly.

"Gee, I'm sorry I got that F, I'll do better next time," he tearfully apologizes.

But homework is rarely done. Books and assignments don't come home for study and grades continue downward in a never ending plunge toward FAILURE.

Unmoved and unmoving, Paul passively withdraws to the television screen. He is immobile and unresponsive when his mother calls him to his homework. He stares intently at the TV as her normally quiet tone escalates. He blinks his eyes as mother's shouts pervade the room. Finally, when mother screams in desperation, he apologizes for not hearing and asks what she'd like him to do. When she suggests homework, he lies assuringly and says that his homework is all complete and retreats to the screen in further absorption.

Mother, frustrated and despondent, is reassured by dad that Paul must certainly have done his homework, so "why not let him watch TV?" and they too settle comfortably in front of the tube — until the next teacher conference.

Perfectionist Pearl

Neat, tidy papers. Neat, tidy desk.
Perfectionist Pearl always does her best.
Handwriting's A, Spelling's OK
But Pearl can't get her work done today.

Today Mrs. Jones has assigned an original story. The other children started 20 minutes ago but Pearl doesn't have a word down on her paper, not even a title. Finally, she raises her hand timidly. "Mrs. Jones," she whines, "I just don't know what to write about." Mrs. Jones is perplexed. How can Pearl, who is so bright, who completes workbook pages so perfectly and uses impeccable grammar, not be able to think of a topic for a one page imaginary story? Mrs. Jones makes several suggestions and Pearl listens quietly. Tears glaze her eyes and she explains, "Mrs. Jones, I don't see how I can write a story if I can't find a perfect topic."

Pearl's problems have just begun. In grade three she is still a very fine student. As long as her work assignments are concrete and specific she performs well. However, when she needs to think abstractly, to come to conclusions based on reasoning, to originate her own ideas, or to take a small risk she is paralyzed by fear of failure. Her grades and confidence begin their decline in middle school. Gifted Pearl who began school in the top reading and math groups moves steadily toward classroom mediocrity.

At home Pearl's room is neat. She is obedient. She causes no problems. She is the perfect child - until adolescence. Adolescence brings a strange rebellion. Anger, eating disorders and feelings of depression appear. Pearl searches for ways to control a small part of her life perfectly, since for Pearl the alternative to perfection is failure. She sets impossibly high standards and feels helpless in her search for success.

Jock Jack and Dramatic Dick

Captain of the football team, blue ribbon swimmer, trumpet soloist, or star of the school play, Jack and Dick share similar characteristics. They thrive in competitive activities and are personable and socially adept as well. They have assets such as general attractiveness and excellent muscle coordination and they are natural athletes, charismatic actors, or talented musicians. They seem to be propelled toward success. As high school seniors they give their parents great joy. At the athletic, music or drama awards banquet, parents and children alike feel great pride as they experience the thrill of receiving awards for excellent contributions to the team, drama club or band. Why is this a problem? Actually, it may not be, but one needs to look carefully — because the Senior High Awards Banquet may represent the peak achievement of these young persons' careers.

Why are they underachievers? These young people who are the pride of their teams and their families may have reached the high point of their lives at that senior banquet, despite the special talent and competitive spirit that have served them so well. If you look carefully at their activity selection, you may discover that they participate only in activities in which they are winners. They select sports if they will be captains, drama if they will be stars, band if they will play first chair, and social activities if they can be leaders. Although they actually have excellent scholastic potential (they must be bright, how else could they learn all the lines for the play), they claim that schoolwork has never provided a satisfactory competitive challenge; but perhaps it provided too much competitive challenge. They didn't select academics because their drive to win, encouraged first by their parents and then internalized, automatically eliminated activities in which they could not attain "first place'. They became just average students because they did not see themselves as winners in academics.

Now as they graduate to life-after-high-school, they may join a traveling dramatic troupe, organize a musical group, or go to college to play football, but they will discover that hundreds of "stars" are competing with them and they are no longer outstanding. Worse, their history of academic underachievement has narrowed their career options. They will wander and search. If they are fortunate, they may find a community, or a career field, or a school environment where they can again be stars, big fish in little ponds. If they do find such a haven, they may be successful; if they do not find a niche that accepts their leadership, they flounder and dissipate their many undeveloped talents.

Taunted Terrance

Terrance is a fag, Terrance is gay,
Push him down, beat him up,
Don't let him play!

Notice Terrance on the playground. He wanders alone, watches the ball game and maybe talks to other kids, but he usually leaves the group being teased or taunted. He says he doesn't have any friends, but really doesn't want any. After school each day he sits at the kitchen table with mom, whining and complaining about the "mean kids at school". Mom seems to understand and wishes that the teacher would protect poor Terrance or that the kids wouldn't be so mean. Dad says that Terrance needs to learn to "play baseball". He tries to teach sports to Terrance but ends each attempt with angry scolding. The ritual also is punctuated by Terrance's return to mom with complaints that "Dad doesn't understand me." A mom and dad bru-ha-ha terminates most father and son activities. Dad gives up and mom wonders what she has done wrong. She feels sure that Terrance's problem is caused by her husband or the school or the other kids.

In school, Terrance doesn't finish assignments. He works slowly, daydreams and sometimes brings his work home to finish with mom's help. He works at the kitchen table so that mom may alternate stirring the soup with doing fourth grade math. Terrance may manage to do a few problems on his own, but he doesn't really see how he can do any work without his mom. When she's not home, he doesn't even start. "Why try?" he thinks to himself. He needs help. Mom must tell him what to do. Big sister should protect him from the kids at school. Why do the kids pick on him all the time? Why is he so weak and small? Why can't he do anything on his own?

"Don't give up, Terrance. Try the computer," and Terrance does. Terrance loves the computer, and the keyboard doesn't require social conversation. Terrance can control the computer. It responds predictably. Everyone knows that Terrance is terrific with the computer, and although all agree that he is somewhat weird, Terrance is at last a hero! His assignments continue uncompleted.

Rebellious Rebecca

Rebecca's bedroom door is locked. She has closed herself off from her parents. She no longer wants to hear their scolding, their reprimands, their continuous criticisms. In her determinedly messy bedroom, her telephone, her stereo and her journal writing protect her from the anger she feels toward her parents, her teachers, her minister and the rest of the whole establishment world. Sometimes she gets depressed and feels alone as though she has no goals or purpose. Her friends, her smoking and her drinking may help her to temporarily not feel the emptiness. She doesn't know what she's for, but knows for certain what she's against. She labels her parents' way of life as narrow, empty and hypocritical. "You should see the way they really are," she complains to the "shrink" to whom they've sent her.

In school, her once consistently good grades vacillate between A's and F's. She tells the guidance counselor that "school is irrelevant" and asks, "Why should I bother studying for geometry since I'll never use it anyway?" She definitely sees no purpose in going on to college. She works well for the teachers she likes, but proclaims that "I can't get along with Mrs. Smith, the Spanish teacher, because she doesn't like me no matter what I do." So there isn't much sense in studying Spanish.

At the last dance Rebecca seemed drunk or high. She was with Director Dan, the Student Council President. They are a nice couple and seem so right for each other. Why do we feel uncomfortable about their relationship? Rebecca says she has finally found someone who really loves her. By senior year she is pregnant. That may be followed by marriage or, just as likely, abortion. The smoking, drinking, drugs and "sleeping around" alternately feel to her like expressions of her individuality and her desperation. Her Underachievement Syndrome is minor in the constellation of much more difficult problems.

Bully Bob

Bob's temper tantrums have controlled the family since before he was two. Bob learned that he could get exactly what he wanted instantly if he lay on the floor and kicked his feet or held his breath until he was blue. Candy at the supermarket, sister Mary's toys, or going to town with mom were all at his command if he protested loudly enough. So he did. When father told mother she was spoiling their son, she insisted that dad was just too hard on little Bobby and needed to be more understanding. So dad tried.

By age seven, when Bob's shouting wasn't effective enough, he tried throwing things — just pillows and soft stuff at first, but then a jar or a dish. That showed his mom and dad that he was serious. Crashing vases are intimidating. The family learned to exercise care so that Bob would not become angry, so he didn't have to resort to throwing often. Verbal threats kept his parents and siblings under his control.

Homework, studying — why should Bob do his schoolwork? Who was going to make him do that boring math anyway? Certainly not his parents. Why should he care if he gets poor grades? He knows he can do that easy stuff without all the studying. Why do teachers give so many assignments? To no one's surprise, Bob's grades are poor.

Bob does have one complaint. He says the kids don't like him, they're always picking on him and he has no friends.

Teachers on the playgound break up Bob's fights almost daily. He loses his temper if the guys don't play his way and throws the bat if he strikes out. "The ref should have called a ball," he shouts angrily. When the kids call him bully, he retorts, "They started it. They just don't like me!"

Manipulative Mary

Mary: Ms. Sally, you know that D you gave me in math. Do you suppose you could "up it"just a little. I'm afraid to go home. I've never had a D before. My father will kill me! I promise I'll work harder next quarter.

Ms. Sally: (Aside) Mary seems so worried and frightened. I wonder if her dad will beat her. She did promise to do better next quarter. I guess I could give her one more chance. (To Mary) Well, I guess I could change it to C- if you're sure you'll get all your homework done next quarter.

Mary: I promise. Thank you so much, Ms. Sally. I really do appreciate your kindness. Yes, I will try harder. Gee, you really saved me!

The next quarter brings a repeat performance. Can her dad really be so mean?

As a matter of fact, Mary twists dad around her little finger too. Although occasionally he or mom catch onto Mary. They rather enjoy her charming persuasiveness and can't really say 'no" to her. She is a good, sweet kid who is helpful and obliging and it just may be, they admit, that they spoil her just a bit. She's always had lots of toys and clothes, and, no, they really can't think of anything she has wanted that she hasn't received. Mary's request for possessions is endless and her specific "need" for designer labels is becoming outrageous.

Mary's social behavior at school is a significant priority compared to her study habits. She chatters incessantly and buzzes around the playground from friend to friend. Despite her apparent conversational ease and sophisticated appearance, her friendship circle is unstable. Her peers avoid close alignments to protect themselves from being overwhelmed and manipulated. Can it be true that she pays $2.00 for swing rides to maintain their friendship?

Ms. Sally wonders why Mary is so insecure. "It must be that her parents are mean," she reasons.

Mom wonders why Mary is so insecure. "It must be that the other kids are jealous," she believes.

Dad wonders why Mary is so insecure. "It may be that school is too demanding," he concludes.

They all resolve to provide Mary with extra affection to compensate for her poor self-concept. Mary manipulates on.

Adopted Annie

Adopted Annie is a specific example of a Manipulative Mary. She differs mainly in that she was a long awaited child. Mom and Dad knew from the start that they loved her more than they could possibly love a child of their own, precisely because they had waited so long to adopt her.

Annie was adored and adorned and denied almost nothing. However, Annie occasionally misbehaved so mom or dad might scold her. Strange, this Annie. When scolded she withered. Tears clouded her eyes.

"Mom," she whimpered, "Don't you love me? Is it because I'm adopted?"

"No Annie dear, I love you so very much, even more because you're adopted. We waited so long for you and you're so special to us. We couldn't love a birth child any more than we love you. I'm sorry I scolded you, but I only wanted to help you..."

The sermons of devotion proceed *ad infinitum* and Annie bathes in assurances of love despite the naughtiness that initiated the scolding.

In school, her bid for affection and protection begins the first week. She confides to Ms. Sally, "My parents don't really love me because I'm adopted."

Solicitous Sally stops her work immediately. She puts her arm affectionately around Annie and assures her that her parents really do love her.

Adopted Annie's social and school patterns are precisely like Manipulative Mary's, but teacher and parent conclusions are somewhat different.

Ms. Sally assumes, "I guess her parents don't love her because she's adopted."

Mom and dad wonder, "How can we convince Annie that we truly love her. Will she never feel secure with us?"

The neighbors conclude, "Adopted children just never work out. They must have bad genes."

Sick Sam

Mom: Sammy, are you up yet? Time to wake up. Time for school.

Sam: (Silence)

Mom: (5 minutes later) Sammy, it's past time to get up. You'll miss the bus.

Sam: (Weakly) Mom ...

Mom: Yes, dear, what is it?

Sam: Mom, I don't feel so good — got a bellyache.

Mom: Sammy, your stomach hurts again? Maybe you shouldn't have eaten that pizza. Try to get up and walk around a little, you might feel better.

Sam: (More weakly) But mom, it hurts so much I can't move!

Mom: All right. I guess you'd better stay in bed. Go back to sleep. It must be your allergy.

Sam spends the morning in his bed, but by eleven, he's up and feels much better. Mom cooks him a "nice wholesome lunch" and keeps him company as they sit at the kitchen table. They chat and giggle and she assures him that he's a wonderful, talented boy, and if he could only stay well, she's sure he could be an A student. Sam agrees and laments on how hard it is to keep up with schoolwork because he's missed so much school. He protests to mom, "It just doesn't seem fair that the teachers pile on all that make up work. How do they expect me ever to catch up?" Mom sympathizes and assures Sam that she'll talk to his teachers about the problem. "Don't worry Sammy," she comforts. "Just stay well. Why don't you go in the living room now and relax and watch television."

And Sam does.

At two o'clock the telephone rings. The principal, Mrs. Smart, is on the line. She expresses concern about Sam's frequent absences. Mother details Sammy's maladies, his allergies, his asthma attacks and his digestive problems. Mrs. Smart explains to Sammy's mother how these illnesses may be psychosomatic and that they could be caused by tension. She suggests finding out the reasons for Sam's pressures. Sam smirks to himself as he snuggles under the afghan, watching his favorite soap, and listens to his mom's response.

"Mrs. Smart," she blusters, "if those teachers would just stop giving my Sammy so much homework, maybe he could relax a little and feel better." But although mom sounds convincing on the telephone, she can't help but wonder to herself if Sammy really is sick.

Torn Tommy

Today is Tuesday. Tommy was at his dad's last night. He looks a little sleepy and a bit more rumpled than yesterday. Wednesday will be another bad day, but Thursday and Friday will be better. Next week Tom will also have two sleepy days, but we're not certain which days. The two visitation days vary from week to week. Other things change for Tommy too:

At dad's house the family has fun; at mom's house he has to do homework and chores.
At dad's house he does his homework in front of the TV; at mom's house he has to work at his desk in his room.
At dad's house he can stay up with his dad and dad's girl friend until he gets tired; at mom's house his bedtime is 8:30.
At dad's house he takes exciting vacation trips; at mom's house it's boring.
At dad's house no one makes him study; at mom's house he listens to nonstop sermons on the importance of schoolwork.

Dad often calls mom. They argue on the telephone. Tommy hates it when they ask him where he wants to be for Christmas. If he chooses dad, the gifts will be bigger but mom will be sad. If he chooses mom, dad says he won't be mad, but inside Tommy knows he will be angry. Tommy wishes he didn't have to choose.

Tommy loves his mom and his dad and every night he prays they'll get back together. If they don't, he wonders if maybe he ought to move in with dad. After all, when he grows up he wants to be a man like his dad and have fun. There isn't much sense in study, study, study anyway. Just when Tommy thinks he has things all figured out and is about to say to mom that he'd like to move for a while, he finds her in the kitchen crying. She says she's so lonely, and she wishes Tommy would be happy at her house. Then Tommy feels sad and feels sorry for her and he knows he can't leave her. He assures her that he'll try to be good and to help her. He shuffles up to his room, slouches at his desk and stares distantly at his math book, wondering if other kids feel as mixed up as he does.

Academic Alice

Extraordinarily gifted. IQ 155. Alice learned to read when she was three — spontaneously. She did double digit addition in her head by four. Her extensive vocabulary and high level reasoning captivated and entertained adult friends and relatives. "Surely she's a genius," they declared.

A four point average, academic acceleration and rank number one in her small town graduating class of 300 established Alice as an achiever. At graduation ceremonies she received awards, honors and scholarships. There was no doubt about Alice's bright future. She was university bound and planned a career in medicine.

Alice does not have Underachievement Syndrome. How did she get into this book? Let's look further. She's a freshman now at a prestigious eastern university, taking her premed classes — chemistry, calculus, biology and English Literature. There are four to five hundred students in each of her lectures and many of them also ranked first in their graduating classes. Some have had two years of chemistry, calculus and advanced biology before they entered. Alice wonders, "How do they know so much? They seem so much brighter than I. How can I compete?" Her fears are confirmed on her first exam grade, which is a B instead of the usual and expected A.

"Why do I feel so depressed?" she wonders. "After all, a B is a good grade and there's plenty of time to bring it up to an A." Alice resolves to study harder. She spends many hours preparing for the second exam. However, she finds it difficult to concentrate on the course content. She feels tense at the thought of the test and is obsessed with worries of how she will perform. Nevertheless, she is reasonably confident that she has mastered the information - until the morning of the exam. As she stares at the first question, the words blur. She feels nausea. She can't remember ever seeing that concept. Could she have missed it entirely? "Relax, Alice," she tells herself as she skips down the page to look at the other questions. Some she feels confident about; others she knows she has studied but is not sure of the answers. Fifteen minutes have passed and Alice hasn't marked a single answer on her paper. "Can anyone see how nervous I am," she wonders. "So this is test anxiety," she concludes, and then determinedly begins responding in the best way she can. She's run out of time and has five more questions to go. "Darn," she slumps in her chair, "that's probably a B again! Oh, well, I guess in college I'm a B student."

Five days later the test grades are returned. She has a C —the first C in her entire school history. How can she tell mom about this? How can she get into Med school? Maybe she isn't as bright as they told her. Her friends are getting A's — what's happened? She'll study harder next time. The material is so complex. It seems so irrelevant. "How will calculus make me a good physician?" she asks herself. "What a stupid way to select doctors! Why am I here? Should I quit? Should I change my major? My parents will be so disappointed; they'll never understand. How can I have become such a failure? Failure...failure...failure..."

What happens to Alice as the tension builds? There are certainly many possible outcomes, some positive and some negative depending on how creatively she handles her dilemma. Alice may adjust to the tension and bring her grades back up to A's. She may learn to live as a B student and continue her medical direction. She may find that she's an A student in psychology or literature and that she prefers an entirely different career than the one she originally selected. There also are less favorable outcomes — dropping out of college, psychological and psychosomatic illnesses, and in a few cases that most distressingly final solution, suicide.

Alice was an achiever and her Underachievement Syndrome came late in her education. Young adulthood is a difficult time to deal with competition and with one's first failure experiences.

Creative Chris

"School is boring. What's the purpose in teaching me to read and do workbook pages at this simplistic level when I'm capable of reading far above this level?" Chris challenges his third grade teacher. She can tell he's going to be a problem. She must keep him busy. She assigns more workbook pages. Chris schemes and plans, "How can I avoid all this dull stuff?" He slows his work. He daydreams. He creates reasons why he should not have so many assignments. He brings his rationale home to mom and persuades her to go to school to argue for him. She becomes his advocate. He is now excused from his assignments. He can read a library book instead, but he must stay out of trouble. That wasn't exactly what Chris or mom had in mind for academic challenge, but it seemed better than "busy work."

Chris reads extensively and continuously. When there are chores assigned at home, Chris is reading. When the teacher explains math, Chris hears only half the lesson because the book on his lap absorbs the other half of his attention. His literature teacher expects eight book reports each year. Chris reads 30 books but does not complete a single report.

"Chris," mom queries, "you enjoy reading so much, why won't you write those book reports?"

"Because, mom," Chris retorts, "I shouldn't waste good reading time writing the obvious. My teacher knows I've read the books. I see no reason to give her written proof."

"Yes, I guess that does make sense," mom acknowledges.

By sixth grade Chris and his teachers are in full battle. Chris will not do his assignments. His teachers insist on giving him poor grades. Chris argues that he knows the work and can pass every test, and he does. His exam grades are B's and C's without any effort. His teacher averages these with F's for his missing assignments and so his report card reads C's and D's.

As Chris's psychologist I ask, "Chris, can you explain why you're doing so poorly in school when you are so capable and are so interested in learning?"

"I could get A's if I made the effort, I just don't care about grades," he defends himself.

"Chris, are you sure you could get A's if you put forth the effort?" I question further.

A silence follows.

"No, I guess I'm not sure — probably only B's. I start to listen to the teacher explain the math and it seems so easy and boring, so I get back into my book. Then I guess I must miss some small explanation so that when I look at my homework assignment, I'm not sure I understand it. I feel too dumb to ask questions since maybe the teacher explained it while I was reading, so I just don't do the math. By now, I suppose there are quite a few gaps, so maybe I could only get a B. I usually get a C with no work, so why should I bother? Even when I do make the effort, the teacher doesn't notice. I guess C's are good enough. It's more important to learn and be creative than to get good grades anyway."

And mom agrees, Chris is just too gifted and creative for typical schools.

In addition to Chris' vast reading experiences he writes poetry and short stories. He adds unique comments to classroom discussions and delights in drawing original cartoons. However, he is determined not to conform and so he receives little academic credit for his creative contributions.

How To Determine If Your Child Has Underachievement Syndrome

The children I've described may be familiar. They may resemble some that you know. More likely, the child you suspect is an underachiever will be a blend of several of these descriptions. For example, Rebellious Rebecca is often the adolescent stage of the child Manipulative Mary. The characteristics of Sick Sam and Taunted Terrance may be blended in one child. Many Passive Pauls and Perfectionist Pearls may be more or less extreme than those described here.

You may find that your child exhibits some of the habits or behaviors described, but you are uncertain as to whether these indicate a problem. It is true that achieving and happy children show many of the same characteristics as do underachievers. The main differences are in the degree to which they show the characteristics. All children, all people, achieve less than they are capable of some of the time. It is only when underachievement becomes a habitual way of responding in school that it should become a serious concern.

For many children, and for their families and teachers, Underachievement Syndrome is a serious problem. In our society, it sometimes appears that Underachievement Syndrome has reached epidemic proportions.

2

There is no Gene for Underachievement– Early Hallmarks

Psychologists and educators argue endlessly about the nature/nurture basis of intelligence, the extent to which genetics and environment contribute to cognitive ability. However, there is nothing in the psychological or educational literature that suggests underachievement is inherited. There is no genetic theory to explain why many children who have obviously good abilities do not perform well in school. Therefore, in identifying the causes of underachievement we must look toward learned behaviors.

Children learn to underachieve and the habits and skills may be mastered very early, before they enter school. Their first teachers may be parents, grandparents, siblings, babysitters or important others who impact on their environment during infancy and early childhood. The behaviors that are likely to result in underachievement are not seen as problems during those early years. Sometimes they originate by reason of a particular set of circumstances for a specific child in the family while in other cases they stem from the overall child rearing philosophy of the parents. In the first circumstance only one of the siblings may be adversely affected; under the latter conditions, several or all of the children may be affected, although not necessarily to the same extent.

Let's look at those early symptoms of later problems. Preschool environments which predispose a child to Underachievement Syndrome fall into several categories, including the overwelcome child, early health problems, particular sibling combinations, specific marital problems and giftedness. Each will be explained separately. While none necessarily result in underachieving children, all provide facilitating environments which increase the risk of initiating family configurations which support underachievement.

The Overwelcome Child

We have long recognized that the unwelcome or rejected child is likely to have adjustment or emotional problems. However, parents are rarely admonished about overwhelming their child with too much attention. Although occasionally someone may suggest that parents ought not to "spoil" their child, it is more in vogue to recommend that parents not worry about their excessive demonstration of love. Present folklore holds that one 'can't love a child too much'. While it is true that extraordinary love in itself does no harm, excessive attention is a hallmark for later underachievement and emotional problems.

These paraphrased statements provided by parents of underachievers are examples of "overwelcome" children who are at risk.

> We waited so long for Mary. We knew she'd be the perfect child. My pregnancy was difficult. I had three previous miscarriages. We were so thankful that she was healthy and alive. She became the center of all our thinking. Since she was the first grandchild in our family, grandparents, aunts and uncles helped us to admire and care for her.

> We had tried for ten years to have our own child. Then we waited three more years before all the adoption papers were accepted. When we saw Debbie, we were immediately in love. We knew she would be more precious than even a birth child could be.

> I wanted so much to make Jeffrey perfectly happy. When he whimpered I was there to comfort him and hold him, rock him, feed him or change his diaper. I was so happy to be a mother. I decided to devote all my days to helping Jeffrey develop into whatever his potential would allow.

> Bobby couldn't sleep so we took turns rocking him until finally he would fall asleep in our arms. We couldn't leave him with babysitters because he would cry until we returned. It was almost as if he knew how much we loved him.

> I had read about the research on early infant stimulation and I was determined to encourage Matthew's abilities. I would climb into the playpen with him to talk to him and to teach him how to play with his infant toys.

Ronnie was premature and spent his first four weeks in a hospital incubator. When we finally got him home to ourselves, I was devoted to caring for him. He almost never cried since I perceived his needs before he began to feel uncomfortable. He was a perfect baby.

John and I had such difficult childhood. Our parents were poor and we had so many brothers and sisters that few of our material or affectional needs were met. As we looked at John Jr. we made a commitment together to provide him with both the affection and material possessions we both felt were lacking in our own childhoods. We had much and we wanted to give our all to that beautiful new baby.

The inherent danger that comes with this extraordinary commitment to the new infant is that it previews other behaviors, including overindulgence and overprotectiveness. The child for whom all is accomplished before any effort is exerted is not allowed to take initiative and thus to build confidence. These parents often couple this intense investment of self with unrealistically high expectations, because the success of that new infant becomes an extension of the parent's own personal aspirations. The infant, almost from birth, is viewed by the parents as the long-awaited answer which gives meaning to their own lives, to their own sense of fulfillment.

Of course, new babies should be welcomed and loved. Parents surely must make extensive commitments to the wonderful being they have created. It is only the exaggeration and the extreme of parent personal investment that may steal from the children their own sense of efficacy and competence. Doting parents confer on their children extensive power to manipulate their adult world before they have the knowledge, wisdom and maturity to wield such power. These children learn very early how to get important people to do their bidding. They expect their needs to be gratified instantly by others and they literally become addicted to continuous and immediate adult attention. They are not permitted to struggle to accomplish the personal challenges of early childhood.

Early Health Problems

Allergies, asthma, congenital birth defects or physical or mental handicaps may lead to a unique relationship and commitment by one or both parents (usually the mother) to an infant or preschool child which potentially could have a debilitating effect on the child's growth of self-sufficiency. The child's temporary requirements may put so many obligations on the mother that she is required to forgo her own personal, social, intellectual or career interests in order to minister exclusively to the overwhelming demands of the child. She thus invests herself almost totally in the child and makes her *raison d'etre* the alleviation of his pain, the development of his full potential, or his adjustment to the nonhandicapped world. The kinds of commitments these parents make are reflected in the following paraphrased statements.

> Barbie was hospitalized 12 times in her first four years of life. She had surgery five times to enable her to walk. Then there were other emergencies -pneumonia twice and a routine tonsillectomy which became complicated. Nothing seemed simple for Barbie. Several times I believed we might lose her. Bob managed the rest of the children or they stayed with my sister, but I was near Barbie during all her illnesses. I spent many nights in hospital chairs suffering almost as Barbie suffered, dedicating those years to keeping her from death's door. Now when I see her in such good health, I feel comforted to know that all my efforts were worthwhile and I only want to help her to catch up with her schoolwork and adjust better socially.

> Our pediatrician shocked us completely when he revealed to us that our beautiful baby in the hospital nursery was a Down's Syndrome child. Bob and I struggled with the decision as to whether to place him in an institution or keep him at home. After as much research and deliberation as time would allow, we decided that it would be best for Matt to develop in a normal family setting. As I rocked my infant in my arms, I determined in my own mind that I loved him as much as I could a normal child and that I would dedicate my life to helping him to achieve all that he could despite his limitations.

> Ronny had continous food allergy problems and I monitored his diet carefully. I breast fed him until he was 2 1/2 years old because there was so little he could eat. At three he began having asthma attacks. I slept in his room so that I could be near him if he wanted me. John, my husband, said he was too dependent, spoiled and babied. However, I felt that John was much too impatient with Ronny and was pressuring him to grow up too soon. John thought he should be a "jock," but Ronny was just too small and sickly for sports. John seemed to not want me to mother Ronny, although that was exactly what I wished to do. I loved my new mother role and Ronny really needed me.

These cases all begin with a child's unusual physiological or psychological need and a loving parent responding totally to the child. However, as the parent narrows her own life and withdraws from her own goals in a sacrificial attempt to "save" her child, the child's wants supersede all else. The relationship becomes a symbiotic, mutually dependent one. Although the child's biological and educational requirements are met, his feeling of well-being is tied to immediate gratification and positive feedback from the parent. In turn the parent measures her own personal success almost totally by the health and learning gains of the child.

Initially the relationship is synergistic and mutually beneficial. The child's gains go beyond what physicians have predicted. The parent's satisfactions exceed what she had expected and she feels that her Great Commitment is well rewarded. The preschool years thus are dominated by sacrifice and hard-earned success. This pattern may continue into the early school years or as long as the handicapped child's demands can be met on a reasonable and tolerable basis. But sooner or later the child must be weaned from this dependence or the relationship becomes pathologically parasitic. The sacrificing parent wearies of the extensive commitment and now views this same child as hopelessly demanding, rebellious and no longer within her control. Further, she has constricted her own life to the extent that she has lost many potential opportunities for growth and she has strained her marriage beyond repair. Although she now sees the importance of initiating new, more independent goals, she remains limited by the demands of her manipulating special child and her own guilt. She reminds herself frequently of the special commitment she made to him or her as an infant, but she questions how long she must continue this encompassing and consuming obligation.

Particular Sibling Combinations

Birth order and sibling rivalry affect all children. For example, studies have found relationships between birth order and IQ scores and birth order and achievement (Bossard and Ball, 1955). Other studies describe typical characteristics of oldest children, middle children and the "baby of the family" position. And beginning with Cain and Abel, history and literature frequently document cases of extreme sibling rivalry.

There are specific sibling combinations which predispose children toward underachievement. The underlying reason for this predisposition is that the particular combinations are inherently more competitive than usual, and that one or more of the siblings are disadvantaged by this competition. Many families learn to minimize sibling rivalry or at least assist siblings in dealing with their irrational competitiveness. However, in these special combinations, the parenting job is extremely challenging.

The combinations which seem unusually difficult include very close-aged same-sexed siblings; younger siblings of an extremely gifted child; the youngest child in a large family of children who are considerably older; and the sibling of a child with extreme physical or mental health problems. Some examples of each of these combinations will be described.

> Our boys were only 11 months apart. Since they were so close in age we made a special effort to give them the same privileges and responsibilities. They shared their room, their toys and their clothers. Despite the similarities in the way we treated them, Troy, the younger of the two, always complains that we are unfair. The boys argue intensively and almost seem to hate each other.

In the case where two close-aged same-sexed siblings are treated similarly, both children are likely to feel more competitive pressure. Since they are expected to act the same, the age difference typically puts stress on the younger one to keep up with the older one, causing the younger one to often feel inadequate. The older one also may feel some frustration because he or she does not receive special privileges which go with age. Since the older usually outperforms the younger sib, he or she will appear confident unless the superior ability is threatened. The child then may become defensive. Both siblings also are likely to compete for a close relationship with the same-sexed or most powerful parent. Recognizing individuality by acknowledging privileges of age and differences in interests and abilities tends to relieve some of the competitive pressures. However, parents can expect to feel frustration as they try to deal with two competitive brothers or two hostile sisters who should be such good company for each other.

> Bridget, our older daughter, is extraordinarily gifted. She's cooperative, pleasant and a high achieving student. Bobby, her younger brother, has an equally high IQ, but we have never managed to get him to achieve well in school. He learned everything quickly but was sloppy, careless and oppositional from first grade on.

When the first child exhibits unusual talent, he or she is likely to be the recipient of special parent and school attention, unusual educational opportunities and a multitude of honors and awards. This child thus becomes the pacesetter for the siblings who follow. High standards are set and younger siblings believe that in order to earn equal recognition they must achieve a similar level of success. Even if they are very capable they are likely to view such an accomplishment as quite impossible. Since they want to establish an individual and respectable place in the family, and since they view themselves as unlikely to compete successfully, they select a different and sometimes opposite direction for achievement and attention. If the family can support the unique intellectual or artistic activities, the child may develop both competence and confidence. However, if the oldest sibling's accomplishments are significant, it often is difficult to convince younger children of their own talent. In such cases they may resort to nonaccomplishment for attention seeking. Their failures and their behavior problems may thus become their route to family recognition. These may not be highly rewarding for them, but they believe they have no alternative since they can find no other effective way to get family consideration. They attain "equal time" by manipulating family members to attend to their problems, thus setting an underachieving cycle in motion.

Another option available to a second child, who may also be a middle child, is social success. If the intellectually gifted or achievement oriented first child is not particularly socially competent, then middle children like Mary may compete by being friendly, likeable, and brilliantly social.

> Mary is our social butterfly but we can't seem to motivate her to do any work. John, her oldest brother is really into science, but he is a loner. Pammy, the baby of the family is an excellent reader, a good musician and a serious student. Mary seems too preoccupied with her friends to consider school important. The telephone and parties continue endlessly, but study never really begins regardless of how much we emphasize the importance of schoolwork.

The birth place as "baby of the family" may initiate a special style of Underachievement Syndrome. The youngest child is by no means always an underachiever. As a matter of fact, youngest children are found to be second only to oldest children as achievers. However, if youngest children are either overindulged or overpowered by older siblings, they will be in the very same situation as the "too welcome" child discussed earlier.

Older children may treat their youngest sibs almost as toys and do so much for them that they are prevented from developing their own ideas and activities. In this case they become dependent on the positive feedback from older siblings and they may become fearful of assuming responsibilities or initiating creative activities. The youngest children see little likelihood that they can be as competent and successful as their older siblings, and besides, it is much easier to get any help that they need from the collection of "big" people around them. How can they develop self-confidence if they do not attempt challenging tasks? Fear of failure and a habit of taking the path of least resistance prevent them from trying to achieve in the classroom. Annie is an example.

> Annie is five years younger than her brother Bob. The other children, Ron, Ruth and Bob, are close in age. Annie has always been coddled and spoiled by her older brothers and sister. Although we all acknowledge that Annie probably always gets exactly what she wants and manages to evade household chores and responsibilities, everyone adores her. School is easy for her, but although she's very bright her grades are poor and teachers always tell us she's working far below her ability.

The sibling of a handicapped or physically ill child tends to have unusual competitive difficulties. For example, Kim's parents described her problem behavior:

> We can never seem to satisfy Kim. She always claims that Jeff has more privileges than she has. Jeff has been sick most of his life and has so many other problems that of course we do special things to help him. Kim is well and popular and bright and she does get almost everything she asks for, but if we say "no" to her about anything, she loses her temper and blames Jeff for her problem. Despite her good ability, her schoolwork is disastrous.

Kim's problems are analagous to those of the siblings of the unusually gifted child. Jeff's continuous illness, surgery and hospital stays have provided him with constant sympathy from parents and relatives. Although Kim surely could see his real physical suffering, she also was aware of the special encouragement, support and praise which only he received. How was that unfair competition? There was really nothing positive that Kim could do which would bring her the extensive and loving attention that Jeff received. Thus Kim's continually unreasonable demands of her parents reflected competition for attention equal to that which Jeff receives. Since Jeff's health problems require so much solicitude, there will be no end to Kim's demands. As her parents feel more frustrated and angry with her unpleasant and inconsiderate actions, and express that in the form of reprimands, Kim's oppositional behavior will increase and her parents will find that there is little positive behavior to praise. Kim's complaints will become accurate descriptions of her problem. Her parents will become unfair and antagonistic toward her, and neither she nor they will quite understand how family life became so unpleasant. Kim's Underachievement Syndrome then is a result of her efforts to attract her parents' notice.

Specific Marital Problems

An early broken marriage or out-of-wedlock birth creates a situation in which a child develops a very close one-to-one relationship with his or her mother, which may predispose the child toward Underachievement Syndrome. The mother usually is in a highly stressful situation in which she may feel rejected and is likely to question her life-style and, indeed, whether life is worthwhile living at all. At this vulnerable time in mother's life she may decide, at least temporarily, that her child is her only purpose for living. As she dedicates herself to the child's needs, she may, as in the case of the overwelcome child, do too much for him or her, thus preventing the child from taking initiative. Alternately, she may treat the child almost as a spouse or partner, thus giving the child too much power. The child learns to expect this power and is not willing to give it up to conform to the requirements of peers or school.

Other risks for single parents are their dependence on surrogate parents during working hours. Typically a grandparent is called upon. Grandparenting is often comparable to overwelcoming the child. Grandparents are more likely than parents to give too much attention, and to do too much and buy too much for the child. The child feels loved by many adults and doesn't need to share this attention with other siblings or children. He or she learns to relate to adults in either a too dependent or else too powerfully manipulative way. Mother may feel caught in both a social and financial bind and can find no alternative to bringing her child up in a world of two generations of parents. She may hesitate to ask her own parents to change in fear of hurting their feelings in the midst of the appreciation she feels for their help. Alternatively, she may argue with them frequently about child rearing, which leaves the child confused by the opposition between his or her care givers.

Children in such adult settings tend to develop verbal abilities early and express themselves well orally. They may look for adult help and attention when effort is required. They also may emulate adult power struggles with their adult-like vocabularies and reasoning styles.

Marriages which stay intact but have a pervasive oppositional style also may cause children to have Underachievement Syndrome. In such marriages, although there are two parents they may have "agreed to disagree" on most everything. Typically, child rearing techniques will be an important area of disagreement. The children in such a family are continually surrounded by power struggles. They may pick a favorite parent, but usually try to please both parents. As the parents struggle for power, they pull and tug at their child who vacilates between them. If you can visualize one parent tugging at one arm of the child while the other pulls the other arm in the opposite direction, you can sympathize with the child who may feel literally suspended in midair. The child cannot move in either direction, but neither can he or she move forward.

The oppositional nature of such a marriage, or of a divorce if parents continue embattled, is likely to set off Underachievement Syndrome for children of any age. Even as late as senior high school formerly excellent students suddenly may change their achievement direction, triggered by the sense that they can no longer please either of their parents, or else by their concern for pleasing the parent with whom they are no longer living. The discussion of divorce-precipitated Underachievement Syndrome will be described further in a later chapter.

The Gifted Child

Why is the gifted child so vulnerable to underachievement? Their susceptibility stems both from their early childhood home environment and from their school experiences. While this is not a debate on genetic theories of intelligence, our clinical experiences with gifted children strongly support an important early environmental influence on the child's giftedness. That is, virtually all of the gifted children seen at Family Achievement Clinic had at least one adult who made a major time commitment to enriching the child's early years. This does not rule out a genetic contribution, but only states that early enrichment is very important for intellectual development.

Within that early enrichment are the same risks which are involved in other close one-to-one relationships: that the child will become too dependent on a one-to-one adult relationship or that the child will become too powerful because of the authority granted by the adult. For the gifted child there are added risks. A large vocabulary, "cute" comments, apparently mature reasoning, or musical or other talent, all attract the attention of surrounding adults. Grandparents, friends, parents, teachers and even strangers applaud the child's unusual abilities. The child thrives on the audience's encouragement and becomes addicted to it.

Gifted children's early school experiences are either full of nonlearning, since typical work is not challenging or they find that teachers, principals and parents take action to provide a special, individualized program for their needs. The first discourages these children's initiative since the academic environment requires no effort and is indeed boring. The second flatters them into believing that their special talents are extraordinary enough to permit them to change an adult-managed system. This is impressive power for a five or six year old, even one who is known as the "brain" among peers.

In sum, the risk for these gifted children comes from both attention addiction and too much power. They may learn to expect both uninterrupted applause and complete freedom of choice in their education, but neither are possible regardless of their intelligence.

Conclusion: Dependence and Dominance

Although there are multiple high risk conditions in early childhood learning which can initiate Underachievement Syndrome, they can best be summarized as a basic control problem. There are a great many appropriate ways to bring up children and there is surely a range of structures, for example, liberalism versus conservatism and dependence versus independence, that are satisfactory for child rearing. However, the previously described early childhood situations, some within the control of parents and some outside of their control, frequently have the effect of throwing even the best intentioned parenting into an imbalance state in which a child learns either a ritual of unusual dependence on or dominance over adults.

Neither of the two extremes appear to cause a major problem at home during the preschool years. Parents become accustomed to either the dependent or child dominant relationship. Occasionally they may label their dependent child as somewhat immature, but they assume that the child will outgrow the problem. They also may acknowledge that their too domineering child is a little bit spoiled, however, they have reasonable confidence that their child's problems will be resolved by his or her entrance to school. They believe that teachers and the school structure will help the too powerful child to adjust.

Dependent and dominant children have practiced their control patterns for relating to adults for several years before they enter school. These patterns seem to work well and they know no others. They carry them to the classroom and expect to relate to teachers and peers in the same ways. Teachers may be effective in changing some of the children's ways of relating. However, the more extreme the dependency or dominance, the more difficult the modification. Further, the dependency pattern is often masked as insecurity, immaturity, hyperactivity or even a learning disability. The dominant pattern sometimes may not show itself in the early elementary grades, since the child may feel fulfilled by the excitement and power of school achievement. Dominance may also be exhibited as giftedness, creativity or not-so-positively as a discipline problem. Even if some teachers manage these children well in school, the underachievement pattern may continue to be reinforced at home. If so, it will surely surface in a later year when the school or the child can no longer keep the pattern under control.

3

Underachievement by Imitation

Children may learn to underachieve by copying their parents. They may acquire the Underachievement Syndrome by imitation even though their parents are achievers. Unconscious copying begins between ages two or three by a process known as identification. Children copy a parent or both parents because they see themselves as like that parent. You will recall the identification process easily and will be able to determine which parent is the identification figure if you can remember your children walking around in a parent's shoes pretending they are that parent. Rocking a doll, talking on the telephone, driving a bicycle to work or doing chores around the house are all typical identification activities that you no doubt have observed in your own or others' children.

Identification with a same-sexed effective and achieving parent encourages, but does not guarantee, achievement in a child. The identification research clearly supports the significance of children's identification with good parent models as an important family factor in high achievememt; and the lack of that identification, or the identification with a poor parent model, increases the chances of underachievement. Parents who view their own lives as interesting and successful and who model an equitable and respectful husband/wife relationship provide optimal role models for both male and female children and thus increase the likelihood of good educational achievement.

Research by Mussen and Rutherford (1963) and Hetherington and Frankie (1967) found that the parent model chosen for identification and imitation depends largely on a combination of three variables: (1) similarities between the parent and child, (2) nurturance, and (3) power. The first variable that affects whom children identify with is related to the similarities the children see between themselves and a parent. This similarity provides a strong basis for sex role identification. High similarity between mother and daughter and between father and son strongly support same-sexed parent identification, given that nurturance and power of the parents are equal. However, unusual similarities in appearance, abilities, interests or personality between boys and mothers or girls and fathers frequently contribute to cross-gender parent identification, imitating the opposite-sexed parent.

The nurturance variable simply says that the child tends to identify with and copy the behavior of the parent who is highly nurturant. The parent may not be particularly warm and loving in general, but there may be an especially warm, loving relationship between the parent and a particular child or children in the family. If that parent is an achiever, the child may adopt a similar achieving attitude.

The power influence on identification refers to parents' power over a child's life. Sometimes a parent may appear to be powerful because he or she makes decisions about politics or finances. However, the child may or may not perceive that parent as powerful depending upon whether the decisions impact on the child's interests, needs and discipline. Since power is an important variable which affects identification, and since routine observation of power in a family, even one's own family, may be misleading, power patterns will be discussed in more detail later.

In noting who your children or your students are copying, it is important to be sensitive to all three variables, similarity, nurturance and power. Identification with a parent may not be constant. It can be different when children are younger than when they grow up. Identification actually may change several times and, in addition to parents, can include grandparents, older siblings or other persons in or around the home.

Positive and Negative Models

Obviously positive models for children are fathers and mothers who feel good about their accomplishments. They value education and hard work and receive intrinsic as well as extrinsic rewards from their efforts. They respect and value each other, and their children see them as supporting partners in a noncompetitive marriage enterprise. They help each other to grow separately and they share in building a life together which includes achievement-oriented family activity. Neither parent is all powerful, and their lives fit together to make a total family picture like pieces of an interlocking puzzle. There is a sense of progress as a family unit, a respect for the value of education and a family solidarity that provides a clear model which is readily emulated.

So much for idealism. Love, virtue and achievement continue, however, rarely as flawlessly as this ideal picture. Problematic patterns also occur, sometimes deliberately, but more likely not quite in conscious control. Unfortunately, by chance or poor luck, parents at varying times in their adult development and married lives act in ways which provide models for underachieving. Recognizing these life-styles as models for underachievement is the first step in correcting them, and thus beginning the cure of a child's Underachievement Syndrome.

Remember that, as parents, you are a model for your child only part of the time. That is, the productive work you do in your job and the loving words you pronounce to your spouse in private are unobserved by your child. However, the tired sighs at the end of the day and the angry demands you make of your spouse are heard very clearly. Your first task is to become more aware of the times and ways in which your children see you. It may feel a bit like play acting, but the little person you are influencing can see you only when you are on the home stage.

Examine the following potentially harmful model scenarios to see if they seem familiar. You or your spouse may feel some guilt as you see yourself as a negative model which will harm your children's achievement. However, the purpose of these messages is not to communicate guilt but to recognize problem behaviors that can be changed. None of us are perfect; all of us can do better. If you find that you are blaming yourself for your childrens' problems, please remember also to take credit for their good qualities. That will help you to put their Underachievement Syndrome in perspective while considering the changes that you may want to make in your own lives.

I Didn't Like School Either

School has not been a positive experience for all children, and you as parents or teachers may indeed have sad memories of your childhood education. In your efforts to empathize with your struggling children you may think it helpful to share with them your unfortunate memories. You may describe the humorous times you outsmarted your teacher, the pathos of your boredom, your criticism of the inadequate education in your school, or the problems caused by your own underachievement. While confiding these stories of the past may help you and your children to feel closer, they also convey a message of expectation. A gifted, high-energy six year old who had just completed his second day in first grade summed it up succinctly: "My grandpa hated school, my dad hated school, and I hate school." Obviously, his family influence and his identification with his father have not contributed positively to his attitude about learning. His father is a teacher and he rationalized his dad's career by adding that being a teacher was more fun than being a student. His oppositional statements repeated in the classroom would certainly antagonize even the most devoted teachers, and because he was extremely gifted and outgoing, he would certainly be destined for underachievement had the family not come for help.

Telling your children about the similarities between yourself and them enhances identification. However, tell them only that part that provides a positive model. Save the remaining more problematic details for later when they have established their personal identity as acheivers. If you've already told them all, try to undo the damage by emphasizing your positive accomplishments and indicating that you hope that they won't repeat the errors which truly complicated your life and made it more difficult. Since they listen more to what you say about yourself than to your lectures, cut down on the latter and give only positive partial views of the former. There is no advantage to either you or your children in exaggerating your skills as an underachieving troublemaker, though it may seem good material for family humor.

The Disorganized Home

Disorganization is a key characteristic of underachievers. Often, although not always, they learn this disorganization from parent models. Some parents pride themselves on their disorganized life-style; others fall into disorganization out of despair. The young mother with three children in diapers and two in school may have given up trying to keep order in her home and may settle for soap opera escape. The father with two jobs, three children and four parents to support may be floundering for a framework to support his busy work schedule. Families sometimes choose a frenzied life-style for their children, for example, one which includes ballet, piano, Little League baseball, scouts and half a dozen other activities. The frantic taxiing of children and themselves between involvements leaves little time for structure or clear expectations and responsibilities.

Some persons assure me that they prefer disorder. I try to persuade them that it is not rigidity that I want for their children, and that "flexibility" could be a reasonable compromise. I persuade them that their children require a reasonable framework for their lives. They frequently remind me that creative people prefer disorganization. In turn, I point out that truly creative persons feel comfortable in some disorganization, but make meaning and order out of chaos. They find orderly patterns and explanations in places where no organization or explanations existed previously. I even point out to these persons, who are usually successful in their own jobs, that in areas where they are successful and have made personal contributions, their efforts and abilities have been highly organized.

Children must have some organization; they need structure and routine so they can understand their limits and explore the space between. They must adapt to the organized life-style of a school program that requires orderly desks, reasonably neat assignments, homework deadlines and rules of discipline. Adaptation to this routine is accomplished more easily if it is reflected in their home environment by parents with whom they identify.

Passive Aggressive Parenting

This scene may be familiar. Father is lying comfortably on the couch, relaxed Z's emerging from his solemn lips. His passive position does not automatically emit a sense of power. Mother stands nearby and in anger and frustration demands for the tenth time, "Would you please fix the screen door?" "Z's" continue to emerge. Father does not move. Mother leaves the room muttering and sputtering. Father is passive, but he is also powerful. He is very much in charge of the situation and he is an unfortunate model for his son. Note this conversation with fourth grade underachiever Mike.

Dr. Rimm: Mike, who do you think you're most the same as, your mom or your dad?

Mike: (Without hesitation) My dad.

Dr. Rimm: How are you the same as your dad, Mike?

Mike: When my mom calls my dad to do something around the house, he doesn't answer. And when my mom calls me to do my homework, I don't answer either.

Passive aggressive behavior is characteristic of many underachievers. The "I forgots" and "I don't knows" and "I have no homework" are all forms of passive aggressive behavior. The child is in power without appearing to be, but parents and teachers are powerless. What can you say to the child who solemnly admits that he's forgotten?

The situation described above could be the fault of either the wife or the husband. It may indeed be true that the wife cannot get her lazy husband to do chores around the house. Or it may be that the husband has just returned from a full day of work, and if his nagging wife would give him just a few minutes to rest, he would be pleased to take care of the chores. Regardless of where the blame falls the modeled behavior is problematic, and if it represents typical behavior that children view, it is problematic modeling.

It is not males alone who model passive aggressive behavior toward their spouses. Females, too, do their share and since it is powerful behavior, either male or female children may imitate it. The most typical female modeling of passive aggressive behavior comes in the once traditional style of family where dad is ostensibly dominant. In this family if wives resent their lack of power, they may not openly discuss their feelings in fear of aggravating an already difficult situation. Instead, they may use passive aggressive approaches. For example, if spouse wants dinner ready by 6, it is never ready until 6:30; or if he has asked specifically that she buy a particular food he enjoys, she always "accidentally" forgets to buy it. When the frustrated husband comments on her lack of effort to please him, she shrugs and mumbles some reasonable sounding excuse — "I was busy, I forgot."

Passive aggressive behavior never improves marriage relationships, but it does provide an obvious model of underachievement that is difficult to modify. Furthermore, it is frequently passed from one generation to the next as an acceptable mode of behavior. One father asked me this question: "Do you mean that if I just volunteered to do things around the house without my wife nagging me that it might make a difference in my son's schoolwork?"

You can guess the response.

Overworked Parents

If passive, lazy or disorganized parents are inappropriate models, then surely hardworking industrious parents must be positive models. Not necessarily. Overworked fathers and mothers who come home exhausted, who complain about the stresses of their jobs, the unfairness of their salaries, or the unjustness of their bosses are modeling negative attitudes about the world of work. Furthermore, if one spouse complains about all the work done by the other spouse or if either spouse finds no time for play or pleasure, they are modeling an image of work as an area to be avoided by children. In elementary school these children will only complain about all the hard work their teachers (bosses) give them. By adolescence they censure their parents as "doing nothing but working" and insist that it certainly is not the life-style they wish to emulate. A virtually certain way to prevent a son from respecting his father is for his mother to complain during his entire childhood about how she hates his father's career.

How can we hardworking parents manage to change that model for our children when the requirements of our job do consume so much family time? Since I have a busy career and one daughter still at home to whom I must model, I've learned a few tricks which may be helpful. When I return from my typical ten hour day to my teenager impatiently waiting for one or both parents, I (usually) gather up all my energy and my positive recollections of the day and greet Sara with, "Sara, you just won't believe what an interesting day I had today..." I continue with a description of the latest child I've helped (no names given, of course) and we share insights on our cases. I say "cases" because Sara has learned to share with me her own psychological insights on friends and the children she babysits for or tutors. Discussing an insight on teenage rebellion, Sara says "she's born into it."

It doesn't really matter to me if Sara decides to become a psychologist, but I want desperately for her to know how satisfying I find my work to be. An interesting and unexpected side effect is that I feel much less tired and much more satisfied at the end of each day. It has actually become a rather good habit. If the daughter-like-mother story sounds familiar, it may only be a reminder of the old style country doctor whose son traveled with him as he visited his patients. It wasn't unusual at all for a son to follow in his dad's footsteps and choose medicine as a career which he had learned to respect. In Sara's words, "he was born into it."

The Post-Divorce Parents

Divorce has a special impact on child identification. Both the period prior to and after the divorce present modeling and identification dilemmas for parents and children. The pre-divorce problems are an extension and exaggeration of the oppositional relationship which took place earlier in the marriage. For example, if the boy identified with an aggressive father and the father remains in a powerful position, and furthermore is obviously disrespectful to his wife, the boy may copy his father and also become belligerant toward mother. He will be, at least temporarily, a behavior problem at home and school, imitating the aggressive style of his father whom he views as his model. The actual behavior may vary considerably, depending on the age of the child, the modeled father, and the child's prior experience. Outsiders see this situation as the son being most difficult toward what appears to be the wronged parent.

If the son has identified with a passive aggressive mothering style he may continue in this style until he finds a different male model or until his mother changes to a more assertive life-style. If he accepts his dad's behavior as negative, as described by his mother, when asked whom he is most like, he may indicate that he is more like his mother. In this case he prefers to deny any similarity to a father who has been described as a "bad guy." In one family where, prior to the divorce, the father had been particularly obnoxious, each of two boys separately indicated that they were more like their mother — although they each concluded that their brother was like their father. It was obvious that neither cherished the image of a lazy, inconsiderate, alcoholic dad as an appropriate model.

For the girl who identifies with her mother, the identification is likely to continue after the divorce and will largely reflect the kind of adjustment to the divorce that the mother makes. The girl may, however, feel a sense of rejection by her father if her mother shows such feelings. If the daughter does feel rejection, her anger may be addressed toward her mother, whom she may see as the cause of her feelings of rejection.

After the divorce there can be some other difficult effects of identification patterns. If both parents are nearby the children are likely to continue identifying with the same parent they identified with previously. However, their view of that model may change and may distract them from school achievement. For example, the visitation father whom the child sees two to four times a month will typically take on the role of providing "fun and games" for the child. Since he does not see his children frequently, he is determined to make the meeting enjoyable. He plans dinners out, movies, baseball games, and so on.

While that sounds fine, we need to look at the message this communicates to the child who identifies with him. That child never sees his father in a working role but always sees his mother in a working role. He also knows that his father makes no educational demands of him, since he is not required to do schoolwork during visitation. Mother, whom he lives with during the school week, expects him to do homework. Is it surprising that he fights with his mother continuously about his school responsibilities? If he sees himself as like his dad, and if his dad's modeling is one of fun and games, it certainly does not make much sense to him to bother with homework.

Of course, if the post-divorce period is dealt with constructively, this kind of nonwork message can easily be clarified for everyone. Dad must communicate to his child his schoolwork expectations and his interest in the child's achievement and study habits. He also must insist that the son be thoroughly respectful to his mother. If parents are aware of the messages they are communicating and if they are sufficiently concerned about the child to forego their own power struggles, they can make a dramatic difference in that child's achievement direction.

In one case where we clarified an achievement message from father to son, on the few occasions where the son regressed to his old rebellion-toward-mother behavior, it took only a brief telephone call from father to remind son of his study obligations. It is important that both mother and father agree on the same educational message and that the parent identified with makes a strong effort to reinforce that message by interest and example.

After multiple separations and divorces, the messages become even more confusing. David, a gifted fourth grader with an IQ score of 135 was underachieving. He had a series of important adults confuse his academic direction. First, there was his birth father, whom he never actually lived with but visited fairly regularly. Second, there was the father whom his mother married shortly after his birth and who took the fathering role during his preschool years and until he was in second grade. Third, there was a father-to-be, the man his mother was going with very seriously after her divorce from father #2. Finally, there was his mother who had stayed constant during all his life. David was an only child and was receiving school related messages from all four adults. Birth father #1, whom David visited approximately once a month, believed David should study hard and get good grades. However, all of the other adults in David's life put father #1 down and so he was considered a "bad guy." Father #2 was David's identification figure. David visited with him two or three times a week. Although he felt school was important, he also gave David the message that he was satisfied as long as David earned average grades. David easily was meeting his expectations. Father #3 was not giving specific school messages yet. Mother realized that David was underachieving and did try to encourage him. However, she was anxious not to put too much school pressure on him, which really was the equivalent of communicating to David that perhaps he could work only a "little" harder.

The key people here were obviously the initial two fathers. The first, whom David was taught not to respect, was giving the appropriate school message. David was hearing and following the advice of the second father whose message was truly one of underachievement. It was easy enough for David to follow his father #2's lead but he was developing some very poor study habits in the process and not bothering to learn some critical skills. When the situation was clarified, all adults were willing to change messages to make them consistent; and with a little perseverance on everyone's part, David raised his school expectations and his achievement.

Prior to or after a divorce, consistent school-related messages by all important adults are critical to a child's school achievement. Those messages should be modeled as well as spoken. Continuous power struggles between parents through children is likely to result in the child's not knowing how to please both parents and in his taking the "path of least resistance." This places him in an underachieving mode. The resulting child of such modeling I've called "Torn Tommy."

Cross-Gender Identification

Cross-gender identification takes place when a boy identifies with his mother or a girl with her father. How does this affect school achievement?

If a boy identifies with his mother, it frequently has a negative impact on school achievement and is likely to cause at least some temporary problems. He tends to exhibit fewer male stereotyped behaviors and more typical female interests. If his school environment supports a "macho" image of males and an emphasis on team sports and physical prowess, as it usually does, the boy is unlikely to be accepted by his peers. This rejection typically takes place between grades three and six during what Freud called the "latency" period of development. The impact of this period on children's behavior is readily obvious in viewing the typical elementary school playground at recess. Most girls will be playing with other girls, jumping rope, swinging, or just talking to each other. Most boys will be playing more rough and tumble kinds of games and sports. If a teacher asks a girl to hold a boy's hand, the girl is likely to say "yuk." If a boy is asked to play with or choose a girl, he may be likely to mutter "girls are poison." At this time the boy who is not sufficiently masculine may also be labeled by boys as "poison," or "fag," or some similar term or ridicule for being effeminate. On the other hand, since girls see him as obviously not one of them, he remains "yuk" in their eyes.

Being "yuk" or "poison" has the effect of making our mother identifying boy feel isolated and lonely. In his wish for friends, he may fall into a trap of inviting teasing or ridicule as a substitute for a more positive relationship which he doesn't feel capable of attaining. Alternatively, you may see him walking on the playground alone, unless he has been fortunate enough to befriend a few others with similar interest who will prevent the loneliness. One such fifth grade boy communicated to me his sense of being different in the following way:

> If you could look down at our playground from an airplane you would understand what I mean. The boys are playing baseball and the girls are jumping rope or on the swings. You would find me with two friends just walking around the playground, talking. We're not part of any group or game. We're just different.

That sense of being different, of not being acceptable, at least temporarily seems to have a depressing effect on achievement. Perhaps the sense of feeling socially different makes these boys feel that they also should be academically different. They tend not to carry through their academic assignments or hand in homework, and they seem to find special difficulty with mathematics. Their self-esteem is low and they feel unaccepted by their peers.

There may be several other reasons why these boys who identify with mothers become underachievers. The boys fall into two patterns of identification, although the two categories often overlap. One group of boys who identify with their mothers are very dependent. Their identification begins in that very close one-to-one relationship that originates with an early divorce, a father frequently away from home, or early illness that causes the child to become accustomed to a one-to-one dependent life-style with mother. Mother dependence results in school underachievement, passivity and poor self-esteem.

The second type of mother-identifying boy is found in an oppositional marriage where the mother models passive aggressive behavior toward the father to avoid the father's control. The boy emulates this pattern by not doing the schoolwork expected of him by his father and by his school, thereby also avoiding father's power. Mothers usually are not aware that they are modeling this behavior.

Identification with mother may cause other emotional problems for boys such as insecurity about their own masculinity. However, many boys change their identification pattern as they mature. They may follow their father's model or copy male teachers, older brothers, neighbors or other significant males. If boys identify partially with both parents it does not seem to cause social or emotional problems. It is important only to have some, not necessarily total, identification with male figures.

The cross-gender identification of a daughter with her father typically is not problematic for her school achievement or social adjustment. Our society is much more tolerant of assertive females than we are of effeminate males. Actually, in one study of female mathematicians (Helson 1971) the author found that more creative mathematicians were those who identified with their fathers. As long as father gives an academic, pro-school message to his identifying daughter, she is not likely to have a school or career related problem.

If the girl identifies with a dad who portrays a "tough" anti-school image, then the girl may develop school related and/or social problems. She is likely to be the tomboy girl who wears the oldest torn jeans and the dirtiest sweatshirt, uses tough language and plays with the boys. She may indeed be determined to do no schoolwork at all. This pattern is relatively easy to change if it is identified early. However, as in most Underachievement Syndrome, it is very resistant to change if not discovered until high school.

If parents are supportive, the early change can be made by the father deliberately giving a positive school message and showing an interest in the child's learning. These will improve her school attitude and skills. An effort to "clean up the girl's act" in terms of slightly more appropriate dress and attempts to teach softened language will ease her acceptance into the world of females and she will be more comfortably accepted socially.

Some of the problems related to cross-gender identification are related to the sex role stereotypes which continue in our society; some are more directly related to achieving. As society becomes more tolerant of sex role differences the first type of problem may diminish. Certainly classroom teachers and parents can help children be more concerned with individual differences regardless of sex. The second type of problem, however, will continue to be an achiever problem — that is, dependence on a parent, passive aggressive oppositional behavior and not valuing school.

There are some characteristic skill patterns of most cross-gender early identifiers that are predictably and consistently found among the children who are evaluated at our Clinic. Boys who identify with their mothers typically show higher verbal scores and lower performance scores on the WISC-R (Wechsler Intelligence Scale for Children-Revised, 1974) than those who identify with father. They also tend to score lower on the Arithmetic Reasoning subtest than on the other verbal tests. There are some exceptions to this finding. If mothers are strong in math, mother-identifying boys tend not to exhibit the typical pattern; they score high in Arithmetic Reasoning and in the Performance subtests. Girls who identify with father frequently show the opposite pattern — higher performance than verbal scores and stronger math skills than verbal skills.

When we try to separate genetic and environment contributions to intelligence and achievement, it is tempting to assume that these children who cross-gender identify and copy the behaviors of their opposite sexed parent are a persuasive argument for the importance of early environmental learning. Although children do learn critical attitudes and skills very early from a parent model, children are also influenced by genetic similarities to a particular parent. Thus the genetic similarity may also be affecting the skills which are so similar to those of the opposite sexed parent.

The power influence on identification yields some strange patterns which may cause children problems. I call these sabotage rituals because one parent actually sabotages or destroys the other parent's power. The saboteur typically does not view his or her own actions as damaging to the spouse or the children, but instead sees them as appropriate to being a good parent. Although child development books frequently describe sibling rivalry in families they seldom touch the subject of parent rivalry. Parent rivalry for the love of children is usually only attributed to divorced parents, when in fact it frequently also takes place in intact homes. Parents involved in the rivalry seldom admit or address the issue.

In a rivalry situation there must obviously be winners and losers. In this case, the losing parent becomes less powerful in the sense of influencing the child by identification. The sabotage rituals caused by this rivalry cast one parent in the role of good or smart parent, and by comparison the second parent is described in less complimentary terms, mainly bad or dumb. I call these sabotage rituals "Ogre" and "Dummy" games. They may be directed toward the mother or the father and they may be played out separately or together. In some especially oppositional marriages, all four rituals combine to cause mother and son and father and daughter to team up against each other. Descriptions of the individual rituals and some examples will make them more clear. One important effect of these rituals is to reduce the chances that the children will identify with the same sexed parent. However, even if they did identify with that parent early, by adolescence they will typically compete with him or her.

Father Is An Ogre

In this family the father is objectively viewed as successful and powerful, the mother as kind and caring. Often a closer view of the home life shows a father who wears a big No on his forehead. That is, he firmly prohibits many of the activities the children wish to pursue. However, the children learn to bypass his authority by appealing to their kind, sweet mother. Mother either manages to convince dad to change his initial decision, or surreptitiously permits the children to carry out their desired activities anyway. Children quickly learn the necessary manipulative maneuvers. The ritual becomes more extreme because as the children grow older the father begins to recognize his lack of power over his family. He becomes more authoritarian as he tries to cope with his own sense of powerlessness. In response to his increasing authoritarianism, mother feels even more obliged to shelter and defend her children. In her desperation she invents new approaches to sabotaging her husband's power in the belief that she is doing the best thing for her children. She literally encourages her husband to become an ogre. Although girls in this family are likely to be achievement-oriented because they see their mother as powerful, boys will tend to underachieve. They see no effective model in their father, who appears both mean and powerless. They may fear and resent him, but are not likely to want to emulate him.

When we look to the history of this marriage it fits what one usually thinks of as a traditional marriage, with father serving as breadwinner and making all major decisions. Although mother accepts his power initially and is not likely to pursue a meaningful career, she does define her role as "in charge of the children and other household tasks." The final word over the children initially is also dad's by agreement and by appearances. However, mother's feelings of powerlessness cause her to personally decide that, in fact, she should be the children's protector and guide.

The scenario looks like this. Johnny, as a little guy, is into a bit of mischief. When dad finds him playing with some of his tools, he makes it very clear, in a booming voice, that those tools are his and that Johnny is not ever to touch them. Mom assures dad that Johnny is just curious and that he should not get so angry over so small a problem. The next day Johnny is "coincidentally" playing with the same tools. Now dad is livid. He has just scolded Johnny and has been ignored, and so he decides that what Johnny should have is a "good spanking." Mother watches in agony as dad spanks. Johnny is sent off to his room screaming and crying. However, the act does not end yet. Scene two is Johnny's bedroom. Mom is holding him comfortingly in her arms and reassuringly explains, "It's all right dear, daddy didn't mean to hit you. He just doesn't understand you. You're such a good boy — you were just curious."

Thus begins a long line of sabotages which mother thinks of as protections for her child from her husband's wrath. She wishes he wouldn't lose his temper so easily and that he would be more understanding of his children. But alas, over the years the father/son relationship worsens. Father never does learn to talk to his son and Johnny feels no respect for dad, only an awesome fear and a determination to never grow up to be as mean as he. By age 16, the act has solidified to a persisting ritual. Here is an adolescent example.

> It's homecoming weekend at Smalltown High School and Johnny has arranged for a date and pre-dance dinner. Naturally he's short some money. He isn't really worried but he does need to go through a three scene drama to get the necessary funds.

Scene 1: Johnny Prepares Mom (Kind Mom)

Johnny: (Confident and assured) Mom, could I borrow $15 for the Saturday night Homecoming dinner? I'll pay you back next week.

Mom: Sorry dear, you know that's dad's decision. Just ask him. I know he'll help you out.

Johnny: Gee, mom, you know dad will just say I should have saved it up.

Mom: Well, Johnny, you'll just have to ask him anyway.

Scene 2: Johnny Asks Dad (The Ogre)

Johnny: (Hesitant, trembling, speaking quickly as if to get it over with) Dad, could I please borrow $15 for Homecoming? I promise I'll pay it back by Friday. I'm just a little short because I didn't realize that dinner would be quite that expensive and...

Dad: (In customary booming voice) Absolutely not! You get an allowance. You'd better save it next time. (Returns to newspaper)

Johnny: (Retreats silently, head down, relieved to have completed the unpleasant chore.)

Scene 3: Johnny Collects (Wonderful Mom)

Johnny: (Head is still down with tear suitably placed on cheek.) Mom, dad just doesn't understand me. (He knows that for sure since mom has told him that for 16 years.) Even though I said I'd pay him back, he wouldn't give me any.

Mom: (Withdraws money from apron pocket and gives it to Johnny with kind smile.) It's all right dear, here's $15. Have a wonderful time but don't tell dad. It's from my grocery money. You know, Johnny, your dad really loves you. He just doesn't understand teenagers.

Johnny: (Hugs mom briefly) Gee, mom, you're just great! Thanks a lot!

What has this kind, sweet mom done? She has literally made her husband into an ogre — and a powerless one at that. Why would Johnny want to be like dad? What son would respect a mean father who doesn't truly have the respect of his own wife?

When Johnny was little he said he was more like his mom. As he got older and it became uncomfortable for him to acknowledge similarity to mother, he preferred to think he was like neither. "I don't really know who I'm like," he says. As a matter of fact he doesn't really know what he wants to do, where he wants to go to school, or what he'd like to major in. He just can't seem to find any direction. But that's all right, mom will probably help!

There are variations in the ways that mom "tries to help" but inadvertently makes father into an ogre. For example, she points out to son that dad works much too hard and she doesn't see any reason for him to devote so much of their family life to work. The underlying subtle message to son is "don't be like dad — don't work so hard — life without all that work is more meaningful." The son's application of this concept and his response to his parents by the time he gets to high school, or possibly earlier, is "I don't see why I need to do this work at school. It's really only busy work and has no relevance for me. There's much more to life than just schoolwork anyway."

Mom, does it sound familiar? You did give him that message. Unfortunately, he no longer listens, even to you, when you now tell him to do his homework.

Here's another part of the same ogre sabotage ritual. Dad would like his son to take challenging courses and would like to encourage him in the direction of his own career. Mother protests that son has the right to choose his own courses, his own career and to "do his own thing." Furthermore, she puts down her husband's career as one that requires too much travel or too much time away from home or too much arguing or doesn't produce enough salary. The indirect message to son is "don't be like your father" and "don't do the things he recommends." The words of the adolescent son come out as "I want to do my own thing." He's not sure what that is and he prefers not to hear what it is. He wants to find out for himself about "his own thing." He knows what he is against: his dad, his dad's career, his dad's course choices and his dad's "establishment." He must choose something that is different in order to establish his uniqueness. There is a vacuum — he says he must "experience living." He can't take advice from anyone (except from those who are also doing their own thing — his peers). So he grows long hair, experiments with drugs, or maybe he even joins a religious cult. If he is not permitted to please the people he loves, then he must find some other person or group that accepts and notices him. By this time mother is not happy either. Yet she unwittingly denied her son an ideal model, the man she loves and chose to marry, her successful husband, his successful father. She made her husband into the man her son must rebel against instead of a model he could learn from, and now neither mom nor dad understand their son.

Mommy Is An Ogre

Equal time for both sexes! Now we will look at the way in which the husband makes his wife into an ogre. This ritual creates underachieving boys and girls. It includes a kind, sweet husband who would be viewed by women outside of the family as "perfect." He's generous, loving, warm and even likes to discuss feelings. He enjoys his parenting role and considers himself a good, fair father.

He rarely loses his temper and frequently discusses differences of opinion with his children. They know they can count on him to talk things over and to understand them. It never occurs to him that rivalry exists between him and his wife.

Of course there should be some discipline in the home. Children must be guided. Since father is the "good guy" he recommends to his wife that she be in charge of the rules for the children. Mother clearly sees the need for guidelines for her children and so she establishes the rules. Now here is the catch: She makes the rules — and he breaks them!

An example:

Scene 1: The rule is: Children are supposed to do their homework before they watch television. Mother and father agree to this rule. The rule is made on Sunday. Now it's Monday. Mother walks into the living room to find Matt watching Monday night football.

Mother: Matt, have you done your homework?

Matt: (No response)

Mother: Matt, have you done your homework yet? Matt, remember the new rule we made.

Matt: Yeah...just a minute. Gee, mom, this is an important play.

Mother: (Leaves the room and returns in a few minutes.) Matt, is the play over yet? You have to do your homework.

Matt: (Looking up briefly) Dad said I could do it after the game — this is really an important game.

Mother: (Leaves room discouraged) Dad said, dad said — so what can I do?

Scene 2:   Game is over. Dad and Matt are sitting on sofa chatting about the game.

Mother: Matt, you said you'd do your homework right after the game. (To her husband) Dear, remember the rule we set up.

Matt: Gee, mom, dad and I are talking. We hardly ever have time to talk. I'll do it in a few minutes.

Father: (To mom) Dear, this should be an exception. Matt will do his work in a few minutes. We were just having a good talk.

Mother: (Leaves room feeling powerless, muttering under her breath) Some rule!

Scene 3:

Mother: (Enters, no longer patient and feeling angry, speaking in a loud tense screeching voice.) Matt, you better do your homework. You'll fail your course. It's ten o'clock. You can't talk all night...

Matt: Gee, mom, what are you yelling about? I'll get it done. It's too late to concentrate now, I thought I'd go to sleep and get up early and do it in the morning. (In a loud rebellious voice) Don't worry about it, it's my homework and I'll get it done!

Father: It's okay, dear, no reason to lose your temper. Matt will do it in the morning. He'll get it done and it will go much faster after a good night's sleep. (To Matt in patient voice) Good night son. Have a good night's rest. Be sure to do your work in the morning.

Matt goes off to bed thinking that his mother is really a nag and resolving to do his work in the morning. Father settles down in front of the TV wondering how his wife became such a shrew.

Mother sits down with him in front of the TV feeling drained, angry at herself for losing her temper, wishing she could get her husband to help her and sensing that somehow she is powerless. She knows for sure that Matt will not do his homework. When the alarm goes off in the morning, he'll go back to sleep. Even after the snooze alarm goes off twice and she calls to him three or four times he will barely be able to pull himself out of bed; and when he whizzes down to "just miss the bus" dad will offer him a ride to school on his way to work. She feels exasperated. She knows she will attend the next parent/teacher conference without her husband and again hear the teacher say, "Matt is such a bright boy. If he could only use his brains to do his work instead of figuring out ways to avoid it, he'd be a great student." Matt becomes a bright underachieving mystery to his teacher, to his mother and, much later, to his dad as well.

The "Mommy is an Ogre" game fosters Underachievement Syndrome in boys and girls. Girls underachieve in this family because they see their mother as powerless and an ogre, certainly not an appropriate model. They would prefer to be "daddy's little girls" and effortlessly please daddy. The boys in this family are happy to identify with their father. They like being "powerful and kind." Unfortunately the message they receive from dad does not encourage achievement. It is a passive aggressive message to ignore mother, to ignore teachers, and to ignore rules. It is a message to "do your own thing" and to procrastinate until you feel ready. The readiness rarely comes.

Daddy Is A Dummy

This ritual is a slight modification of the Ogre play and is found mainly in homes where mothers are psychologists, educators or have taken a parenting class. Their husbands, on the other hand, may be doctors, engineers or truck drivers but have not taken any parenting courses. The main difference, of course, is that mother has learned the "right" way to bring up the children and the father hasn't. Therefore, mother decides that it is her responsibility to give father directions on how to rear Bobby correctly.

Mother knows for sure that boys need their daddies as appropriate male role models, so she explains this to her husband.

He is delighted. He has visions of him and his son going off on fishing trips together and watching football games every Sunday. Initially, he is told he must play with his little boy to get the good positive relationship started. So he does. He coos and goos to him; he feeds him and he even changes his diapers on occasion. Sons are fun! So far things seem to be working out well. Father is delighted and pleased that his wife knows all about child psychology.

Somewhere around age two the problem begins. Dad is in charge for the day and he finds Johnny exploring and destroying his books and papers. His work is in a shambles. Father loses his cool. He picks up his little boy and spanks his bottom half a dozen times and puts him in his crib screaming and crying. Mother enters to find the living room strewn with papers, father distraught and her angelic son screaming desperately in his crib. She begins step 1 of her first aid psychology by immediately taking Johnny out of his crib, comforting his hurts and explaining that everything will be all right and that daddy just lost his temper. "Poor daddy."

Johnny is calmed down so she moves to step 2, which is to explain to father a better way to handle this kind of dilemma in the future. She indicates that he must explain to his son the appropriate behavior and refrain at all times from scolding or spanking him, because punishment is harmful to his self-concept and will cause his son to resent him. Father listens patiently as he applies his own first aid to his strewn and crumpled papers that cover the floor. He wonders why he lost his temper and he feels terrible about possibly damaging his son. He is most willing to try again and he resolves to use only positive reinforcement. After all, his wife took the parenting courses and she should know.

Dad tries again. And he tries again. Each time he seems to lose control. Each time he ends up "damaging his son's self-concept." 'Maybe," he thinks, "women are just better at bringing up children. If he could only put off playing with his son until the boy is a manageable size, he could probably do better. Perhaps he'll go back to school at night anyway and get another degree, or he should certainly devote more hours to his work at night. If he worked on Saturdays that surely would improve his opportunities for promotion and he could earn more money and, in the long run, he probably could do more for his son."

Dad's conclusion: I'll work hard now and play with Johnny when he's older.

Mom's conclusion: I wish John wouldn't have to work so much, but he doesn't handle the children very well anyway, so at least I can get them on the right track.

Johnny's conclusion: Daddy's never home. All daddy does is work. That's dumb. I sure don't want to be like daddy.

At about this time, the "daddy is a dummy" tune reverts to the "father is an ogre" melody and the song is played out as it was in the first orchestration.

Mother Is The Mouse Of The House

The dummy ritual for mothers which results in rebellious adolescent daughters begins in a conspirational relationship between father and daughter (Debbie). It is a special alliance which pairs father and his perfect little girl with each other but, by definition, gives mom the role of "not too bright" or somehow "out of it." During early childhood daddy never needs to say "no" to Debbie. She has a special way of winding him around her little finger. Mother admires the relationship, but from early on she doesn't quite understand it nor is she really a part of it. Father and daughter go off hand in hand, looking with wonder at each other. Everyone but Debbie and father agree that she is a little spoiled.

Preadolescence arrives and mother notes a subtle, and sometimes not so subtle, battle taking place between her daughter and herself. She isn't exactly sure why, but Debbie can't seem to take the slightest criticism from her. As a matter of fact, if mother says "black" Debbie says "white," and vice versa. Debbie often goes to dad because she is having trouble with mom. He mediates, smooths things over and helps Debbie to feel better, usually at mom's expense.

Then Debbie enters junior high school, and father begins to worry about his perfect daughter. Dangers lurk in the corridors, in the lavatories, at school dances and at teenage parties. Father begins his tirade of cautions about cigarettes, alcohol, pot, drugs and of course, young men. He must protect his perfect child from the evils of growing up, but Debbie says, "Dad, don't you trust me?" Dad answers that he trusts her but is not so sure about the rest of the world and so he decides it's time for rules.

Rules mean "no's" and Debbie has never really received a no from dad and these no's feel terrible. She appeals to mom, but mom has never really been on Debbie's team so, for the most part, mom agrees with dad. Now mom and dad are on the same team and she stands alone against them. They are saying "no" and even when she does her best manipulating she cannot change their minds. She feels desperate. She can't get them to let her do all the things she wants to do. She needs help. She reaches out to her peers. She finds peers who are having similar problems with their parents. She now has her own team. Together they will prove they can oppose their parents. Debbie tries smoking. All her friends do — the rebellious friends she has gravitated toward.

Now mom and dad are really anxious. Debbie's in with the wrong crowd and they have found cigarettes in her room. How can they trust her? Mom tries to talk to her, but that never worked. Dad tries to communicate their concerns. That's a little better but not really effective because he wants her to stop smoking. She won't. She says she has to be her own person and that her parents must stop being so controlling. Debbie's parents don't agree with her. They believe they should be stricter. They set curfews and Debbie climbs out the window. Now she's smoking pot. She's dating a boy who's a "dirt ball" or "burn out" (another variety of anti-school rebel). Her parents know this because mom reads Debbie's journal that she leaves out on her desk. They also know from the same journal that Debbie "hates" her parents. She's disrespectful, uses foul language, ignores their rules and her formerly A and B grades have dropped to D's and F's. She skips classes and argues with her parents and her most frequent words are, "stop trying to control me." They no longer can control Debbie and they can't understand what happened to that sweet little girl.

The parents bring Debbie to my office. She doesn't want to come. She plops herself down in the chair across from me, determined that I will not help her and says in a disdainful tone, "My mother is stupid. You'd think she was born 100 years ago." "And your father?" I ask, wishing I didn't have to hear the answer. "He's not much better — well maybe a little better. Neither of them know how to live. I really can't stand them. I can't wait until I get out of the house. I'm counting the days."

The rebellious daughter, who had too much power as a small child and whose father unwittingly encouraged her to compete with her mother (who should have been his first love), feels rejected, unloved and out of control. These girls take various paths but they all signal the same sense of lack of power, which they feel mainly because they were given too much power as children. Some girls express their rejection by parents in a pattern of promiscuous sexual relationships. They say their parents (especially their father) do not love them and they must have love. When they are in a man's arms they mistakenly believe that he loves them and it feels good. When he leaves their bed for the next one, they feel rejected and embittered and easily accept the next invitation that looks like love.

Other girls express silent rebellions: Bulemia, anorexia nervosa, depression and suicide attempts are powerful ways of expressing feelings of loss of control. These illnesses leave parents feeling helpless and blaming each other. They put the adolescent or young adult in control of their parents but not in control of themselves. Fathers who conspire with their little girls to put mother down as the "mouse of the house" can expect to suffer through adolescence.

Oppositional Families

I noted earlier that in some oppositional families where husband and wife are virtually always embattled, all four sabotage rituals can take place simultaneously. Although the parents recognize their own marriage problems, they typically do not identify the sabotage effects on their children. However, the children's school achievement and behavioral patterns will reflect the battling parent with whom they identified. In oppositional families there are winners and losers, aggressors and passive aggressors. Sometimes, if the family is very oppositional, all the children are losers, although they may express their losing differently.

The clearest example of an oppositional family where the children of both sexes lose is the one in which the daughter is daddy's little girl, who becomes Rebellious Rebecca, and the son who identifies with his solicitous and kind mother's passive aggressive behavior becomes Passive Paul. In embattled families with all same sexed children, one child takes on the role of one parent leaving to the other sibling the role of the opposite parent. One sibling will appear to be more aggressive; the other passive or, more likely, passive aggressive. Whether the aggressive child or the passive child is more successful will typically be a reflection of whether the aggressive parent or the passive parent is more successful. Some sibling examples:

> Bob, the older son, identified with his mom. Dad was not home very much in his early years because he was concentrating on building his career. Ron, the younger boy, chose dad as his model. Ron and dad were hard workers. Ron was glad to get out and help his dad while Bob preferred to stay inside to read or talk. By the time the marriage fell apart the boys were grown. The father was a successful administrator; the mother was unhappy and felt rejected. Ron was a successful businessman, but Bob dropped out of school, couldn't hold a job and was severely depressed.

> Mary, the oldest daughter, was "daddy's little girl." She began as an excellent student and was musically talented. Jenny, her youngest sister, identified with mom. Jenny was an excellent student too, and had equal musical talent. In adolescence Mary took on the Rebellious Rebecca pattern. Her grades dropped; her interest in music waned. Jennifer continued with her efforts as an excellent student and a fine musician. The father in this family died in a motorcycle accident when the girls were in college. The mother carried on independently and successfully and coped extraordinarily well with the disaster. The oldest daughter struggled through multiple marriages and career changes. The younger daughter continued successfully in more stable relationships and a good career.

In families where there are multiple children, the identification with oppositional parents becomes more complex. The children are forced to take sides because there are clearly two opposing teams. Children who must fight their parents often generalize the battle to fighting the system. Because their most accustomed approach is one of battle, they do not permit themselves to achieve within the educational institution. At some point they feel they must take a determined anti-school position. It is at that point that their underachievement begins.

A basic underlying cause of Underachievement Syndrome is power struggles within the family. The degree and methods of power struggle will heavily influence the achievement patterns of the children, and teachers will have very little control over reversing these patterns without the help and cooperation of parents.

4

Counteridentification: Dependency or Dominance

Parents are rarely certified in child rearing. Their framework for bringing up their children may come partly from books, magazine articles, or occasional parenting courses, but most of all from the evaluations of their own family's parenting during their childhood. By the time you, as parents, first stare with awe at the magnificent new being you have created you have undoubtedly already spent countless hours considering the parenting style you plan to use with that child. As you and your spouse review your own childhood you may conclude that it was basically good and that you would like to provide your children with a similar family environment. However, if either you or your spouse see that childhood as inadequate, you will no doubt consider at length the many ways that you can be a better parent and help your children avoid the traumatic experiences or feelings of inadequacy that you may have experienced in your childhood. As you ponder your own early years and project your emotional experiences into the life of the neonate in your arms, you are initiating the process of counteridentification. It feels to you that you will have the opportunity to "do it right" with this child for whom you feel so much love and commitment; it is almost as if you are part of this child you have created.

The process by which you "identify with" or "see yourself in" your child is known as counteridentification. While it has not been thoroughly explored in research, it appears to make both positive and negative contributions to achievement. When you counteridentify with your children you invest yourself in their activities and empathetically share efforts, successes and failures. The potential for positive contributions for achievement comes mainly from your investment of time and your sharing of skills. In Bloom and Sosniak (1981) study of the biographical characteristics of talented mathematicians, pianists and swimmers, they found that early home learning played an extremely important role in the child's talent development, and that one or both parents had a strong personal interest in that talent field. Bloom pointed out that the parent provided an early and influential model for the child; but it also is reasonable to believe that there existed a high degree of counteridentification by the parent. A familiar example of counteridentification is the vociferous father arguing desperately with the referee at the Little League baseball game as if it were the father who had been unfairly called "out." Another example is the mother who becomes so upset when her daughter loses her first boyfriend that it seems almost as if the mother were experiencing personal rejection.

Since most parents counteridentify with at least one of their children, we know it is not the process itself which causes problems. However, when that counteridentification causes the parents to do so much for the child that the child is not given sufficient independence to develop his/her own initiative or when it leads to the parents giving the children so much power that these children must always be in a controlling position, then counteridentification is likely to cause Underachievement Syndrome. There is a broad range of ways to foster appropriate independence in children. It is only the extremes we should avoid. However, as parents reflect on their own parents' child rearing techniques, they may falsely come to the conclusion that the opposite extreme of the way they were brought up will result in their own children being happier than they were. So in their attempt to be sure to raise their children differently than they were raised they may err in the opposite direction. For example, parents who were brought up with few material possessions frequently are determined to give their children everything. They receive vicarious joy from showering their children with toys and clothes. If parents were brought up with strict discipline they may exaggerate their efforts at being very liberal. If parents believe they received few compliments from their own parents, they may lavish praise upon their children in order to build strong self-confidence. The list goes on, but in each case the counteridentifying parents who cause problems for their child have gone to the opposite extreme rather than using moderation in their child rearing techniques.

Sometimes counteridentifying parents guide their children in a wish fulfilling way which is not opposite from their own childhood. For example, the talented art majors who never fully realized their careers in art may be determined to help their children to develop artistic talents, almost regardless of the children's own interests or abilities. The engineer who wished he could have been a football player, and who fondly remembers his football days in high school, sees his son's talent early and encourages him to train toward being a professional football player. If these parents don't pressure their children too much, and if they don't do too much for them, these counteridentifications may provide positive guidance. However, extreme pressure may again cause children underachievement problems. Understanding the ways in which counteridentification causes problems for children will help parents modify their parenting appropriately.

Dependency

When counteridentification encourages parents to do too much for children, it fosters dependency. Counteridentification causing dependency will be described in three scenarios. The first is called Smothering Mothering.

> Amy is a talented art student. Amy's mother was an art major in college and was also very talented. She did not graduate from college, but decided to get married and have a family instead. Mother provided Amy with plenty of art materials and lots of positive modeling even as a preschooler. She enrolled Amy in a preschool art class at the local art museum and admired her talent as soon as it showed itself, which according to mother was almost as soon as Amy could hold a crayon. Amy is enthusiastic about her art and proud of her talent. Mother, who counteridentifies with Amy, thoroughly enjoys her glory and projects her own unfulfilled wishes for an art career into Amy. Amy begins early to win school art contests, and mother and daughter are delighted. They work together on each contest, with mother enthusiastically contributing ideas and suggestions and Amy excitedly incorporating them into her creations. As Amy wins more and more in competition, she senses pressure to continue to win. The experience of triumph itself creates a strong pressure to continue to excel and to gain recognition even without external pressure from mother. Mother does try not to put pressure on

Amy because she easily empathizes with Amy's feelings of stress. They collaborate on Amy's art work, but eventually it occurs to Amy that she might not be able to win an art contest without mother's help. Now she is distressed and confused. The next contest is important. Amy explains to mother that she must do this painting alone. She is ready to begin, but she can't seem to think of a good idea. She tries for several days, but nothing comes but a bewildering fear that perhaps she can't originate ideas without her mother. Mother tries not to interfere but is also anxious since Amy has not yet started her work. Perhaps, she concludes, she could just give Amy some hints and then Amy could complete the art work on her own. Amy accepts the hints and pretends to herself that the ideas were mostly her own anyway. She works on her painting for a little while, but something about it is wrong. Perhaps mom could help with just a few suggestions. Mother gives those and Amy now feels much more satisfied with her painting and she enters it into the contest. Hurray, another blue ribbon for Amy (and her mother). However, this time Amy really is not sure whether it is she or her mother who has earned the blue ribbon. The succeeding contests find Amy more hesitant and more dependent on her mother for suggestions, less confident in her own ability and even less creative. She has become a talented technician, but not a creative artist. Underachievement? Yes. Mother's counteridentification with Amy has caused her to do too much for her daughter. In the process mother has stolen from Amy her confidence and her creativity, and neither of them quite understand why Amy's early talent has not developed beyond mere mechanical art ability.

The second scenario is called Bothering Fathering.

David was definitely intellectually gifted; his IQ score was around 150. He read before he entered school and understood fractions and decimals by second grade. His handwriting was meticulous and he earned only A grades through fourth grade. In fifth grade there was a change. David wasn't sure exactly what had happened, but he knew that the work was becoming more complex. Sometimes he made a mistake. Sometimes he would get only a B. He decided not to bring B papers home. His mom and dad were so proud of all his A's. He thought maybe if he worked more slowly he could get his work perfect, particularly his math. He seemed to be making too many careless errors. So he slowed down. He slowed down so much that he wasn't finishing his assignments in school and had to bring his papers home as homework. One day he didn't understand his math so he asked his dad to explain it. His dad had a Ph.D. in mathematics. He explained the material to David rather quickly. David thought he understood but he wasn't quite sure and he wanted to be certain to have his homework all right. Dad explained it again. This time dad sat down with David and they worked on math together. Dad was patient and kind. David got all his work done and he and dad shared that nice feeling of companionship. The next night more homework came home and David and his dad spent more time together.

David worked slowly and meticulously. He found it harder and harder to keep up with his classmates, although his grades continued to be mainly A's. Dr. dad spent more and more time helping David with homework. It was difficult to be patient now. He was worried. He certainly didn't want his brilliant son David to bring home poor grades nor could he understand why David worked so slowly and wanted so much help. For David, what had started as the pleasant companionship of his dad had fast become a crutch upon which David had learned to lean and one which he now doubted he could do without. David's Underachievement Syndrome did not show in his perfect report card, but his well-meaning father was increasing David's dependence and lack of confidence nightly.

David was exceptionally bright and it took little effort to reverse his dependent underachieving pattern. However, he is atypical. Concerned parents who do homework for children begin a dependency pattern which may be very difficult to reverse.

Strangely enough the homework dependency pattern often begins in the primary grades on the advice of good intentioned teachers. At an early conference the teacher may caution the parent that their child is falling further behind and needs help with homework. The children soon discover that whatever work they don't complete in class can be taken home where mother or father will give them undivided attention and assistance. More work comes home. Parents spend more time with them. Sometimes father gets upset that mother is spending so much time with their son. Mother and father argue about whether he needs all this help. The children insist that they don't understand the work and will not write a letter or number on their paper without mother's kind supervision. In school these children may be labeled *Learning Disabled* because their achievement falls behind their ability prediction and because they work effectively only in a one-to-one relationship.

> In my evaluation of one such child, his extreme dependency was obvious. Although Brian was a third grader reading a simple self-report inventory, he asked me virtually every word. I explained that I was going for a cup of coffee and, while I was gone would he write down the words he couldn't figure out. Five minutes later I returned to find that Brian had completed the inventory without writing down a single word. He said he had "worked out" all the words.

In the process of reversing Brian's homework dependency, mother needed to sit patiently downstairs and listen to Brian crying for help an entire week before he agreed to do the homework by himself. Now Brian not only does his homework on his own but brings home much less because he finishes most work in class.

The homework location of most homework dependent children is the kitchen, where mother can stir the soup between math problems. Father dependent patterns are more likely to be located in the dining room or den, not too far from the television set.

"Poor Child, Poor Child" is the third and most extreme form of dependency. These are the overprotected children whose mothers wash their hair in eighth grade, help bathe them in sixth grade, or rock them in first grade because mother fears that school makes them tense and anxious. These children get their laundry picked up from the floor, washed and placed neatly in their drawers as if by magic. They come home from school and complain about the hard day they've had, about the kids who are mean to them, the teacher who is unfair, or the principal who picks on them. After the cookie-supported description of problems, they retire to the television set where, they explain to mom, they must relax from their tense day at school. They are too tired to do homework. They can't help with the dishes because they worked too hard all day. They breathe a sigh of relief after a five minute effort at most anything. These dependent children confuse their parents and teachers by their very real symptoms of tension — enuresis, nail biting, hyperactivity, repeated yawning, sighing, wheezing, stomachaches, headaches and tears. Parents and teachers continuously ask themselves if they are pushing these children too hard or expecting too much from them. What actually has happened is that so much has been done for these children that they have not experienced any real effort. All work feels difficult to a child who has never learned to carry through simple tasks independently. These children have not earned the satisfaction that comes from investing energy in an activity. Further, since all work feels difficult, due to lack of experience, they constantly worry that they will fail and not be able to accomplish even simple tasks that their peers seem able to do. Worry about not being able to master a task replaces the activity itself — thus the symptoms of tension.

One favorite example is my own childhood experience of standing before the kitchen sink looking at the stack of dishes that needed to be washed. "I'll never finish," I thought and complained to my mom about the enormous job ahead. She ignored my complaint and simply said, "Do them." I did and the job did seem endless the first time. By the tenth time I wondered why I complained; it was a ten minute job. Suppose my mom had felt sorry for me and done them instead?

The following is a guiding law which will help you identify dependent children who exhibit symptoms of tension:

> Children feel more tension when they are worrying about their work then when they are doing their work.

A corollary to that law is:

> Deprivation and excess frequently exhibit the same symptoms.

Dependent children are aware that they are not keeping up with their peers in the classroom. They also do not have the confidence that they can complete schoolwork without assistance. This causes stress until they actually become absorbed in the task. Symptoms of tension disappear with task absorption. Any adult can identify with similar feelings of tension which feel overwhelming as they face multiple tasks. Adult symptoms also diminish as task engagement begins.

The corollary is even more critical than the law for understanding these dependent children. They continuously seek approval, guidance, help, support and love. It is common for teachers to see these symptoms as indicating lack of love, attention and approval at home and thus ask parents (a) not to put pressure on these children and (b) to be sure to give them more affection and attention. This is exactly the wrong communication to give these parents who have put so little pressure on these children and have lavished them with love and attention.

Our Freudian legacy has mainly given us a message that such dependency symptoms represent deprivation when in fact an excess of attention and assistance produce similar symptoms of insecurity and tension. These dependent children are addicted to attention, affection and assurances of love. This paradox makes it difficult for teachers and parents to determine effective approaches to the identification and treatment of these children.

Fostering Dominance

Counteridentifying adults who feel that their own parents did not give them enough freedom err in the direction of giving their children too much power or control. These parents assume that there is an inherent quality within their children that will somehow light the way for them. If they give their children sufficient freedom, they believe, the children somehow will sense their own direction. The parents see their role as one of facilitating or permitting appropriate independent growth. Further, they consider their parenting to be kind, caring and sensitive. When their children look to them for guidance or direction they are told to make their own choices. Instead of leading, these parents follow their children's direction.

When these children push their parent's discipline limits to determine which behaviors are allowed and which are not, they find no clear limits. Instead, the limits vary with the manipulative ability of the children and with the particular parent or parent mood. They also may be given the message to "be creative" which they interpret as meaning "be different." In the school setting they believe they should not do what teachers require.

These children have become so accustomed to controlling their parents that their habitual way of interacting with peers and other adults is to manipulate them. This extreme habit of control or dominance almost always causes children behavior and learning problems. Sometimes only a fine line separates that kind of problematic control that we call bossiness, compulsive competitiveness and bullying from the more positive forms of dominance known as independence, leadership, political astuteness and creativity. Some case studies will illustrate how counteridentification can cause problematic degrees of dominance.

The least obnoxious, but nevertheless problematic degree of the need for dominance comes from the child whose parent message has been one of creativity. The parents are typically highly creative but view their own childhood home and school environments as not having been supportive of their creativity. These children are admired and rewarded for imaginative ideas, different kinds of thinking, questioning behavior and generally unusual ways of acting. Their parents proudly point out that they "march to the beat of a different drummer." Since creativity is a positive quality that virtually all parents and educators agree should be cultivated, this would not appear to cause any difficulty. But it does, because this child is determined to do only creative work in the classroom and uses "creativity" as an excuse to push all limits. So, for example, "Creative Chris" will write his own stories or plays, will participate in drama and will experiment in science or math. However, he flatly refuses to do any workbook work or drill or rote memory work and insists that it is not reasonable to do such boring or irrelevant busy work.

When first grader Chris puts his hands in a large jar of paste to investigate displacement, his teacher gets upset at the mess and disorder. He argues that the teacher is wrong in becoming upset at his experimenting and his mother urges the teacher to view his exploration as creativity. Fourth grader Chris insists that he sees no reason to learn his mathematics facts since he's already selected his career as a fireman and he only needs to learn the chemistry of extinguishing fires. Sixth grader Chris argues that he is not worried about his F in science, since he received an A in music and that is his career choice. When the question of readiness for other careers is suggested, and the competitiveness of professional performing is pointed out, he argues that he will work hard in music and that if one works hard enough in an area success is sure to come. Tenth grader Chris claims that he no longer measures his success by grades and has now set social skills as his number one priority. Since he intends to excel in social life, he has decided to transfer his creativity to that domain and is indeed being very successful. He wears the most unusual clothes and sponsors the most original parties. High school graduate Chris rejects a scholarship to an excellent college because he is determined to apply his creativity to an experimental drama group or a traveling rock band, each of which will probably survive for six months or less.

The "Creative Chris's" have received competitive messages to be original, unusual, creative and different and to attract attention for this uniqueness. They select an area of expertise which will vary with their age and interest. They use this area of "expertise" as an excuse not to do the routine tasks asked of them, thereby avoiding areas which involve real challenge or the possibility of failure, or chance that they will not receive recognition for their accomplishments. As a matter of fact, even in their area of expertise they may not demonstrate the perseverance, discipline and attention to detail required in a successful creative enterprise. As we see them, Creative Chris's are imaginative, but they use their creativity as a guise for avoiding difficult tasks in exchange for doing preferred activities which bring recognition and attention and which give them a surefire reputation for creativity. They are creative, but not positively productive.

Another degree of excessive need for dominance is exemplified by the people manipulators. These children relate to persons as if the others were marionettes. Their expertise and satisfactions lie in pulling the attached strings. They manipulate parents, teachers and peers and they are especially talented at manipulating key persons against each other to their own advantage. They learn early to blame teachers for their school problems and convince their parents of the accuracy of the blame. They also manipulate the very same teachers against their parents. They are experts at getting one parent on their side against the other parent. They thrive in homes where Ogre and Dummy games are played because their manipulations are encouraged and supported by these rituals. Grandparents become vulnerable to their manipulations when they learn that grandparents may say "yes" when parents say "no." These children also manipulate peers routinely and feel frustrated, angry and unloved when friends will not do as they say. They guarantee disappointment in friendship by defining friendship as a completely controlling relationship. The "victims" of these friendships will say they feel "owned" or like "pawns," a relationship the manipulator views as expected "faithfulness." Friendships are not easy for them since they feel secure only when they completely control their peers.

Manipulative Mark, preschooler, goes into the store with mother and asks her to buy him the very same toy that father had recently denied him. Manipulative Mary, second grader, persuades her dad to let her have a banana split, although mother told her she couldn't have a dessert because she didn't eat her vegetables. Manipulative Mark, junior high school student, persuades his teacher to extend the deadline for a school project because he is working on an extraordinarily large one; but when he finally turns in his half completed project two weeks late, he explains that his mother was too busy working to drive him to the library.

Manipulative Mary in high school refused to accept the temporary "no" her father gave her when she asked to go to the store. He expected her to do her homework first. She managed to get her older sister to drive her to the store and returned to find her father highly displeased with her behavior. He was furiously angry and sent her to her room. She was equally angry and refused to go. He pushed her toward the room, and she pushed him back. In our counseling session she told me he was weak and asked me why I would not expect her to push him. She also told me she got along well with her mom, but poorly with her dad. From mom and dad's perspective, mom said she couldn't control her daughter at all and dad said he could only sometimes. Both parents had said "yes" too often to her when she was little, and neither parent said "no" very often now. When they tried, Mary was an expert at manipulating them to change their decision. Mary was very much in charge of her parents and planned to stay that way. Any sudden effort by her parents to set rules would likely move Mary toward becoming a Rebellious Rebecca.

The third and most extreme form of the too-dominant child is the one in which too much power is not only given but also paired with the teaching of oppositional skill. These parents usually view their own past school experience as unpleasant or inappropriate. Therefore, as they look back to their own childhood they not only feel they were unsuccessful at the school game but also are convinced that the teachers and principals taught them wrong and ran the schools poorly. They are determined that their children will have a better educational experience and are intent on insuring that the teachers don't make the same mistakes with their children as were made with them. The message to fight the system is given early and often, sometimes subtly and sometimes not so subtly; sometimes for appropriate reasons and sometimes quite inappropriately. The power of these children is thus extended even beyond its already excessive level to include what mother or father can accomplish for them in the fury of arguments with the teacher or the counselor or the principal. Indeed, for this oppositional child fighting the system, establishing what you are against, becomes the only basis of building one's self-concept.

Oppositional children find lots of support for their determined nonconformity. Their nonconformity and oppositional attitudes fit well into "ogre" or "dummy" games at home. "Good" mom sets them against tough dad and isolates them from him. "Nice guy" dad protects them against mean disciplining mom. They sense the continued battle and take sides with the parent who most often gives them what they want. Then they enlist that parent's help against their teachers. They compete with teachers and frequently win. They sometimes can even get other children's parents on their side. The final victory is when Mrs. Jones gets fired because she can't control Bobby or the class. These children control peers and parents by bursts of temper or by actually fighting, but more often by debate and argument.

It seems that almost every rule sets off a battle cry and the children's parent or parents ally themselves with them — until adolescence. At this point parents almost certainly become the enemy, unless they say yes to absolutely everything. Parents are now establishment and these oppositional young people, who have become Rebellious Rebeccas and Roberts, join forces with other anti-school youths, the burnouts, weirdos, rebels, anti-war, anti-school, anti-government, anti-poverty, anti-anything groups. Needless to say some anti-groups are worse than others and some obviously have real value. That isn't the point. The point is that the critical component of the group is that they are united by what they oppose, not by what they support. They define themselves by what they are against, what they can beat down, what they are angry about. They may go through years of adolescence and young adulthood bitter at the world because it does not respond to their personal power or the wishes of their group. These oppositional young people struggle through adolescence and into young adulthood. Their identity formation is slowed by the effects of their extreme rebellion, their depressions and their anger. They believe they should have considerable power, yet they feel powerless. If the cause of their opposition disappears, they feel purposeless. Fortunately, many of these young people do build a positive identity out of the ashes of their wars. But the battling is dramatic and takes its toll on them, their schools and their families.

There are many psychologists who believe that rebellion is a necessary style of adolescence. I see such oppositional behavior as mainly nonproductive, and with too dear a price to pay for establishing one's identity. I see it as mainly a response to too much power given to children too early. Note that "if God had meant children to run our homes, she would have created them bigger." (Rimm 1984)

It is possible in reading this chapter that you may interpret my child rearing recommendations as unfeeling, rigid and conforming. They are not intended that way. Children should have help when they need it and parents should be sensitive to their feelings. Children should be encouraged to develop independence and creativity. It is only the extremes that I ask parents to avoid. When children complain, whine or are negative in a way intended to manipulate, or when they request help more frequently than they need it, these are symptomatic of too-dependent relationships. If they are creative mainly for the purpose of being different or if they insist on wielding power without respect for the rights of other persons, then they are too domineering. These extremes will result in Underachievement Syndrome. However, underachievement should be viewed only as a main symptom. Although in this book the emphasis is mainly upon underachievement, they will also have other family and relationship problems. The Underachievement Syndrome must be cured and their dependency or their extreme dominance must also be modified to help them live more satisfying and productive lives.

Identification and counteridentification provide the means by which children learn to relate to their personal environments. If children learn to relate in a mode that causes them too much dependence, they will lack a sense of control. They believe that they cannot achieve, and they will not have the basis for building self-confidence. On the other hand, if they learn to expect to dominate those with whom they relate they will only function where they excel or are in power. Highly competitive children may vacillate between these two extremes of power and tend to feel like either winners or losers. Achievers must learn persistence. Achievers must be problem solvers. Achieving permits the joy of winning and the agony of losing, but requires that the individual be able to emerge from those losses. All children fail at one time or another. It is the way in which they survive the failure experiences that distinguish achievers from underachievers.

The world of sports mirrors how one plays the game. The good athletes stay in and play their best even when that game is lost. They discipline themselves. They practice with grueling regularity the necessary skills for their sport. Education, life accomplishments, creative contributions in the arts, sciences, business ansd government are hard ball games. The competition is keen and there is no place for quitters. Underachievers are quitters. They have given up in the competition or want to play by their own rules, which are much less stringent. Our society is competitive and we must teach our children how to compete. It is the way in which children play the game that makes them into achievers.

5

School Causes of Underachievement Syndrome

Underachievement Syndrome is usually initiated at home. However, schools and teachers can and do make a dramatic difference. Some classroom environments maintain and actually exacerbate Underachievement Syndrome, while other classrooms help to cure it. Some school circumstances actually can become the main cause of the Syndrome. There are a wide range of appropriate teaching styles for guiding children. While teachers may follow many philosophies of education, there are some environments that are extremely problematic for underachieving children. Avoiding the extremes and maintaining a firm positive classroom atmosphere are productive guidelines for all teaching. Some specific examples of undesirable, harmful teaching styles, can provide insights to both teachers and parents.

Structure

Teachers Loose Louise and Rigid Robert provide opposite but equally problematic learning environments in their classrooms. The loosely organized classroom that provides no structure causes underachievers, who already lack organizational skills to flounder. They do not discipline themselves and they habitually push limits. In loosely structured classrooms, they get out of their seats continuously, wander aimlessly, don't complete tasks and get themselves into trouble. Hyperactive children especially, with their unfocused high energy, accomplish little in an unstructured setting. They are easily distracted by the movement and noise level of the class. Teachers often assume that these children must be given freedom to move around. Actually, hyperactive children should know that they are expected to sit firmly in their seats until they have completed their assignments. Also, children who are dependent on one-to-one attention will be at the teacher's desk repeatedly to get help or to ask questions if there are not clear directives in the classroom. My observation of one high energy child in a loosely structured first grade found him continuously out of his seat. The longest time he stayed on task was 70 seconds. A dependent child observed in a third grade classroom went for teacher or peer help 22 times in 30 minutes. In such classrooms, teachers constantly interrupt reading groups to "shush" children working at their desks and there is a general sense of too much sound and movement. These teachers tend to scold frequently, although the repeated reprimand serves to actually increase the noise level. The teacher has little control in such a classroom.

Dominant children become more powerful and successfully challenge loosely organized teachers. "You can't make me do this work, my father's on the school board" or "I can't do my work because the class is too noisy. Why don't you get it quieter?" Obviously this last young man is a major contributor to the tumult. Even children who have no history of previous discipline problems will "act out" in this loosely organized classroom and may well get their start as behavior problems.

Rigid Robert is an equally problematic teacher. The high energy child may actually function better in this class provided Rigid Robert does not overuse punishment. If this child is frequently reprimanded the reprimands may become negative attention, and for this attention-dependent child any attention is better than none and so he will get into further trouble. Dominant creative or oppositional children will struggle for power with a rigid teacher. These children see rigid control as a "call to battle" and they will be determined to win. The struggle for power will be vigorous and the children will rarely defer. Dominant students will correct teachers in front of the class whenever possible. They will argue with them about rules, will not hand in assignments they claim are irrelevant, will question them unnecessarily and will manipulate power struggles between teachers, parents and principals. The teachers' final control of the children comes with grades. However, these children usually prefer to fail rather than acknowledge themselves as losers to rigid teachers. In their battles with such teachers, students may view conforming as causing a loss of face and therefore will continue to refuse to do assigned lessons regardless of threats or grades. In the struggle for power between Rigid Roberts and dominant children with Underachievement Syndrome, neither emerge victorious.

Maryanne, a seventh grader with an IQ score in the gifted range, and especially strong math ability, explained about her F in math to me. She said she understood the concepts and actually did good work on her tests. Her teacher insisted on some very specific formats for writing her name, date and aligning the math problems. He reduced the grade when students did not follow directions. Maryanne pointed out how unfair the directions were and proceeded to explain how she tended to always "forget" one or more directions. The result was that her grade was always reduced. In addition, she saw no reason to do all the busywork required so she only handed in the assignments that were reasonable and refused to do the easy ones when she understood the work. As a matter of fact, she did have very good mastery of the subject and it was a more exciting challenge to see if she could "out-power" the teacher. She was determined not to conform to his rigid standards. In Maryanne's situation, her math scores declined only for a year. A much more flexible teacher in the following year inspired Maryanne back to her former achieving status.

Competition

Underachievers do not handle competition well. They are poor losers. They get angry and quit or they pout, whine, find excuses and give up. They tend to see things in a competitive framework but fear failure because they want so desperately to win. A highly competitive classroom documents their losses. The more frequently they see themselves as losers, the less they try. Even the child who has begun to reverse Underachievement Syndrome will be threatened by excessive competition. Teacher Competitive Catherine is encouraged to maintain a high level of competition in her classroom because of the positive feedback she receives from achieving children. These children thrive and perform at their best with competitive challenge. Underachievers usually are not fully aware of the effect of competition on their performance — but they are likely to dislike the class and the students who always surpass them.

Of course, there should be some competition in the classroom. Classroom contests and games which vary from subject to subject help all children to deal with winning and losing. Practices which should *absolutely* be avoided are the open announcement of individual grades, public criticism of individual children's poor work, announcements of surprise when a child performs well who usually doesn't, the invidious comparison of class papers, and children's criticism of each other's work in the early grades before they are able to handle such criticism. An example of such a situation is described in this observation of Bonnie.

> Despite her IQ in the very superior range, five year old Bonnie's underachievement was encouraged very early by a too competitive kindergarten classroom environment. Bonnie had been a spontaneous and enthusiastic child in her nursery school class, where her teacher had described her as very bright and happily adjusted. In kindergarten she was referred to the psychologist because "she did not like to go to school." Her kindergarten teacher described her school performance as poor. She rarely completed her work, did not seem happy and tended not to participate in class activities. Classroom observation revealed the competitive environment that gave Bonnie her sense of failure and caused her to slow her class pace.

> The children sat on the floor around the chalkboard for their letter-printing lesson. The teacher announced the letter to be printed and some children enthusiastically raised their hands. After the selected child printed the letter on the chalkboard, the children were asked if it were printed well. In chorus, they exclaimed an enthusiastic "yes' if it were and a punishing "no" if it were poorly executed. The teacher would agree or disagree with the children, pointing out the good qualities or the problems related to the printing of the letter. When Bonnie, with her hand barely raised, was selected to perform, the inadequate execution of her letter brought the "no's" that she has come to expect. Furthermore, the in seat handwriting exercise that followed was carefully monitored by open teacher evaluation of each child's performance. It was not surprising to observe Bonnie's very slow performance and her unsuccessful efforts at the perfection which she could not achieve.

> In this highly competitive kindergarten class, Bonnie already was being openly taught that she could not succeed in a classroom environment. Fortunately, in first grade Bonnie was placed with a supportive teacher who fostered a less competitive environment and Bonnie developed confidence and enthusiasm again. The Underachievement Syndrome was reversed by a "good year" (Davis and Rimm, 1985).

Competition with themselves in the sense of individually striving to improve will encourage underachievers to deal with losses in a less threatening way. Recording their own progress and improvement will help children view themselves as competent. Also, classroom contests with other classes will assist them in experiencing winning and losing. This kind of group-level competition helps to foster group solidarity and gives all children reason to want to contribute. Group competition should be directed carefully by the teacher and structured to include all students.

Underachievers' responses to large junior high or middle schools illustrate clearly these students' adverse reactions to competition. Frequently, children who were performing well in elementary school begin Underachievement Syndrome in the larger school setting. When they compare their own performance to that of so many other students, they evaluate themselves as incompetent. They stop making an effort. There are not enough success roles and too many failure roles in this large school environment.

Since our society is highly competitive, it is important for underachievers to learn to function in competition. In the highly competitive classroom or school the underachiever simply does not have a fair chance. In order to learn the competitive process, children should have opportunities to deal with both wins and losses, not just losses. Classroom competition thus should be structured to give all children some of both experiences. Continuous winning or losing is not instructive. It is fun for the winners but disastrous for the persistent losers. Open discussions of feelings about winning and losing will help children understand and deal with their emotional and behavioral responses to defeat. Learning to function in competition is central to achievement. Highly competitive classrooms do *not* accomplish this task well because they document too much failure and not enough success.

Labeling

When a child is achieving poorly in school, teachers and parents alike frequently request help. The child obviously has a need for something different. That "something different" may come in the form of special classes or special assistance from a trained professional. Of course, the extra help costs money. Federal and State governments are very helpful in providing such resources, but in order to maintain accountability, funding is attached to certain definitional conditions. In the process of definition, a name or label for the educational need must be used. These labels vary considerably and are almost always abbreviated with initials. For example, there is learning disabled (LD), emotionally disturbed (ED) and behavioral disabled (BD). The child must be categorized and labeled in order to receive the necessary funding, but in that process there are some real risks. The labels affect self-expectations as well as teacher expectations and in some cases cause peer rejection which causes further problems.

> Ronny had been labeled BD and LD and was placed in a special class for most of his years in elementary school. He hated the label and wanted desperately to be just like other students. He lost his temper frequently in school, did not carry through on assignments and interacted poorly with peers. Each year was a little worse than the previous one, although teachers and parents made continued efforts to meet his exceptional needs. In an effort to reduce the stigma and help him to adjust, he was mainstreamed into his regular class for 85% of the day. Assignments were shortened to help him cope with the material, and he was encouraged to complete his homework in order to stay in regular classes. Although improvement was not entirely consistent and smooth, within one year he was relating well with peers, feeling more confident and completing much more schoolwork. Reading and math skills improved measurably. Ronny continued to get minimal learning disability help, but he was able to function far better in the regular classroom when the labels and the special classes were removed.

Teacher expectations related to labeling are also important. Rosenthal and Jacobsen's (1968) book, *Pygmalion in the Classroom,* as well as the research inspired by that book, found strong support for the effect of teacher expectations on actual teacher behavior directed toward a child. An LD label, which influences teacher expectations, may have a dramatic effect on the child's achievement and self-concept. Estimates vary on the degree of the teacher expectancy effect but 15% decrement in grades has been considered an average impact. Obviously, if 15% is average then we know that in some cases teacher expectations may have a much greater impact than that. Negative labeling of any kind — minority stereotypes, educational categories or grade expectations — may cause problems. Here are some case examples. The first is related to minority expectations.

Carla, a minority student, entered college with reasonable expectations of success. Although she had been a poor student in elementary school, hard work in senior high school showed her that she could do well. Her high school grades were very good and she felt excited about the challenge of college. Based on an English entrance examination, she was placed in a small remedial English class. Most students in the class were on probation and the English teacher made a similar assumption about Carla. When Carla came to me for help, it was because she worried that perhaps she did not have the ability she had only recently come to believe she had. It was the expectations communicated to her in the English class that threatened her precariously held positive assumptions about her own abilities. Fortunately, another teacher had confidence in Carla's ability and convinced her that she was indeed a very capable student, and that it would only take a small compensatory effort to learn some skills she had missed earlier in her education.

It was her minority status together with some very real educational gaps that set the stereotype for negative expectations of Carla. After her confidence was restored, Carla easily learned the necessary English skills and graduated from college as a very successful student (Davis and Rimm, 1985).

The second case is related to the label LD (learning disabled):

Jeff's teachers sat around the conference table puzzling about this eighth grade boy. He had been labeled learning disabled, yet no one was quite sure about him. His WISC-R IQ score was 121 but there was considerable scatter among his separate scores — some were very high, others were below average. Excerpts from a teacher discussion sounded like this:

"Do you suppose I should grade him on a pass/fail criterion since he's learning disabled?" "I'd like to drop him out of band. He's disruptive and prevents other students from learning." 'He's doing a fine job in math. I don't see any real problem." "I know he tested as a poor reader, but today he got a perfect score on a Reading Comprehension test. I thought he might have cheated so I asked him to take the test again." "My concern in social studies is that he doesn't get his homework in. He tells me unusual stories of why he hasn't done it and I don't know whether to believe him or not. He seems sincere and his excuses are imaginative, but he doesn't perform."

His grades are poor. His homework is sporadic. We don't know if he's bright or slow and we're not even sure when he's telling the truth. What do we do with Jeff? He's been labeled LD, a behavior problem, a manipulative child, a lazy careless student and a storyteller. He doesn't fit into this school program (Rimm 1984).

The third case is related to a situation which probably happens most frequently, a teacher determined to convince a parent that her child is not gifted.

Julie's IQ score was 138. Her mother did not know the score at the time of this incident, nor did her teacher. She was a fourth grade student who had been a very successful mostly A student through grade 3. She was, however, very quiet in class and rarely volunteered during discussion. Her mother thought Julie might benefit from more advanced reading material, and so early that year she met with the teacher to advance her suggestion. The teacher seemed somewhat defensive and pointed out that she believed Julie was sufficiently challenged and that her mother was putting pressure on her. The remainder of the year was somewhat of a disaster for Julie. Not only did her grades go to B's and C's to prove her teacher's point, but the teacher confronted Julie with her own conclusion, that she wasn't really as smart as her mother thought. Julie worked very hard that year but she really never found a solution to improving her grades. By the end of the year both Julie and her mother felt frustrated and somewhat frightened. Julie's mother brought her to me for testing and in an apologetic and tense frame of mind, asked if I could at least test Julie to determine what could be expected of her in terms of schoolwork. The IQ scores were consistently high for all subtests of the Wechsler Intelligence Scale for Children-Revised. Her individual achievement tests supported the findings that her skill levels were far beyond grade level. She was quiet and lacking in self-confidence by the time I met with her and I feel sure her achievement would have continued to decline in later years had her mother not challenged the teacher's limiting label.

This last type case has reoccurred with slight variations many times and is particularly frequent among teachers who are hostile toward gifted educational programs.

Any label that unrealistically narrows prospects for performance by a child may be damaging. Peer pressures and lowered parent and teacher expectancy may have a permanent debilitating effect on children's school performance. Although there are some circumstances where labels are absolutely necessary to provide educational support, they should be assigned extremely carefully with consideration to all potential negative impacts.

Negative Attention

As previously noted, children who underachieve often are attention addicted. Their early childhood home pattern has been one of excessive attention and either dependent or domineering manipulations. They are accustomed to relating to people in attention getting ways. They thrive in a one-to-one learning situation but adjust poorly in a classroom environment where they feel unnoticed. They search out ways to gain attention. If positive ways come easily they will achieve, but many of these children find it easier to gain "negative attention."

Teachers Solicitous Sally and Negative Nellie give negative attention freely and thus help maintain underachieving behavior. Solicitous Sally is the trickier of the two to identify because she is typically a very good and devoted teacher. She is, however, so sensitive to children's expressions of feelings that she overreacts to their hurts and calls for help. She does this in a caring way without ever realizing that she is reinforcing an underachieving pattern for the child. There are two main ways she reinforces their behavior, by helping them too much and by providing too much sympathy.

> Diana, a third grader of average ability, was in the lowest reading group in her class. There was no identified learning disability nor any distinguishable reason why she should be reading 1-1/2 years below grade level. She was a quiet shy child and had learned to depend on her mother's help for daily schoolwork. After explaining to her mother how to encourage her independence at home, I took the opportunity to observe her in school. In the classroom she was also quiet and she never raised her hand to volunteer questions or answers. I asked her teacher if she requested more help than most children to which her teacher responded in the negative. She further explained that after giving the class directions on an assignment, she would always go to Diana's desk where Diana needed special help and Diana learned to make the same assumption. By providing daily attention to Diana's helplessness, both mother and teacher inadvertently delivered a message of nonconfidence. Both were solicitous and kind, but neither realized the self-fulfilling prophecy they were communicating. Changed expectations, the encouragement of independence and some accelerated tutoring quickly brought Diana's work grade level where it has remained for the last five years, and she is a much more confident and independent child.

The second trap that Solicitous Sally may fall into is misinterpreting a child's symptom of pressure.

> First grade Barby showed tears in her eyes if she didn't seem to understand directions immediately. Also, she wouldn't finish her work and broke out crying if the teacher made corrections on her paper. Solicitous Sally did not want to put stress on Barby and so she tried most delicately to avoid giving her too much work or correcting her errors. However, regardless of what Sally tried, Barby seemed stressed and fell further

behind her classmates. In the first teacher conference Sally explained to Barby's parents that Barby just didn't seem mature enough to handle first grade work or else it was too difficult for her. My test scores for Barby found her to have high average ability, so her ability did not explain her apparent stress. Further discussion with her parents found her to be a long awaited child and the only child for the first five years of her life. Barby was adored and adorned. Her wishes were always catered to and her cries for help immediately brough a responsive parent. If tasks were difficult for her at home, her parents completed them for her. They dashed to her aid when they noted the least indication of stress. She expected that same kind of response at school. Her parents were quick to change their approach after my explanation and they saw an almost immediate change in Barby.

Solicitous Sally, however, was more difficult to convince because she was truly afraid of hurting the feelings of so sensitive a child. It took about three months of teacher perseverance, with several of my supportive phone calls, before she acknowledged with relief that she could indeed see the difference. She previously had been absolutely convinced that the child was being put under too much pressure at home — when exactly the opposite was the case. Actually, Barby was so unaccustomed to effort that almost any work would have caused her stress. The corollary to the formerly stated Rimm's Law applies here: Symptoms of tension were indications of insufficient inexperience with pressure rather than too much of it.

Another example of inappropriate sympathy is the case of second grader Scott:

In this family there had been family problems and a recent divorce. Initially, Solicitous Sally's concern about the child's stress was appropriate. She explained to Scott that if he needed to talk about some problems she would be glad to help him. Each morning started with a quiet distress story and tears and individual attention before school started. It took several class hours before Scott could put aside his problems and could get on with his schoolwork. Solicitous Sally felt sorry for Scott for a long time before my intervention. A sticker for each happy morning start brought Scott back to his being a bubbly, happy child.

Of course, divorce is always a traumatic event for children and they should have the opportunity to talk about their feelings. However, it is important that they not learn to use their sad feelings in an attention seeking way. Overreactions by teachers cause children to sense that they are expected to feel sad and think sad and act sad and so they actually do. As the behavior continues they get further and further behind in their studies and they feel less and less adequate academically. They worry more and the school anxiety becomes confounded with their family concerns and symptoms of stress become the basis for their attention from adults. They are sad frequently and cry easily. Their manipulations are not intentional but spontaneous. A kind teacher should give a message of brief sympathy but should also communicate confidence that the child is able to handle difficult problems. That permits children to develop the strength that builds confidence and will eventually help them surmount obstacles and deal with other life problems.

In summary, Solicitous Sallys are almost always wonderful and kind people. Their sensitivity and empathy are positive if not carried to an extreme. It is always difficult to determine the fine line between caring and caring too much, but the message that we must all go on with our lives despite problems is critical for achievement and for living fulfilling lives.

Most of Negative Nellie's problems are more obvious and you may have heard or read about them in parenting or psychology classes. However, they continue to require emphasis because negativism remains a problem in many classrooms and is related to underachievement, behavior problems and poor social relationships. Negativism is difficult for teachers to avoid and teachers may not be aware of the frequency with which negative attention causes general classroom problems.

The most obvious form of negative attention is continued and repeated reminders by the teacher to "quiet down" or "pay attention." Generally, the frequency and volume of the reminders increase in a direct relationship to the increasing noisiness of the children. It is tempting to believe that the reminders actually reinforce the poor behavior. Although I have observed many classrooms with this kind of chaos, they mainly exist where there are new or substitute teachers who have not yet learned to control the general class atmosphere. Therefore, this situation is not my major concern in explaining how negative attention affects underachievement. Other more specific kinds of problems will be described below.

When a child misbehaves, teachers typically reprimand the child aloud in front of the class. It simply is more difficult to communicate quiet reprimands or punishment contingencies. Yet both research and practical experience indicate that public reprimands increase the negative behaviors. While both are forms of attention to the negative behavior the peer attention from public reprimands motivates the child to increase his naughty behavior. In elementary school an additional problem plagues the child who is frequently reprimanded by the teacher. He becomes the "naughty boy" of the class and the other children don't want to be friends with him. This, of course, gives him another reason to misbehave as a means of drawing attention. When the child and the teacher are alerted to the problem of how the behavior is affecting friendships, and the teacher arranges a quiet signal with the child, behavior and peer relations improve. In a real sense the negative attention has been converted to positive attention and teacher and child are now on the same team. Perhaps it is not surprising that behavior improves.

If you have difficulty relating to the problem of the "bad boy" in the classroom, think back to your own elementary school days. In my school it was Blair. He was in my class for five years. He licked his lips, chewed his pencils, didn't stay in his seat and wouldn't get his work done. His desk was placed near the teacher's or in the front of the room and he had a regular route between the classroom and the principal's office. Nobody liked Blair. We wouldn't have dared to be friends with him. Blair was bad!

The child who does not complete his work during the school day is almost always reinforced for not doing so by negative attention. Several specific case examples illustrate some cautions.

Ricky almost never completed his math before recess. The class penalty for noncompletion was to remain in the classroom during recess. This was an effective contingency for the other children and rarely did anyone besides Ricky have to stay. There were two reasons this punishment was ineffective for Ricky. First, Ricky enjoyed the personal teacher help and attention he received while the other children were outside. Second, Ricky was often teased by the other children during recess anyway. Thus for Ricky staying in class during recess was a strongly reinforcing shelter. He continued to not complete his math until the reinforcements were changed.

Scott, a gifted fourth grader, never finished his work in school either. He explained his noncompletion this way. "If I finish my work too fast my teacher will criticize and tell me I've done a bad job. If I work slowly she only comes around and reminds me to get to work." In Scott's case both were negative attentions but he selected the behavior that was easiest and caused him the least stress.

Boredom

The single word regarding school that I hear most frequently from underachievers is "boring." Although we all know what boring is supposed to mean, I have learned to reinterpret the word depending on its use by each particular child. For some children it means the work is too hard; for others it means it is too easy. It may mean "I'm afraid to compete" or "the teacher should do it my way" or "I have a power struggle with the teacher" or "I don't like this subject" or "I'd rather be socializing." For only a minority does it mean that the work is actually uninteresting.

Of course, there are some Boring Barbara and Boring Bob teachers. There are, hopefully, only a small percentage of teachers who do not take the initiative to make their classroom activities varied and stimulating. These teachers have an adverse effect on all students, achievers and underachievers. However, in classes where the word "boring" is used as an underachievement defense mechanism, teachers are obviously not at fault. These student descriptions of classes as "boring" would continue regardless of the subject matter, content or method. We will examine the variations of "boring" in order to provide some insight on causes of Underachievement Syndrome.

The most frequent kind of boring, referring to easy or difficult material, does cause underachievers a genuine problem and may be a major origin of the underachievement. Material which is too difficult is an obvious reason for underachievement. If children are expected to learn content for which they are not ready they may feel justifiably defeated and give up. This happens most frequently for a child who has uneven abilities, who finds some subjects relatively easy while others are truly difficult. The teacher assumes that the child is able to handle all tasks well since he or she gives the impression of being very capable. Unfortunately, children who feel defeated in one skill area easily generalize that underachieving style to other subjects where they are quite capable.

Children whose families move and thus must change schools can easily find themselves continuously behind their peers because of school differences. Each new school may be only a little ahead in basic skills compared to former schools, but that sense of incompetence that comes with always finding their schoolwork too difficult may create a sense of defeat that initiates Underachievement Syndrome.

Finding schoolwork too easy is another dilemma. It is a frequent cause of Underachievement Syndrome for the gifted. Some bright children know virtually all the first grade material before they ever enter that grade, and they are legitimately and consistently bored during their entire first years of school. Others may appreciate the positive attention that comes from perfect work and may thoroughly enjoy their early and easy school years. Unfortunately, they learn that schoolwork is effortless. In fourth grade or eighth grade or college when the curriculum becomes challenging for the first time they find they have not learned to study or persevere. Of course, they have never experienced getting less than A grades either. They may label school as boring because of that new sense of effort they must now make or the feelings of failure that come with B's and C's. The source of their problem dates back to the lack of challenge earlier in their school life. Some interesting cases of gifted children can serve as examples.

Greg, a bright five year old, entered kindergarten reading at approximately a third grade level. His mother was hesitant to mention his reading ability to the teacher since she did not wish to be viewed as an interfering parent. At first quarter conference time the main topic was Greg's misbehavior. The parents were so disturbed by those reports that they again postponed discussing his reading skill. Greg continued as a behavior problem during the entire year, and by spring the teacher was ready to recommend retention. In addition to his problem behavior Greg had failed his reading readiness test! It was at the last conference that the shocked parents finally announced to his teacher that Greg had been reading all year. Greg explained that he felt it necessary to circle two responses in test items where a letter or shape looked exactly like the inverted form of the original letter. Of course that misinterpretation had caused the failing test grade. A new evaluation of his reading skill found him to have progressed to a fifth grade reading level. Perhaps it is not surprising that bored Greg was a behavior problem. Unfortunately, although accomodations were made for his reading skill, his behavior problems continued and eventually did lead to Underachievement Syndrome. Certainly we can fault the teacher for not identifying the skill early, but parents too have a responsibility for communication. In Greg's case his reading ability was so good that no reasonable teacher would have interpreted such information as parent interference.

Uneven or inconsistent acceleration may cause gifted children a similar problem. For example, Jean was accelerated one year in math by working independently. As a matter of fact she was so bright she completed sixth grade math in six weeks. However, when she moved to another school district there was no provision for acceleration and so she repeated sixth grade math. Eric, a first grader, was allowed to read with a second grade class since that was his appropriate level. When he moved to another district for the following year, that school would not permit him to work at two different grade levels and so he had to read the second grade material again.

In these two cases "boring" was a result of actual repetition of material by children who had already demonstrated they needed less time than others because of district policies and inflexibility.

In some cases, the forced repetition happens within the same district and even within the same school. It will occur if one teacher views acceleration as appropriate and a second teacher refuses to make exceptions. It may also happen when a school changes from a policy of individualized reading across grades to a within grade reading approach. The reasonable outrage of these children and their parents puts both in an oppositional relationship to the school. This opposition will easily be generalized to other subjects and grades. "Boring" is typically the label that these children decide to use to describe most everything in school. They are certainly at least partially justified.

Jeff, a very bright fifth grader who was having a major problem with math, described his underachievement trap in this way. He said that he would listen as the teacher began his explanation of the material, but as the teacher continued to explain he felt bored because he already understood and didn't really need to listen anymore. His mind wandered and he would think about other things. Finally, the teacher would give the assignment and Jeff would begin his work. Later he would get to a part he didn't quite understand. Because he hadn't listened, he didn't know whether the teacher had explained this material or not and he was afraid to ask the teacher for help. Jeff's options weren't good: He could "bluff" his work, not do it at all, do it with many mistakes, or admit he wasn't listening. He alternated among the first three but wouldn't dare admit he needed help. Although he recognized his own trap, he got further and further behind in math. The skills gaps were preventing his understanding the material and because he needed to "save face" he didn't dare explain the problem to his teacher. Mainly he avoided the confrontation by not completing his assignments and continuing to maintain that math was easy and boring.

Children must learn early that there is a relationship between their effort and the outcome. That creates the sense of internal control that differentiates achievers from underachievers. If their schoolwork is too hard, their efforts do not lead to successful outcomes but only to failures. If their work is too easy, they learn that it takes very little effort to succeed. Either is inappropriate and provides a pattern which fosters underachievement. Teachers should be alert to the skill levels of their students in order to provide the required help or the necessary challenge. There is no guarantee that we can prevent children from describing school as "boring," but at least teachers can insure an appropriate match between effort and outcome.

Individualization Versus Conformity

Classroom environmental causes of Underachievement Syndrome include situations where structure is too rigid or loose, there is too much competition, students are labeled, there is excessive negative attention, and there is boredom related to a mismatch between learning skills and curriculum. All of these problem environments can be reduced to one basic debate: individualization versus conformity. These are value laden words since educators usually interpret individuality as positive and conformity as negative.

The important conclusion of my work with Underachievement Syndrome is that either extreme is problematic. It is obviously wrong to expect extreme conformity since it would obliterate creativity and independence. However, an extreme emphasis on individualization is irresponsible teaching. It makes the assumption that children have innate wisdom which they can depend on to guide them through their education. Certainly they have differing abilities and interests, but they must be guided in order to conform to reasonable educational standards. It is unrealistic to give children the message that education can be tailored to their learning style or their preference for small group or one-to-one teaching. Public education cannot and should not assume that it must be built to serve each child's demands whether the children are gifted, creative or learning disabled. We must enable children to adjust to learning styles and group sizes that are realistic. This is not a call to conformity but a message of moderation. If students are given too much power to dictate their own education, they flounder and fall and have a misconception of their own importance in society. Rigidity is not the solution but firm guidance with reasonable flexibility — the middle range between individualization and conformity — should serve all students well, both achievers and underachievers.

PART II

CURES

6

Parenting Toward Achievement

Parenting toward achievement and good parenting are two ways of describing the same process. School achievement, life accomplishment, and the resulting self-confidence and self-sufficiency are outcomes that all parents wish for their children. There also are many specific agendas that parents value. However, because the focus of this book is school achievement and preventing Underachievement Syndrome, this chapter will provide some general parenting guidelines emphasizing those goals.

Modeling Achievement

The most critical component of parenting toward achievement is acting as appropriate models. Not only should you be achieving persons, but you must share with your children a realistic and positive view of achievement. They must see the components of achievement and especially the ways in which efforts and outcomes are related. They must understand that you sometimes fail, but that you survive that failure to succeed again. They must see both your creativity and your conformity. They must feel your discouragement and your elation. They must view the intrinsic and extrinsic rewards that come with effort. There should be some balance of the positive and negative in their view of you as models. If you are an achiever, that balance probably exists, but sometimes parents unintentionally show a biased and negative perspective to their children.

Parents should also design an "achiever image" of their spouses. There are some common pitfalls for both women and men to beware of. Mothers should avoid continuous complaints about their husband's frequent work. They typically associate these concerns with depriving the children of dad's parenting. They also should not describe his career as a bad one nor blame his occasional loss of temper as related to stress on the job. Mother must be sure to avoid attributing family problems to their husband's boss or administrator or blaming his work for their marriage or economic problems. Instead, mother should interpret to her children the financial and life satisfaction benefits of her husband's hard work. Although she may be honest about the parts of his career that she does not value, she must also emphasize the positive components of that career and explain why dad chose it.

In some circumstances it may seem either extremely difficult or else very trivial to build up father's career. However, parents need to see the parallels between their spouse's achievement at work and their children's achievement orientation in school. The mother who engages in continual tirades about her husband's awful career must be prepared to hear similar attitudes about school from her children. By adolescence she is likely to find the comments quite intolerable. They sound like this:

> I don't see why I have to do all this schoolwork; I need time for fun.

> I'm not anything like my dad and I'd never choose a career like his.

> I don't know what I want to do or be; something where I don't have to work all the time.

> The poor grades are not my fault; that teacher is a terrible grader; he expects too much.

For every message mother has given about her spouse there will be a similar communication delivered by her children about school, because school is the child's work place. There may be times in your married life where it is indeed impossible to avoid negativism and pessimism. However, if mothers can learn to provide a more positive and balanced view of their husband's career, they can certainly expect more positive attitudes about school achievement in their children.

Fathers share the same kind of responsibility for describing their wife's work, whether it is a career outside the home or homemaking. However, the pitfalls are for the most part somewhat different. The common problem that fathers have is that they tend to devalue their wife's contributions. Comments like "Didn't you do anything today?" or "All you ever do is run around and shop" (as the family sits down to a delicious home-cooked dinner in their mother-cleaned home in their mother-laundered clothes) put the unsalaried homemaker into a category of nonaccomplishment. Volunteer activities, which take effort, creativity and responsibility and may make important contributions to the community or to the children, are often described by father as aimless social activities. If mother decides to return for further education, fathers may describe that education as"busy work"or point out that mother's schooling is interferring with the family meals and activities. This puts mother's education in a nonessential, nonvalued perspective. If mother begins a career later in life, because she has waited for the children to grow up, she may have a salary disadvantage related to her late start, her lesser training and experience, her geographic limitations, or to the generally lower salaries paid to women. Some fathers minimize the financial contribution she makes as well as the lesser prestige of her job.

The main danger of father's commentary is in the devaluing or depowering of his wife. Frequently his wife is given the primary responsibility for disciplining the children, communicating with schools and providing educational guidance to her children. Since she has been depowered by her spouse she is indeed rendered powerless to guide and discipline the children. Although father has never directly told his children not to obey their mother, and he actually may be quite explicit about that obedience, he has in fact modeled disrespect without being aware of the seriousness of his communication. Not only has he devalued his wife but he has also underrated all that she represents: caring for children empathically and lovingly, concern with education and learning, and the tremendous initiative it takes to combine education or work with homemaking. His children will view their mother, at least partially, through his description and valuing of her accomplishments. Boys will ignore and put down this mother and will underachieve. Girls will compete and argue with her and will also underachieve. That father needs to explicitly describe his respect for his wife's efforts, contributions, satisfactions and commitments to the community and to education if he expects his children to achieve in school and to respect their mother.

Modeling achievement and describing it in your spouse make a critical difference in your children's achievement motivation. If it sounds idealistic or impossible, listen to what your children are saying about school. You will know that they are watching you, and listening to you and have received your messages about your work and your spouse's work. If you expect them to change their efforts and attitudes, you will want to change your modeling.

Power and Control

You are in charge of your children. Children feel secure following their parent's leadership provided they have become accustomed to that mode. Although they are likely to sporadically "push limits" to determine the extent of their freedom, they will respect the word "no" when it is given firmly and fairly. Children who have not learned to accept limitations in childhood will certainly not accept them in adolescence. Visualize the letter "V" as a model for guiding your children. When they are tiny they begin at the bottom of the V with limited freedom and narrow structure. As they mature and are able to handle more freedom responsibly, the limiting walls of the "V" spread out giving them continually more freedom while still maintaining definite limits. During adolescence, as they move to the top of the "V" they become capable of considerable independent decision making and judgment, but should continue to recognize that there are adult prerogatives in guiding them. They are thus readied for moving out of the "V" into complete independence and personal decision making.

Now reverse that "V" so that it looks like this "Λ." Children brought up at the base of this figure are given much freedom and wide limits. They become accustomed to independent decision making before they are able to handle this freedom responsibly. As they move toward adolescence parents become concerned that their children may misuse this freedom and they worry about the dangers that arise in school and community. Cigarettes, alcohol, drugs and promiscuous sex are perceived as threats from which their children must be protected. So they begin to set limits. Freedoms are now taken away. Adolescents who had much control as children now feel over controlled by parents and their statements echo their feelings of restriction. "My parents are controlling me," they complain. They push all limits and oppose and rebel. Worried parents punish and narrow the limits further, resulting in even more rebellion. Ugly adolescence, with accompanying underachievement, makes the happy home into an armed camp. Once freedom is given it is not easily taken away. The "V" shaped guidance is much smoother and more comfortable for adolescents and parents alike.

Empowering children with adult decision-making provides power without wisdom. It leads to formidable and continuing conflicts between children and their parents as they compete for the power that parents give too early and try to recover too late. The resulting adversary mode may force adolescents to rebel too stubbornly, parents to respond too negatively, and both to lose the positive home atmosphere that can be so valuable in educating children.

Clear Positive Messages

Parenting by positive expectations can be extraordinarily successful in guiding children both in school and out. If high achievement, positive attitudes and constructive behavior are expected and reinforced by parents, they will become internalized by the child, and the need for punishment usually will be negligible. How do some parents guide their children so well without punishment while others seem to use it so frequently?

Between Parent Consistency. Clear and consistent messages, agreed upon by both parents and transmitted to the child, are basic. For example, parental agreement on such underlying values as (1) the importance of study, learning, school, work and responsibility; (2) respect for individuality; and (3) recognition of the need for reasonable amount of recreation and fun seem to underly a positive and achievement oriented atmosphere.

The most valued resource that parents have to offer is their own attention. Children normally prefer positive attention, but frequently develop habits that elicit negative attention. That is, they learn the ways that are effective for getting attention whether or not these habits are good for their own growth and development. If attention to problem behaviors monopolizes the time during which children interact with parents, there is little time left for attention to the positive. They soon lose confidence in their ability to attain that positive notice and never really form the habit of working toward positive parent expectations. More than one discouraged parent has reported that they rarely can find behavior in their children that is worthy of praise. In these cases a negative or punishing cycle predominates and it becomes extremely difficult to motivate their children toward constructive behaviors, namely achievement.

Clear and consistent messages are critical, which sounds much easier than it is. Problems of consistency and clarity originate in many places. Any one parent may not be personally consistent from time to time. That is, parents may change their expectations depending on which neighbor they talked to last or their own changeable mood or their own personal pressures. Parents may not always give clear messages because they may be busy and therefore do not take the time to be clear or because they haven't thought through the message or because they are not sure how they feel about the communication. So, based on one parent alone, expectations may be clouded for a child.

Those complications are compounded when both parents have consistency and clarity problems, and even more complicated after a divorce or remarriage where there may be three or four parents. Of course, the more different these messages are, the more complicated are the directions for the child. The description of Torn Tommy in Chapter One is an example of opposite messages after a divorce. Even within an intact marriage parent expectations may contradict each other and there are absolutely always contradictions in three or four parent situations. If parents are truly concerned for their children, they must truly try to communicate basically similar messages or the children will find it impossible to please their parents and equally impossible to internalize clear directions for positive behaviors. A 17 year old youth described his "Torn Tommy" feelings in this way:

> Tom's parents had been married for 20 years and although they often disagreed and argued he now sensed the severity of their heightened problems. He felt that his father was trying very hard to please his mother. Although she also said she was trying to improve their marriage, Tom felt that she was subtly manipulating him to side with her against his dad. He shared a recent incident in which he had asked his parents if he could drive the car to school. His dad had said no. His mom came to his defense and persuaded dad to change his mind. Dad conceded and left for work. Mom then criticized the boy for not being more assertive toward his dad. Torn Tom left the house in disgust, squealing his tires as he turned out of the driveway. Yes, he wanted the car. No, he didn't expect his mom to talk for him. No, he didn't plan to

start talking back to his dad even if his mom and dad were having problems. His head ached with desperation. How could he please them both? How could he avoid being manipulated by one against the other? How could he prevent the marriage from deteriorating further? He went through his entire school day in turmoil without hearing what teachers or friends were saying. School seemed irrelevant compared to the seemingly unsurmountable problem — learning to deal with two people whom he loved, but who each were calling him to battle on their side against the other.

Seventeen year olds can describe their feelings and talk about strategies for handling two contradictory messages. Younger children feel literally torn apart by the sense of not being able to move forward at all in fear that one of their parents will certainly be displeased. They simply say "they don't care" anymore; it feels completely confusing.

Within Parent Consistency. An example of inconsistency within a particular parent comes in the "Yes-No" message. This confusion typically takes place among parents who are determined to be rational. They assert that they believe that it's wrong to scold children without explaining the reason for the reprimand. They begin very early, attempting the impossible feat of explaining to high-energy two year olds "exactly why they shouldn't be putting a toy into an electric outlet." The children may be bright and may even have excellent two year old vocabularies, but their reasoning ability is far below the abstract level that mother assumes. Their attention spans are brief and certainly do not match the time that mother or dad invest in the explanation. However, they can tell from the parent's tone of voice that they may have done something wrong and that they are loved. The parent may even punctuate the reasonable statements with a hug or two. Assured that they are loved they return to their play and the fun game of inserting their toy into the electric outlet. Mom or dad tries again.

As the children get older and increase the naughty behaviors which have brought them kind voices and hugs, parents become impatient. They lose their tempers; they scold and sometimes even spank. However, since their intent is to be rational, they feel pangs of guilt after their temporary losses of control. So they apologize to the children for their temper or the spanking and explain to them why they, the parents, are misbehaving.

The children don't really understand, or want to understand, if the parent approves or disapproves of the behavior. However, they do learn that the behavior has brought an inordinate amount of valued warmth and attention. Reasonably enough, they increase the kind of undesirable behavior that produces the attention. Punishments are thus punctuated by hugs and affection, and the children, persuaded by a strong basic wish for love, may increase the troublesome behavior in a self-perpetuating, accelerating negative ritual.

Every hyperactive child whose parents have visited me for help had a home environment where at least one parent gave frequent yes-no messages. It may be that the high-energy child's behavior prompted the parent's confused messages. But it appears more likely that the confused messages diffused the focus of attention for the children so that they developed a habit of pushing limits toward their goal of love and attention from a parent. They have discovered quite by accident that troublesome behaviors provide the warmth they seek. They learn no clear limits to what is acceptable and what is not. Unpleasant consequences merge with pleasant ones and permit them to impulsively attempt whatever attracts parents' attention.

As a variation, the children adapt the parent's contradictory pattern as their own and find it effective. As they get older they learn to quickly apologize for their own misdeeds and shorten the time between scolding and affection. These children learn that almost any behavior (for example, ignoring chores, misbehavior, or poor schoolwork) is acceptable. Children who use this strategy can become facile manipulators both at home and at school. For example, after each test they fail to study for, they will have an excuse and an apology that the teacher frequently believes. The same manipulation ritual learned at home is thus transferred to the classroom. The dynamics of the situation confuse parents, teachers, and of course, the children themselves.

Children who are products of this mixed yes-no message may appear to be mild mannered and kind, but their misbehaviors and manipulations may cause themselves and others serious problems. They become expert at irresponsible behavior and avoiding the negative consequences thereof.

The "Beat The System" Message. Adult occupational and financial commitments may not appear at first glance to be related to Underachievement Syndrome. However, they play an important role in communicating messages of responsibility in school. School is the "system" for children, and if they view their parent model as trying to "beat the system" by trying to avoid working, a spontaneous emulation is to try to "beat the system" and avoid working in school.

A gifted high school student who was charming, bright and creative in many ways was an expert at avoiding doing his assignments. He bragged to me about "just getting by." It seemed as if he had made it into a game. His father, in that same counseling session, explained how he was cleverly collecting unemployment benefits, despite possible opportunities directed toward resetting career goals. Dad's justification and rationalizations sounded familiar. Where had I heard similar excuses to avoid taking responsibilities and directing one's personal life? Of course — from his son! If "getting by" is viewed as a parent value, it is translated by children into "getting by" in school. It feels familiar and appropriate to the child to "beat the system" by taking minimal school responsibilities and following his father's model. It is a clearly counterproductive message to children instead of the positive communication that guides achievement.

Referential Speaking

The term *referential speaking* will be used to describe conversation between adults about children within the hearing of those children. Parents frequently speak referentially about children as if children were not listening and with little regard for the effects of the conversation upon them. Parents converse in this way to each other, grandparents, other relatives, teachers, neighbors and even to other siblings. Mothers who are at home with their children probably do it most frequently since child rearing is usually central to their thinking during that period of their lives. Referential speaking is neither bad nor good in itself, but it has the potential for making a negative impact on children and may well be a significant cause of many children's problems. It is a means by which parents inadvertently impart values to their children.

Surprisingly, referential speaking is so automatic that parents are rarely aware of its impact on children. An awareness that these communications are heard by children should encourage parents to be more discriminating of what they say to other adults when children are near. Parents tend to engage in referential speaking more frequently with very young children. They should realize that even very young children tune in immediately to adult conversation which refers to them.

Describing positive behaviors such as kindness, consideration, hard work, independence or effort is likely to encourage children to continue such behaviors. It is reinforcing. The description of accomplishments and achievements are also effective for fostering achievement orientation. However, too frequent comments on accomplishment, high grades and awards may cause the child to feel strong pressure to achieve. For example, bragging to grandma about an excellent report card will communicate your valuing of high grades, which is appropriate. But if the bragging involves descriptions of a straight A record, children may feel they must meet that impossible standard consistently. You may wonder why your children feel too much pressure, since your only direct message to them was to do their best. The answer, of course, is that they were listening when you gave referential messages to important others in their lives.

The most damaging referential messages are the negative communications, and these seem to be the ones I hear about most frequently. Here are a few excerpts from typical mother-to-neighbor messages.

> Peter is so disorganized that even his teacher can't help him with his problems.

> Debbie is so shy that I can't get her to talk to any adults.

> Bob just doesn't seem to care about anything but sports.

> Diane hasn't cleaned her room for weeks. She's just sloppy and I can't seem to get her to take home responsibilities seriously.

> Kevin insists on doing everything his way and I've given up fighting him.

> Mary binges so much, she can't seem to control her eating.

> Ronny is just clumsy no matter how hard he tries.

These negative comments cause children to despair of trying; they feel the impossibility of changing their parents' negative conclusions about their behaviors.

A most common and damaging referential message between parents is a wife's despairing "hello" as her husband enters the door from work. Her tirade on her terrible day often includes how "impossible" the children were, thus dramatizing her own lack of ability to discipline them. It is a communication to the children of her powerlessness and their dominance, and it will serve to encourage the children's control of their weak mother. It would be much better if she could tell her husband about their accomplishments. They would then greet their dad determined to prove how good they could be. Telephone calls between spouses when one is traveling or working late have the same powerful effect. Parents should not communicate their feelings of helplessness when children might be listening. It has a guaranteed adverse effect on their behavior.

One of the most difficult forms of referential speaking comes typically from adults other than parents. It is the reference to looks or beauty, which is a much valued attribute in our society. The beautiful child receives frequent admiration, with comments typically directed to the parents about the child and within the child's hearing. This continuous message of beauty, particularly if it is acknowledged by the parent or originated by parents and relatives, may easily be the basis for internalized pressure relative to appearance. Beautiful children do not necessarily grow up to be beautiful adults. Dealing with social pressure for good looks is frustrating for the majority of society who do not fit the guidelines of Fifth Avenue glamour. The beautiful child, who is surrounded by referential descriptions of his or her delightful appearance, has encumbered an impossible adult burden which may lead to the threshold of eating disorders and to an obsession with fashion and appearances. For this child or adolescent, school or career achievements fall far behind in the list of priorities.

Of course, referential conversation among adults is spontaneous and normal. Parents enjoy talking about their children to other adults who show an interest. Unfortunately, it is too easy to engage in adult conversation as if the little folks playing nearby are too busy to hear the discussion. Please recall these words of your grandparents: "Little pitchers have big ears."

Competition - Winning and Losing

The ability to function in competition is central to achievement. Underachievers have not learned the techniques of competing. Although they win happily, they have not learned to recover after losses. They lose their temper or sulk or quit or don't take the risk of playing unless they are certain to win. Parents should teach children how to deal with a competitive life-style, since functioning in a competitive environment is synonymous with achieving.

Gail Sheehy (1982) in her book *Pathfinders* discussed differences among adults in handling their own developmental crises. In comparing adults who viewed themselves as successful and who led reasonably fulfilled lives versus those who saw their lives dominated by frustration and failure, she concluded that the main difference was the way in which they dealt with their failures. "Pathfinders," the term she used for the more satisfied persons, experienced just as many failure experiences as did the others. However, they were able to use those failures to grow and move forward. On the other hand, the less satisfied persons came to identify themselves as failures and remained in their less-than-satisfactory life positions.

Children establish similar patterns. Those who are achievers, creative and success oriented view their failures and losses as learning experiences (Covington and Beery, 1976). When failure occurs, they identify the problems, remedy the deficiencies, reset their goals and grow from the experiences. Failure is only a temporary setback, and they learn to attribute their failure to lack of effort, the unusual difficulty of a task, or perhaps the extraordinary skill of other competitors. As coping strategies, they may laugh at their errors, determine to work harder, and/or redesign their achievement goals. Most important, they see themselves as falling short of a goal, not falling short as persons.

Other children usually take one of two main paths. Some children will persevere in the same direction, disappointed by their performance but determined to achieve that initial goal. If the goal is realistic, the renewed effort and determination may produce satisfying success and they may feel like "winners" in the competitive game. However, if the goal is unrealistic their continued efforts will fail and produce continued frustration.

The other path is even more destructive. With failure, they become failure oriented (Covington and Beery, 1976). They come to view school as a competitive game in which they are incapable of winning, so they logically decide that there is little purpose in playing. They learn to give up easily and to "get by" with a minimum of effort. The skill deficits increase, and these children become underachievers who have little or no confidence in their ability to successfully compete in the education game.

To help their children cope with failure, parents should first examine their own competitive style; children may have learned maladaptive responses to failure at home. For example, parents may model an attitude of quitting too quickly if a problem gets difficult, of avoiding any type of competition, or of habitually blaming external sources for one's own shortcomings or lack of effort. A possible restructuring of parent attitudes and expectancies, therefore, may be the first priority for helping children who are not achieving well in school.

Children should be taught to identify creative alternatives for their losses or failures. For example, they should recognize that normal people — even very talented ones — cannot be "Number 1" in everything, but that every person has areas in which they are talented. The child should not feel insecure or threatened by an occasional setback. Note, however, that a discussion of a child's failure may need to wait until after the emotional tension is reduced in order to avoid defensive behaviors. Parents cannot expect rational perception or logical thinking during the immediate stress period following an upsetting defeat.

A questioning approach, rather than a lecture, may better help children understand that (1) they cannot always win, (2) disappointment does not mean they are failures, (3) the particular experience simply was not as successful as they had hoped it would be, (4) everyone would like to be smarter than they are, and especially (5) the main goal is to play the learning game at their best performance level, regardless of their competitive ranking. Effort counts.

It is important for parents to send a clear and direct message to their children about the central role that school learning plays in their life. Indeed, if children are to succeed academically in a way that capitalizes on all of their abilities and optimally prepares the child for higher education, then the "learning game" should be played above all others. If parent messages stress that winning — regardless of the game — is all important, then winning at tennis, on the swim team, or in popularity contests may become too crucial to their children. Young adults in their 20's or 30's, whose peak life achievement was election to their high school class presidency or being star of the basketball team, probably feel unfulfilled by adult standards. Their competitive strivings helped them perform at their best, but in areas which were peripheral. Of course, high school should not be all drudgery. However, students should be aiming at higher education and building long-term goals, and their academic education should not be secondary to socializing or athletics.

Although children must learn to function in competition, and especially to emerge from failures and losses, they should also become involved in noncompetitive activities which are intrinsically reinforcing — interests which they enjoy for personal and not competitive satisfaction. If all of a child's activities are tied to recognition or competition, he or she may be unprepared for relaxation and an absence of constant activity or social contacts. Children who have not learned to enjoy noncompetitive activities will feel boredom and depression when they are not accomplishing something or moving toward a goal. Certainly achievement motivation is critical, but even high energy achievers need relief from a compulsive activity level. Intrinsically motivated noncompetitive activites provides an important diversion that makes competition meaningful. Children and adults ask similar inevitable questions. Why are we working so hard? What is the purpose of all this activity? In addition to goals for achievement, they must value living goals which are not competitive.

Grades and Rewards

Many parents ask if they should pay children or give them rewards for good grades, usually A's. They actually may think that paying children for good grades will motivate them to achieve. Children typically will work for A's if they believe they can achieve them. A core problem is that underachievers don't really believe that their hard work will help them get good grades. If you ask them what grades they would like, most will admit with a smile that they'd like "all A's." When you explore further, they typically acknowledge that they don't see A's within their reach and that they really don't see much value in working hard to achieve only B's and C's. The rewards for A's, which they see as unachievable, therefore do not motivate them. The unattainable rewards may, in fact, serve to further confirm their inadequacy. Although parents ought not expect to reverse underachieving patterns with rewards for A's, such rewards are not likely to harm an *achieving* child and thus can be used without harm (or major benefit) if parents choose.

There is an important place for reward in curing underachievement. In order to begin the reversal of the pattern it is frequently effective to use a temporary extrinsic reward system. A suggested reward system will be described in a later chapter.

Grades are important and parents should communicate their concern for good grades. Grades, in one form or another, will always be used to evaluate performance whether they are A's and B's, S's, E's, I's or verbal comments. They are a shorthand method of communication and they serve their purpose with reasonable effectiveness. Children will always be able to control their grades to some extent, but never completely. The vicissitudes and differing standards of teachers and evaluators will always influence the outcome. For example, some teachers rarely give A's; others give only A's and B's. Such information is important for the interpretation of the letters and words. Children should be expected to earn the best grades of which they are capable, but allowances must be made for both teacher differences and ability differences.

Generally, parents should have some indication of a range in which they might expect their children to perform. Of course, past performance is a helpful indicator. However, if students move from a less to a more competitive school, the differing levels of student achievement will be an important consideration. Thus the parents of the A student who moves from a small rural elementary school to an upper middle class suburban middle school should make some changes in grade expectations.

Liberal parents, who may have experienced academic pressure as children, frequently give their children the message that "grades don't count as long as you're learning." If they communicate this message, they should be prepared for poor grades in junior high school and a similar defensive response from their adolescents. They will explain that there is no reason to do the daily assignments and "busy work" (which causes the D's and F's) since grades don't count and they are learning. They refuse in righteous indignation to prepare class work, from which they are not learning enough for the purpose of grades alone. There is no need to argue — they'll quote their parents.

Organization

Disorganization is a frequent symptom of Underachievement Syndrome. Most underachievers appear to be purposely disorganized. For some, the disorganization shows itself in messy desks, messy papers and messy rooms. Others seem unable to plan their time and thus hand assignments in late or not at all. Still others seem unable to organize their talking and thinking and, although they are vocal their conversation changes continuously from one topic to another. Concomitant with the disorganization patterns are statements which typically are not entirely honest, such as "I forgot," "I didn't know I had any homework," "I didn't know today was the deadline" or "I thought I had already completed the assignment." Although some students will admit that such statements are excuses, others will swear that the statements are honest and accurate. They seem like declarations of opposition to organization and commitments to nonconformity.

Two main parenting styles seem to foster disorganization patterns. One style mentioned earlier, which is obvious, is the family that advocates a disorganized life style. They value disorganization as synonymous with freedom and creativity and assert openly that they prefer a disorganized life-style. The children thus emulate the parents and have never learned organizational techniques. Disorganization feels natural, right and creative and remains for the whole family a preferred approach to daily life. Extreme disorganization, however, is dysfunctional for achieving in school.

The second pattern is much more common and more difficult to identify. In this family situation, one parent uses disorganization as a passive aggressive power play in an oppositional marriage. One parent typically is a perfectionist, or very structured, and apparently the more powerful parent. The second parent cannot assertively or rationally deal with his/her sense of powerlessness, so he/she uses passive aggressive techniques like forgetting things, not preparing things on time, not accomplishing tasks requested and ignoring responsibilities. Although this spouse feels powerless, he/she may be viewed as powerful by one or more of the children. Those children will emulate the passive aggressive parent in opposing the demanding, more structured parent. Disorganization relative to school work becomes the power weapon for the child.

Living with a small amount of chaos or tolerance of ambiguity seems healthy and may contribute to creativity and a noncompulsive life-style. On the other hand, rigidity and perfectionism are likely to interfere with school and life achievement. Reasonable structure and organization are necessary to school and life accomplishment, and it appears again that moderation is more effective than extremism. Parents must take the initiative to model and teach reasonable organizational techniques as they relate to home and school responsibilities.

Order At Home. Let's begin with order at home. One of the most frequent complaints I hear from parents is "they never make their bed." Making beds seems clearly to be a symbol of children's rebellion against order. I recall as a child wondering why my own mother put so much value on getting a bed made. As I listen with concern to the "unmade bed" symptom described by so many parents, I find myself wondering about the state of my own bed for the day. Whether I managed to hastily arrange the covers and spread varies with the time of my first commitments of the day and my last appointments the night before. I never feel great concern for my client's unmade bed; I know that children and parents will survive that degree of disorganization. However, if children do not assist with home responsibilities willingly and are not required to maintain their own rooms to at least minimal standards, then I believe that home responsibilities are a problem. For example:

Bobby said, "I believe I have a right to have my own room exactly as I like it, and I prefer the mess." Bobby's parents concluded, initially, that he should be allowed this freedom. However, they soon began feeling concerned. He slept without sheets rather than make his bed. Crumbs all over the floor attracted ants. He picked up his laundry only when he was out of clothes, and he stopped inviting friends to their home because he was ashamed of his room.

Bobby's room has progressed beyond reasonableness. So has his school-work. His parents kept a very neat household. His father is a perfection-ist; his mother a passive aggressive individualist in response to her husband's demanding power. Bobby, in symbolic rebellion with his mother is determined to hold his room as a bastion of power (and mess).

The younger children in our clinic are treated to a series of group therapy sessions in which we spend at least one session on family cooperative effort. A song which delights them all from the musical *Free To Be You and Me* (Harnick, 1972), is one which acknowledges that those "ladies on TV" who smile when they are doing housework are actresses and are paid for those commercials. Further, it points out that everybody, including mom and dad, hates housework. In the final appeal of the song it says:

Little boys, little girls,
When you are big husbands and wives,
If you want all the days of your lives
To seem sunny as summer weather,
Make sure when there is housework to do
That you do it together.

The song is followed in therapy by asking that children devise ways in which they can be of help. We introduce cooperative statements which they have rarely used but which have been a humorous standby at our own home. "Sure, mom, I'll be glad to" or "sure, dad, I'll be glad to" take on special meaning when family members attack some of our more odious tasks like retarring the blacktop or mopping up the flooded basement floor. They surpass "do I have to?" or "why doesn't Johnny have to do the hard work that I have to?" The song and the discussion send children out of our therapy sessions offering to do household tasks, to the surprise of their parents. However, I wouldn't dare collect data on the continuity of their willingness. Parents do need to cultivate and even insist on a sharing of household responsibilities. In addition to teaching cooperation, parents, you are teaching organization.

How to do it? It isn't easy! These tasks are not fun, but really must be done. Again, personal attention is your most powerful reinforcer. You can best teach your children good work habits in one-to-one partnerships. If they share a job with you or your spouse, you model the skills, show your appreciation for their cooperation, and give them a sense of importance and self-confidence that come from completing a difficult task. If you can establish that pattern early, they will be willing co-workers and will eventually move toward independence. Early parent patience results in cultivating good organizational and work habits.

Giving two siblings a task to share is their invitation to compete. Either they will compete to make one the "goodie" and the other the "baddie" or they will vie for who can get away with the least work. Don't expect motivation or cooperation. Sibling chore efforts have a hidden agenda. Getting away with as little as possible is the typical goal.

What quantity and quality of work do you insist on? Do you pay for chores accomplished? Please don't expect your own personal standards of excellence: something below what you'd expect for yourself is reasonable and fair. Regarding payment, paying children for working is debatable and optional. Certainly some tasks should be done without salary as part of family responsibility. If you do pay them, use children's standards for salary. (Too much money is more than they can manage.) Savings accounts are a good and positive diversion for their funds.

Mom and dad, avoid getting into a nagging mode. Two reminders are enough. Beyond that, children aren't listening. Use a written checklist and clear consistent consequences. For example, rooms can have Friday inspections before weekend activities are permitted. As children develop reasonably good and regular organizational habits, such consequences and inspections won't be necessary, but you may want to use them to get the turnaround started. Most important, stay with the promised negative consequences if tasks are not completed. They can be removed immediately upon completion of the assigned tasks, which should prevent children's resentment. Children may resist at first, but parent persistence pays off in reasonable orderliness. The orderliness generalizes to school organization and will be helpful in promoting children's achievement.

Communication With Schools. Organized communication with schools in order to monitor children's progress may seem to be the school's responsibility. Obviously, such communication is partially a school's task. However, whether your children are in public or private schools those schools have a much larger adult/child ratio than you have at home. Therefore, despite good intentions the risk of their not communicating problematic underachievement patterns is high. Children falling through cracks is a somewhat stereotyped but appropriate visual image for what easily happens to those whose parents do not take an active and orderly approach to school communication. I emphasize *orderly* here because sporadic overreacting may seem like communication, but it is not nearly as effective. Parents frequently feel threatened by teachers and vice versa, and so both may tend to wait for an emergency before communication begins. Certainly emergency communications sometimes are necessary, but it is the steady persistent efforts of parents to stay in touch with teachers that is most helpful. Teacher conferences have a purpose and parents (both of them, if possible) ought not to miss a single one. However, if you suspect even minor school problems, one or two conferences are not sufficient.

Four to six weeks into the beginning of the school year is an appropriate time to call a teacher if, for example, your children have a history of not completing assignments or any other underachievement symptom. By that time the "fresh beginning" is wearing thin and your children may be resuming some old habits that are unsatisfactory. On the other hand, they are not so far behind that they can't catch up. The early call to the teacher also is appropriate if the children's comments about school cause you to suspect a problem. Explain that you are mainly concerned with your children's working up to their ability and that you wonder if he or she is noting any problems. If the answer is "no" but you're still convinced a problem exists, you might then specify the previous problem area or the specific difficulty the children may have mentioned. If things are going well, you need only thank the teacher and ask that she or he notify you if a problem appears. If the teacher does indicate a concern offer to meet at the teacher's convenience. Most teachers will appreciate your interest, and it can be the beginning of a good teacher/parent relationship — one which is important for preventing or curing Underachievement Syndrome.

Your first regular conference should include some specific questions to assure yourself that your children are working up to their ability levels. If children have been underachieving for sometime, it may be impossible for the teacher to assess their abilities. Further, if they tend to be quiet and lacking in confidence, the teacher is less likely to expect as much and you may actually be a better judge of ability than the teacher. You've obviously known your children for a much longer time. Ask specifically about which reading group they are in and the grade level at which they are reading. Many reading series have multiple levels which are not so apparently tied to grade level, but the teacher can interpret that information to you very specifically. Similarly, you should ask the grade level at which the child is doing mathematics. Some teachers are more eager to tell you about particular skills mastered. However, it is much harder to assess whether your child is underachieving using that criterion. Also *grade level* of performance is not the same as *grade equivalent test scores*. The latter may be quite misleading. The former is necessary for unambiguous assurance of your children's success in school.

Teachers frequently assume, mistakenly, that you're putting your children under pressure when you ask for specific achievement information. You can reassure them this is not the case. Admittedly, such assurances may not be effective, but take courage, many of them also are parents, or have been, and hopefully will identify with your reasonable concern.

Homework and Study Habits. Homework and study habits should be structured for students who lack organizational skills. The tools for that structuring should be familiar to most parents. Assignment notebooks are a must. Use large ones rather than small ones. Small ones get lost. A separate folder and notebook for each subject are helpful. A backpack or school bag which is prepared for school at night before bedtime will help their organization. A place to deposit the school bag and books close to the back door will help keep books and bags from cluttering the living room, kitchen, bedroom and family room and will help to make organization a habit without nagging. Insist from the start that the place of study must be quiet, alone and at a desk or table — no siblings or parents and no television or stereo until the work is complete. If your children are achieving well, quiet music is permissable, but studying in front of a TV is never effective. Anything but leisure reading should not be done on the floor or bed. Reclined positions are not conducive to concentration, despite your children's arguments that they prefer such comfort. If you insist on organized study, your child will develop automatic responses that are conducive to learning. Children who organize their work and are achieving well won't need these structured guidelines from you, since they probably have developed most of them on their own.

Under no circumstances should your children expect to have you or your spouse sitting next to them at homework time. Don't let them convince you that they cannot work without you. The focus of your attention should be directed to the completed assignments. It is reasonable for parents to provide children with occasional help or explanations. These should be brief and given only after they have tried understanding the work on their own. If they have studied the material first, parents can quiz their children or give them a trial test. However, if performance is poor children should return to their desk for independent study. Parents can't be expected to study for their children; however, parents can recommend learning strategies that may be effective in particular situations.

In providing structure for your children, they will surely debate you. Your argument should be firm. When they achieve well they may do it their way; if they have not been successful using their own style, they must change to yours until they are clearly achievers for at least a full year.

The Indulgence Traps

The ways in which some family patterns result in Underachievement Syndrome were described earlier. There are some tactics that parents may use to diminish risks in these special situations, starting with avoiding overindulgence. Doing too much for children almost always causes them problems. What is 'too much"is so hard to define that parents easily fall into this trap without realizing the harm they've done. Here are the main risk categories for overindulgence:

The Long Awaited Child. This is the child born after miscarriages or difficulties in becoming pregnant. The child who is adopted or the first born to a couple late in life may also fit this category, as does the premature child whose trip home from the hospital seems a medical miracle. These long awaited children dramatically affect the parents entire life-style. They will exclaim to each other, and to me, how dramatically they have altered their life to center it on their beloved new child. This child is the focus of all of their conversation, all their planning, their hopes, dreams and activities.

The Only Child. Much has been written about the only child. This child is at high risk for overindulgence because, with a two-to-one ratio, it is likely that the child will receive too much attention, much more than society away from home can offer. Attention is addicting.

The Grandparented Child. Children who are born to parents whose first children are already grown up may be treated as if they were grandchildren. Grandparenting carries with it certain privileges in our society. Grandparents give their grandchildren more material things, more privileges and more desserts than "regular" parents do because, by and large, grandparents are temporary visitors. They shouldn't have to be burdened with the every day discipline that goes with guiding children through the many years of growing up. If however, grandparents have the main responsibility of rearing the children, or if parents have their children so late in life that they fall into a pattern similar to grandparenting, they must temper their treatment of the child with the wisdom that should also come with years.

If you are reading this book as parents, and you recognize that your children are victims of these overindulgence traps, you may yet be able to redirect your child despite your former errors of too much giving and doing. First you must convince yourself that under many circumstances saying "no" may be kinder and more loving than saying "yes." This is important because you have so far defined doing things for your children and giving things to them as love and kindness. Depriving them of anything makes you feel guilty, so you try not to if you can avoid it. One father stated it this way:

"Do you mean that after working so hard to finally earn sufficient money to provide well for my son that I have to say NO to him when he asks me for material things that I can now afford and that I would like to give him?"

It was difficult for me to explain to this warm, generous father that in giving his son so much that he was depriving him of the very quality he valued so much in himself and others — the willingness to take initiative and follow-through in working for something. He was stealing from his son the privilege of achieving and earning for himself.

My suggestion to this father, and to you too, who want so much to give so much to your children, is to "match efforts." Matching their efforts and funds provides a practical basis for avoiding doing too much, at the same time rewarding children's efforts. You can use it to guide you in helping them with household tasks and schoolwork, as well as with the purchase of material things. If children put forth approximately equal effort or money, they gain an appreciation for their own contributions as well as your efforts. They earn the confidence that comes from challenge and you can feel the pleasure that comes from giving of yourself. If you give too much your gift is rarely appreciated because the recipient becomes accustomed to lavish material possessions. If you reverse your earlier generosity and not give at all, your children are likely to feel angry, resentful and deprived. The matched effort compromise permits a phasing in of initiative and provides your vote of confidence for your children's efforts.

Overindulgence traps usually include giving too much praise and attention as well as too many material things. Praise which suggests to children that they are best or "smartest" is the most damaging. Though children may recognize that they are, indeed, not the best nor smartest, that message of comparative praise communicates to them that their parents have set competitive goals for them. They may internalize these as impossible perfectionistic pressures and, therefore, assess even their very adequate accomplishments as failures. Certainly, praise and positive reinforcement are important for achievement motivation, but their too frequent use causes children to become dependent on continued compliments. They will not perform in the classroom environment without it.

Reducing the amount of praise should be accomplished gradually, so the children can move from dependence on outside reinforcement to rewards that come from feelings of task accomplishment and personal achievement. Praise should never be entirely removed. If you feel you are lavishing too much praise on your children, begin by tallying the number of times you praise them each day and set as a goal about one half that number. Reduce the praise gradually so that the children don't begin negative acting out to receive attention. You can also reword your praise so that it is positive without being exaggerated. Emphasize correct learning processes and efforts, and be sure not to praise the children when they have made little effort. They should earn your compliments.

It is difficult to measure what is "sufficient" but not excessive reinforcement. Most adults can recall during childhood being exposed to a "gushing" adult who praised continuously. At first, you were impressed by the continued compliments, but you later realized that they were meaningless since they were given so freely and were unrelated to efforts or outcomes. You, as overindulgent parents or teachers, may not be quite that overwhelming, but if you continuously tell your children how wonderful they are, it is a good idea to reduce the praise to a more realistic quality and quantity. It will be valued more if it is not exaggerated.

If you are not guilty of such overindulgence, but the children's grandparents are, please copy this special *open letter to all grandparents.* Before giving them the letter, remind them that you are sharing this because you know how much they love their grandchildren.

Dear Grandparents:

Grandparenting is fun! You may enjoy these children of your children with the more relaxed perspective that parents rarely have. You can be more patient, loving and giving than you had time to be when you raised your own children. Please remember your own parenting days. You wanted to bring your own children up by your own rules. You believed in firm discipline and you knew the children were easier to manage if you were consistent and did not always give in to them. When you were parenting your own children you taught them not to expect an endless stream of material possessions. You expected them to take responsibilities, to show effort and to persevere. The children you parented have grown up responsibly. You must have done many things right. Now we ask you to permit your children to parent by their own style and standards. Support and encourage your children as parents. It is tempting to play the "good" grandmom or grandpop, but don't do that if it makes your children into "bad" parents. If you overrule your children's discipline of their children, your grandchildren will not respect their parents and eventually will not respect you either. Consistent discipline is a key to your grandchildren growing into fine adults. Give love, give attention and yes, give gifts — but please don't give so much of any of these that you steal from your grandchildren their initiative, self-discipline and self-confidence. Moderation, giving less than you would like to give, is a better guide than the generosity that I know you feel. This is a hard message to give grandparents that love so much, but somehow I know you will understand because at one time you were parents too.

A note of caution: The child you indulged too much may be beyond the stage of receiving too much positive attention and may already have become dependent on negative attention — such as continued scolding, nagging, arguing and reminding. Note that your individual attention remains their most critical motivator. You will need to use one-to-one personal attention to reverse the negative pattern, and you should key that attention into the change to positive efforts. More specific guidelines for this approach will be described later.

Nontraditional Parenting

So many children are brought up in nontraditional families that in many neighborhoods a majority of children may not be living in what we used to think of as "typical" families, that is, one birth mother, one birth father and the natural children of these parents. Children with a single parent or remarried parents are no longer unique. Nonetheless, *all* of the school age children I have seen, as well as most of the adolescents, express the wish to have their original intact two parent family. They usually will add parenthetically, "without the fighting, of course." Since children overwhelmingly voice a similar sentiment, one can hardly ignore the special demands and pressures on them and their parents in these nontraditional families. Although many children lead productive lives despite these pressures, many others experience severe emotional trauma. Underachievement is a visible symptom of their stress. The following are prototypical family arrangements and suggested ways for avoiding typical pitfalls.

Single Parenting. Parenting alone is undoubtedly the most difficult form of child rearing. Usually women have this experience, but cases of men receiving full custody are increasing. Ideal conditions for single parenting exist when the parent has a positive career goal, when there is a second parent for visitation who is supportive of the single parent, when a regular reliable babysitter is available and when the parent is managing to maintain his or her own positive adult social life. Children are thus given consistent parenting, they view their parents as achievers who are supportive of each other, and they are treated as children (not adults) with reasonable amounts of attention and independence. Unfortunately, this ideal is rarely achieved immediately and usually not at all. More typically, the single parent is a victim of rejection, feels little confidence about personal achievement and may be dependent on his/her own parents. Children may have multiple care givers, grandparents, available babysitters, or Day Care Centers of varying quality. The parent, in his or her loneliness and guilt, may smother the child with affection and overprotection as he or she sees the child as the only reason to go on living, thus causing the child to become too dependent.

Alternatively single parents may take the opposite approach. Because of their loneliness they may treat the child as an adult, sharing confidences and status and sometimes even an adult bed, thus moving the child into the dominating mode that comes from giving too much power. These one parent children are frequently surrounded by a variety of adult caretakers and soon develop people sensitivities. While they become talented at sensing adult moods and emotions, their habits cause them classroom problems. They push limits to determine each caretaker's response, and they behave inconsistently, depending on their estimation of what each adult will accept. These children tend to underachieve in school and may exhibit the unfocused high energy that is often termed hyperactivity. It is almost as if they move without direction in a continuous search for teacher and peer attention. As they move they touch and hit others and clumsily drop materials. The more active they are, the more difficult it is for them to focus on productive effort. They receive continuous negative attention from teachers and fellow students.

As a single parent are you destined to have a problem underachieving child? Of course not, but your job is more difficult. Here are some simple rules to guide you — simple only in that they are few and straightforward. In reality they are terribly difficult for single parents to negotiate. Pat yourself on the back for each successful day, you deserve it. Now the rules:

1. Find a career direction for your life to give you a sense of purpose and to build your self-confidence. Making your children your only purpose gives them power and pressure that will be too stressful for them to manage.

2. Find some adult social outlets for yourself. Don't feel guilty about enjoying yourself as an adult.

3. Find a reliable babysitter or Day Care Center facility for your children. Consistency in care givers and surroundings is very important for young children.

4. Treat your child as a child — not a toy to be played with nor an adult to be depended on. Do not share your bed with your child (except during thunderstorms). That is an adult status that you should maintain should you remarry.

5. Take time (I know you have little) to enjoy your children's achievements and encourage them to take responsibilities.

Now two special rules for single mothers parenting boys.

1. Boys should have an older male to serve them as a model. Find effective role models for your boys — uncles, grandfathers, teachers, Boy Scout leaders may all be helpful to your son in learning to be comfortable with his masculinity.

2. If you do not view your children's natural father as an effective role model, absolutely do not tell your boys how much they look like and remind you of him. Also, avoid power struggles with him. If he mistreats you and shows open disrespect, your son is likely to imitate this powerful, but disrespectful behavior.

The rules will sound simplistic to some and impossible to others. They may be difficult for a single parent to live by, but they are effective for parenting your children. Tape them up on your refrigerator.

The Recreated Family. Remarriage brings stepparents and stepsiblings, new rules and new relationships. Children who have accustomed themselves to one parent are now faced with a multitude of new adjustments and emotions. In what ways can parents and stepparents make these transitions smoother? How can they give a consistent message of achievement so that children clearly know that all parent figures expect them to achieve in school? How can parents avoid their children's manipulations?

The remarried family, where the special parent-child comradery is disturbed by the parent's adult relationship with a new marriage partner, elicits conflicting emotions in the children. They recognize the appropriateness of feeling happy for their parent, but they feel disappointed at the loss of attention that previously was all theirs. Their feelings toward the stepparent may also be mixed. They certainly may resent this parent displacing their own birth parent, but they also may be happy to have both a mother and father at home. If the single parent previously conferred too much power on children and has been unable to manage consistent discipline, they are likely to see the new parent as an intrusion and recognize that their former power will be diminished. The children will certainly not welcome the new control.

There are guidelines which will be helpful in the new family setting. For example, husband-wife regular communication time to discuss parenting adjustments are a high priority. The communications should take place daily at first when all children are away or asleep. The emphasis in the discussions should be fairness and consistency. Children should not be involved in these talks. It becomes too easy for them to become manipulators of their birth parents, and the main purpose of these daily discussions is to avoid such manipulations. You may benefit from meeting with a counselor to mediate the "my children, your children" problem, if this particular difficulty becomes stressful.

Family meetings, which include some or all of the children, can also be arranged to provide an opportunity for children to help determine study places and times, household responsibilities, and social guidelines. The balance of control between children and parents in these meetings will certainly vary with the age and responsibility of the children, but final decisions should be made by the parents, with consideration to other birth or stepparents.

Although there is a temptation to believe that both families will be able to participate in all activities together, in actual practice it seems more effective for birth parents to continue to have some alone time with their own children. It is also important, especially for boys, to have some one-to-one time to develop interests with their stepfathers. Developing shared interests outside of school will help children to accept school achievement messages when they are communicated. Stepparents should certainly become involved in children's school related activities, but should avoid setting unreasonable expectations or reinforcing dependent behavior.

The greatest problem in recreated families will come in the children's wishes to maintain close relationships with their birth parents by eliminating their stepparents. They will look for ways to complain about their stepparent, and birth parents are very vulnerable to these manipulations. School work and discipline are the main areas of manipulation and dramatic underachievement becomes a common and powerful tool. Daily communication rather than crisis oriented overreaction can prevent this most exasperating problem.

The Visitation Family. The typical arrangement for children after divorce includes living in one parent's home and visiting the other on weekends and for longer periods in the summers. Since most school day time is spent at the first or main home, the parent carries the main responsibility for supervising homework and school-home communications. Therefore, this parent is the most important communicator of school related messages.

The visitation parent is usually cast in the model of providing fun, games, trips and gifts. There seems to be little time for school discussions during visitation time. However, if children are to achieve in school, they must have clear messages from their visitation family about the importance of good study habits and school achievement. Visitation parents must commit time to discussions about grades, projects and activities at school. They should make an extended effort to support the home based parents' study expectations. Despite any animosity they may feel toward their former spouses, the two parents should come to a clear agreement on school expectations. The "Torn Tommies," children whose parents voice different attitudes related to schoolwork and achievement, rarely achieve well in school until they are able to address school responsibilities in a way that pleases both parents. Visitation parents should become actively involved in setting achievement expectations for their children and communicating these regularly. These messages can be very effective because the school expectations are paired with the brief and happy stays during visitation.

What happens if the expectations of the visitation parents are greater and more realistic than those of the home based parents? Obviously, the visitation parents will feel much frustration and will truly be limited in what they can accomplish without agreement and commitment by the home parents. If visitation is weekly or bimonthly, then visitation parents may set weekly goals and responsibilities for their children which they may reinforce with positive activities on the weekend. It will be difficult to monitor progress, but teachers may be cooperative if parents ask for regular feedback.

In difficult cases, clinical help and some private schools will also be effective in helping underachieving children who receive different achievement messages. Psychologists and private school teachers will be able to contribute more time than regular teachers and can become effective mediators between the two families for clarifying school progress and requirements.

This chapter has thus far emphasized some general parenting patterns which encourage achievement and should prevent Underachievement Syndrome. Recommendations for curing underachievement will be more specifically discussed with step-by-step instructions in later chapters.

7

Curing Underachievement Syndrome: A Trifocal Approach

Underachievement Syndrome is cured most effectively by a TRIFOCAL approach. Our clinic psychologists reverse underachievement in approximately four out of five children by focusing on the child, the parents and the school. Parents and teachers, without a psychologist, can prevent many underachievement problems and can cure some underachievers at less severe stages. Many parents who have attended my lectures have frequently noted that by following my suggestions, they have corrected problems and have improved their children's achievement without needing further consultation. Teachers also have indicated that my workshop presentations have been practical and effective in helping them to reverse underachievement in their students. Although it is possible for each to work alone, the most effective strategy is for parents and teachers to cooperate.

The trifocal model will guide you, as parents and teachers, in curing Underachievement Syndrome in your children and your students. You will recall that the characteristic behaviors of the Underachievement Syndrome were learned. The cure will therefore involve new learning for children, their parents and their teachers. The TRIFOCAL MODEL includes six steps; the first five of which apply to all underachievers. You would select one of the three branches of the last step. Plan to be patient and persevering for success. The average cure time at our clinic is six months. The time varies with the intensity of the problem, the age of the child, and most importantly, with the consistency and perseverance of parents and teachers. Figure 7.1 illustrates the TRIFOCAL MODEL which includes the following six steps:

1. Assessment

2. Communication

3. Changing Expectations

4. Role Model Identification

5. Correction of Deficiencies

6. Modifications of Reinforcements

Assessment will be described in this chapter. The next four steps of the model will be explained in Chapter 8. A separate chapter will be provided for each of the three subsections of the final step, modifications of reinforcements. Chapters 9 to 11 specify recommendations for conforming and nonconforming dependent, conforming dominant, and nonconforming dominant underachievers, respectively.

Assessment

The main purposes of the first step, Assessment, is to determine the extent and typology of children's Underachievement Syndrome. There are formal and informal methods of assessment. The formal approaches include group or individual intelligence and achievement testing, and creativity and underachievement inventories. Informal evaluations involve the questioning and observation of children by their parents and teachers. The formal assessment approaches will be reviewed first.

Formal Assessment

Formal measures of underachievement can be divided into two categories, those which measure the extent of the problem and those which provide the typology. The extent of underachievement can best be evaluated by reviewing all IQ and achievement scores to date and having a psychologist or teacher administer a test battery at this time. The Wechsler intelligence tests have been the most effective for measuring variability in

Figure 7.1

TRIFOCAL MODEL FOR CURING
UNDERACHIEVEMENT SYNDROME

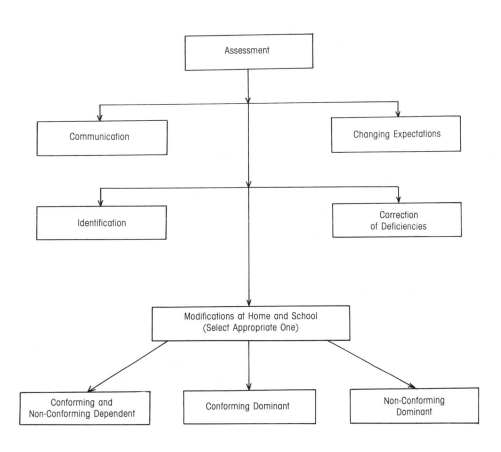

skills and aptitudes. These must be administered by a psychologist. Other individual and group intelligence and achievement tests which may be given by teachers can also be helpful. How can you review these test scores to determine the extent of your children's underachievement? The following are some guidelines to aid you in reviewing the available data.

Complete the chart on next page based on all test scores and grades available and ask the following questions:

1. Have IQ scores, either individual or group, declined ten or more points during the child's educational career?

2. Is there a difference of two categories or more between IQ and achievement tests?

3. Is there a difference of two categories or more between individual and group intelligence tests with individual tests being higher?

4. Is there a difference of two categories or more between intelligence tests and school grades?

5. Is there a difference of two categories between achievement tests and school grades?

If your answer to at least three of these questions is "yes," the child is certainly underachieving. If there is more than a ten point decline in IQ or if the differences between variables go beyond two categories then the degree of underachievement is greater. You may look at underachievement in this way for only one subject or for all subjects. The magnitude of the problem increases with the number of areas of underachievement as well as the extent of that underachievement in any one area.

Other formal assessments which provide help in identifying underachievers include parent and child self-report inventories which have been developed and researched by us at Family Achievement Clinic. They are helpful in understanding the underachiever and his/her typology of underachievement. A description of these instruments follows:

FIGURE 7.2

CHART FOR ANALYSIS OF TEST SCORE AND GRADE DATA TO DETERMINE AREA AND EXTENT OF UNDERACHIEVEMENT

Child's Grade	Individual IQ Test Scores	Individual Achievement Test Scores	Group IQ Test Scores	Group Achievement Test Scores	Grade Point Average
K					
1					
2					
3					
4					
5					
6					
7					
8					
9					

Use the following word categories to describe test scores and grades.

Word Categories	IQ	Achievement Tests Percentiles	Achievement Tests Stanines	Grade Point Averages
Far Below Average	Below 80	0-15	1 or 2	F
Below Average	80-89	16-29	3	D
Low Average	90-94	30-44	4	C−
Average	95-104	45-54	5	C
High Average	105-109	55-69	6	C+
Above Average	110-119	70-79	7	B
Superior	120-129	80-89	8	B+, A−
Very Superior	130+	90-99+	9	A

Achievement Identification Measure. An objective parent report of typical student behaviors based upon findings from interviews with parents is entitled *Achievement Identification Measure* (AIM; Rimm, 1985). It serves to standardize, objectify and shorten information collection. It includes 78 items which can be answered on a continuum including *No, To a Small Extent, Average, More Than Average* and *Definitely.* Items scored vary slightly for males and females with 74 and 66 items being scored, respectively, for each gender. The slight difference in inventories is based on the statistical item analysis which showed that some questions were appropriate for males but not for females, and vice versa. Parents answer all items regardless of the child's sex, but computer scoring is different for males than for females. Reliability and criterion related validity have been established for AIM.

AIM is in regular use at the Clinic and is extremely helpful in communicating to parents the characteristics which their children exhibit relative to achievement motivation. It's ideal for parent teacher conferences because it identifies the syndrome and its main symptoms. Factor analysis yielded five dimension scores which match closely the main problems that characterize Underachievement Syndrome. The dimensions include *Competition, Responsibility, Control, Achievement Communication* and *Respect.* Table 7.1 presents a description of each dimension. Sample questions from AIM are included in Table 7.2.

Group Achievement Identification Measure. A student self-report form known as *Group Achievement Identification Measure* (GAIM; Rimm, 1986) is presently being researched. Items will follow the same pattern as the parent report. Additional items which are similar to things that students say about themselves are also included. The dimension scores will focus on the pattern of underachievement as well as providing a total score.

Group Inventory for Finding Creative Talent and Group Inventory For Finding Interests. Creativity self-reports for schoolage students which use the "characteristics" approach to identifying creativity include *Group Inventory for Finding Creative Talent* and *Group Inventory For Finding Interests* (GIFT; Rimm, 1976, 1980), (GIFFI; Davis & Rimm, 1979). Numerous studies indicate high reliability and satisfactory

TABLE 7.1

DIMENSIONS FOR
ACHIEVEMENT IDENTIFICATION MEASURE (AIM)
(RIMM, 1985)

Dimension	Explanation
Competition	High scorers enjoy competition whether they win or lose. They are good sports and handle victories graciously. They don't give up easily. Low scorers get depressed, cry, complain or lose their temper when they do poorly at something. They tend to brag as winners. They are not skillful in peer relationships because they want to be in charge or prefer not to play.
Responsibility	High scorers are independent and responsible in their schoolwork. They tend to be well organized and bring activities to closure. Low scorers depend on adults for help and attention and do not plan or organize their school responsibilities. They may also misbehave in attention getting ways.
Control	High scorers are comfortable in school or home settings without dominating or manipulating parents, teachers or peers. Low scorers tend to be dominant or controlling children who have typically been given too much power as preschoolers by one or both parents. They expect to be the center of attention and to be in control of their peers, their classroom and their family and feel angry and out of control even when they are subjected to reasonable discipline.
Achievement Communication	Children who score high are receiving clear and consistent messages from parents about the importance of learning and good grades. Their parents have communicated positive feelings about their own school experiences and there is consistency between mother and father messages. Low scorers have parents who give contradictory or negative messages about achievement in what they do and/or in what they say.
Respect	High scorers are respectful toward their parents and other adults. Low scorers are rebellious or disobedient and ignore their parent's requests and requirements. There is frequently inconsistency in the discipline philosophy of the parents.

TABLE 7.2

SAMPLE ITEMS FROM AIM

I help my child with his/her homework.

My child had many health problems as a preschooler.

My child is considered bossy.

My child does schoolwork at a reasonable speed.

My child enjoys competitive team sports.

My child blames others or finds excuses when he/she loses at something.

My child is anxious to be as similar as possible to friends.

My child forgets to do homework assignments.

My child has an older sister who is a high achieving student.

My child loses his/her temper at school.

My child usually obeys his/her father.

My child is very like his/her mother.

My child is perfectionistic.

The father in this family liked school.

My child can get one parent to say "yes" after the other parent has said "no."

The father in the family is a more rigid disciplinarian than the mother.

(statistically significant) criterion related validity using teacher ratings of creativity and ratings of children's stories and pictures as the criteria. The inventories have been validated for specific populations in this country, including rural, urban, suburban, Black, Hispanic and Native American, learning disabled and gifted. They also have been validated internationally in Israel, Spain, Australia, France, Canada, Taiwan and Germany. Dimension scores based on factor analysis include *Many Interests*, *Independence* and *Imagination* for GIFT; and *Art and Creative Writing*, *Challenge-Inventiveness*, *Many Interests*, *Confidence* and *Imagination* for GIFFI I and GIFFI II. The dimensions are described in Table 7.3.

TABLE 7.3

DIMENSIONS FOR
GROUP INVENTORY FOR FINDING
CREATIVE TALENT (GIFT) AND
GROUP INVENTORY FOR FINDING
INTERESTS (GIFFI)

Dimension	Explanation
GIFT	
Imagination	High scorers are curious, enjoy questioning, make believe, and humor.
Independence	High scorers enjoy aloneness, prefer challenge and are not afraid to be different.
Many Interests	High scorers are interested in art, writing, and many hobbies.
GIFFI	
Creative Art and Writing	High scorers enjoy creating art, stories, poetry and music.
Challenge-Inventiveness	High scorers enjoy difficult tasks, taking risks, inventing, and thinking of new ideas.
Confidence	High scorers are independent and view themselves as creative and have good ideas.
Imagination	High scorers are curious, enjoy questioning, aloneness, imaginary ideas, and travel.
Many Interests	High scorers have many hobbies and interests. They enjoy drama, literature, and learning about many things.

The characteristics approach is particularly appropriate for psycho-educational assessment, since it identifies particular areas of strength and weakness as well as providing an overall score. GIFT and GIFFI are brief and easy to administer. They permit discussion of interests with the child and do not involve the pressure of typical testing. They are remarkably effective in identifying the creative underachiever who may easily be overlooked by teachers and parents who may mistakenly tie creativity to achievement. Sample questions from GIFT, GIFFI I and GIFFI II are included in Tables 7.4, 7.5 and 7.6, respectively.

TABLE 7.4

SAMPLE ITEMS FROM GIFT

I like to make up my own songs.
I ask a lot of questions.
*Making up stories is a waste of time.
It's all right to sometimes change the rules of the game.
I have some really good ideas.
I like to paint pictures.
I like things that are hard to do.
*A picture of the sun should always be colored yellow.
I like to take things apart to see how they work.
*I'd rather color or paint in a coloring book than make my own pictures.
*Easy puzzles are the most fun.
*I wish other children wouldn't ask so many questions.
*I would rather play old games than new.

*Negatively related to creativeness.

TABLE 7.5

SAMPLE ITEMS FROM GIFFI I
(GRADES 6-9)

I have a good sense of humor.

I have had lots of hobbies.

I like to take things apart to see how they work.

I like to write stories.

I like to invent things.

I would like to know more about things like flying saucers, witchcraft and ghosts.

I like to try new activities and projects.

I often think about what is right and what is wrong.

I make up games, stories, poems or art work more than other students do.

*When something I want to do gets hard, I give up and try something else.

*I always like to play with friends, but never alone.

I have taken art, dancing or music lessons outside of school because I wanted to.

*Negatively related to creativity.

TABLE 7.6

SAMPLE ITEMS FROM GIFFI II
(GRADES 9-12)

I am very curious.

I am quite original and imaginative.

I enjoy trying new approaches to problems.

I am a risk taker.

I would like to be hypnotized.

I am confident in my intellectual ability.

I am able to work intensely on a project for many hours.

I am witty.

I am very aware of artistic considerations.

I try to use metaphors and analogies in my writing.

I have engaged in a lot of creative activities.

I often think about my personal values.

Informal Assessment

The informal approach to assessing underachievement in your children may be apparent. If your children's teachers have told you for years that they are "not working up to their ability," you can safely assume that the problem is real. If you as teacher see students who rarely pay attention in class, do not do homework or complete assignments and do little or no studying, you can be virtually certain that they are underachieving. If these same students complain that most teachers don't like them or that much of the work is boring or irrelevant or that grades aren't important, these statements are probably coverups or defenses for their underachievement. If they are preoccupied with social life, athletics, drama or music to the exclusion of academic responsibilities, academic underachievement is almost always taking place. Although you can easily determine if your child is underachieving, the characteristic patterns or typology may be more difficult to identify. Careful observation, at school and at home, will probably reveal that.

The earlier descriptions of underachievers may have helped you to determine your children's patterns of underachievement. Figure 7.3 also will aid you in locating patterns in terms of the children's attention reinforcement. Children located in the dependent quadrants manipulate persons in their environments in ways which require more than the typical assistance and encouragement. Children in the dominant quadrants relate to persons in their environments more assertively. However, since they function comfortably only when they feel that they dominate a situation, they feel out of control and dependent when they are not in the dominant mode. Thus they tend to move back and forth between the two halves of the pictograph. Children who exhibit mainly the dependent characteristics may be classed as dependent, while those who show both groups of symptoms are usually dominant. Differences between categories and prototypes are not discreet but may blend. Nevertheless, identifying the main symptoms will help to determine the best approach to modifying reinforcements.

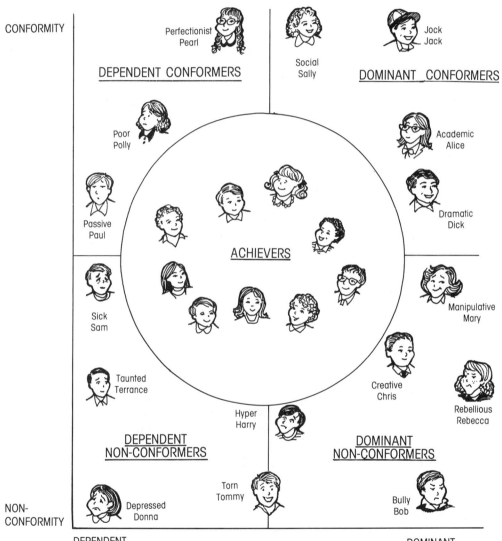

Figure 7.3

THE INNER CIRCLE OF ACHIEVERS

AIM, the achievement inventory described earlier, will help to confirm your suspicions. Dependent children have low scores for Responsibility, but average or high scores for Control and Respect. Dominant children have especially low scores for Control and Respect. Competition and Achievement Communication scores may vary for either group.

Separating conforming underachievers from nonconformers is easier and less important. Conforming underachievers are less visible. They tend to mask their problems. You may be assuming that they will outgrow them. Therefore, they are less likely to be identified as underachievers. It is important to be aware of their characteristics because they are at high risk of moving to the nonconforming state. If your children are nonconformers, they are in a more intense state of Underachievement Syndrome and you can be more certain of their problem. They are also more difficult to cure.

When parents and teachers observe their children at home and in school, it is most important to note how and for what behaviors children gain adult and peer attention. Underachievers are "attention addicted" and want more than their normal share of being noticed. A knowledge of those behaviors used to attract persons to them will help you to discriminate between the two groups. For example, if they continuously ask for help, act very passive, sad or shy, work slowly and don't complete assignments, they are exhibiting dependent behaviors. If they achieve attention by bragging, losing their temper, arguing, or assertively manipulating, they are more likely to be dominant. The usual pace of dependent children is slow and cautious while dominant children are more likely to be speedy and impulsive.

In order to help you confirm the prototype and main direction of underachievement, summaries of each quadrant of Figure 7.3 and of each prototype, as well as typical manipulations, will be described. Each child is truly individual and the labels are used only to focus on a main problem. The titles communicate in a few words multiple behaviors and attitudes. They are shortcuts, and parents, teachers and students themselves may find them helpful.

Dependent Conformers. These children are quiet and pleasant and manipulate adults in covert ways. They seek to attract help with their work because it takes more effort than they are accustomed to. They tend to get along well with others although they are rarely leaders. Parents will describe them as especially sensititve. They cry and are frustrated easily. They whine and complain and report headaches, stomachaches and injuries that are not visible. They exhibit little energy and attract attention at home by their minor illnesses, sadness and calls for help. At school they ask questions and have trouble following directions. They tend not to complete work although the quality of that work may be very good in elementary school — less good in junior and senior high school. They definitely prefer easy tasks and will manipulate persons in their environments in order to avoid pressure or tension.

They may not be noticeable as underachievers in early grades, but their manipulations begin then. Teachers tend to move them to lower reading and math groups to avoid pressuring them. They usually don't like to write because it is "too hard." They may not appear to teachers to be as bright as they really are. At home, parenting usually includes at least one parent who is doing too much for them, overprotecting them and serving as a shelter. If one parent acts as shelter and the second as ogre, the dependent pattern is stronger because the children covertly manipulate one against the other. That gives these children more power. They usually identify with the sheltering parent.

Dependent Nonconformers. Nonconformers differ from conformers in the greater magnitude of their dependency. Thus they are more readily identifiable. They attract more attention to their problem because they are more visible. They are noticeably and typically sad and lonely. Their illnesses and psychosomatic complaints are more frequent and cause them to miss more school. They are teased by other children and use their victimization to attract adult and peer solace. Their problems are more difficult because their sadness is real, and their role of "victim" is less likely to be within their control. As ninth grade Depressed Donna explained it, "No one is nice to me except when I'm really sad and upset. Then I can usually count on my friends to be helpful and supportive." She was mature and introspective enough to understand that although her sadness was effective in attracting friends temporarily, at the time of her emergencies, those same friends would not stay if she continually misused her depressions. However, she also assured me that her feelings of sadness felt very real.

Dependent Prototypes. Dependent conforming and nonconforming prototypes will be reviewed to emphasize the main characteristics of each.

Perfectionist Pearl. Pearl is determined to be a "good" and perfect child. Pearl is usually a "daddy's little girl." Sometimes she is the favorite child of multiple admiring adults. As a child she may manipulate her environment so subtly that no one realizes she has any special problems. As an elementary school student she achieves well. Her underachievement begins at junior or senior high school where for the first time she may find herself "second best." She is addicted to continued positive feedback and since perfection is not as clearly defined in creative enterprises, she typically prefers objective assignments where she can be assured of receiving A's. It still is difficult to identify her as having a problem since she seems so well adjusted. The tears which come if she is corrected or criticized are the first hint of that too strong inner pressure to be perfect. The tears prevent adults from being too critical and keep her feeling precariously perfect. Her main dependent manipulation involves functioning in a way that causes adults in her environment to say "yes, you are a wonderful child." Any attempt to say "no" which cannot be changed by quiet persuasion is met by tears, fears and anger. As Perfectionist Pearl becomes a teenager the tears and anger may be accompanied by feelings of inadequacy, lack of control and depression.

Poor Polly and Phil. These sad little children find a sympathetic ear among parents, teachers, and eventually their teenage friends. They claim that schoolwork is difficult, peers don't accept them, or they are afraid to try particular new experiences. They seem to thrive on anticipating negative outcomes and on persuading persons in their environment to reassure them about their intelligence, their social skills or their wishes for more self-confidence. Parents and teachers, who do much of the early reassuring, comment on the children's low self-esteem, but do not realize that by giving so much attention to their avoidance techniques, they are preventing the development of confidence.

Continuous attention to the child's negative anticipations provides a double problem message. First, the frequent, sincere and kind attention teaches children that self-doubt and feeling sorry for themselves are effective ways to elicit assurances of support and love. Second, the attention often protects them from attempting risk-taking activities that would help build their self-confidence. While solicitous adults truly are attempting to provide kind assistance to these children, that assistance prevents the growth of self-confidence and encourages the avoidance behaviors that maintain their underachievement.

Passive Paul and Paula. Overwelcomed and overprotected, Paul and Paula are at great risk of becoming dependent, daydreaming, and lethargic. When they were tiny tots, parents, grandparents and older siblings clustered around to bathe, feed, dress, entertain and of course, baby them. When these children enter school, adults also try to learn for them or at least provide the easiest way for them to learn. These are the children whose parents sit with them to help with homework and remind them not to get too upset during exam time because "no exam is worth the stress." These parents also help them with shoe laces and hair washing and check their ears to be sure they're clean until they reach adolescence. The parents and solicitous teachers express their loving and caring relationships with these children in ways intended to help them avoid struggle. They are successful in their mission since these children rarely struggle. Rather at the first sign of impending effort they call for help and find it. At the least bit of stress they stop their effort and prevent the uncomfortable feelings. They are protected from thoughts of anxiety but, unfortunately, also from work and from dealing with realistic stress. They have poor self-concepts and often admit that they feel dumb. They try not to dwell on these problems. Instead they escape to television, computer games or sometimes to books and imagination. A parent or grandparent, and sometimes a teacher, will shelter them from the strain that would remove the pain.

Sick Sam and Sara. Dependency is accidentally initiated for Sam and Sara by early physical sensitivities such as allergy, asthma, ear infections or surgery. Actual physical suffering puts children into situations where they are surrounded by adult caretakers who, in their solicitous and sympathetic treatment, unintentionally addict these children to adult attention of their health problems. When their health improves and they receive less attention, they feel ignored and neglected. When adults are not focusing on these children's needs or when they face a challenge, they regress to their habitual way of attracting assistance. Headaches, stomachaches, sore throats, vomiting and asthma attacks are effective in bringing loving adults to their side.

Are the physical symptoms real? Some truly are, but some do mysteriously disappear if a pleasant alternative activity is substituted. It is truly difficult for caring parents and teachers to discriminate the real from the imagined, and frequently it is not clear since to the child the symptoms are true illness. Stressful events certainly aggravate the illnesses, but the illnesses may also serve as an avoidance technique for dealing with normal tensions.

Tormented Terrance. Terrence is a more extreme and more obvious manifestation of Poor Polly. As in the case of Sick Sam, some real problems often have initiated the pattern and it is difficult to separate the real from the imagined; to determine who is instigator and who is victim. If Terrance is handicapped or a minority group member, the accurate recognition of cause and effect becomes even more problematic. Terrance is often alone and typically the last to be chosen for any team. That final choice is accompanied by nasty remarks and sneers or comments on the misfortune of the team. He gets teased and made fun of and sometimes is beaten up. Yet even observant teachers aren't sure whether Terrance is causing his own problems. Terrance's tears elicit considerable sympathy. Since he doesn't know how to become accepted in positive ways, being noticed in negative ways is better than feeling ignored. It is difficult to change Terrance's dependency without changing his peer environment, since peers and parents have set expectations, traps into which Terrance easily falls.

Depressed Donna. Donna's childhood and adolescent sadness can be the result of a more extreme form of any of the dependent patterns described above. Depressions can also come when a dominant child feels he or she has lost control. The main characteristic of depressed children is feelings of inefficacy. Thus the passive children who have escaped so much from stress or effort may feel depressed at their extreme inadequacy; and the perfectionists who see no way to accomplish perfect goals may feel equally depressed. Children who feel in control only when they dominate their environment may feel depressed or out of control if they can't persuade parents of friends of their point of view. The specific causes of depression may be varied, but the displayed characteristics are similar. Sadness, tears, frequent sleeping or sleeplessness, binge eating or noneating, preoccupation with sad themes or suicide are all symptoms which can alert parents to their children's cries for help. Depressed children should have professional help; they have reached a stage beyond which parents or teachers alone can treat them. Identifying the symptoms and recommending help is an important job for both parents and teachers, since symptoms may show up at home or school, but not necessarily in both environments.

Torn Tommy and Tammy. Children who are literally shredded by pre- and post-divorce problems may be either dependent or dominant, which is why Tommy is pictured on the line between the two quadrants. The key to their dependent manipulations is that they do not believe that positive, achievement oriented activity will be as successful as "poor me" symptoms in attracting the attention of one or both parents. Sometimes they believe that getting their parents to feel sorry for them may actually bring those parents together again. If the divorce has been finalized, expressions of sadness bring immediate attention from caring teachers, concerned family doctors, dentists, and even neighbors. Messages of deprivation at one home may bring gifts or compensating love and attention from the other home. For dependent Tom or Tam, sorrowful eyes are more effective and easier than positive effort and in the confusion that surrounds divorce, it becomes a habit that traps them into a dependency pattern.

However, Torn Tommies are not always dependent. They may just as easily take on a dominant manipulative pattern and then will function much like Manipulative Mary, Rebellious Rebecca or Bully Bob. With each parent trying to become a good parent, frequently at the price of making the other into a villain, dominant manipulators can acquire amazing power. If they manipulate in a dependent way, the chapter on dependency is most useful. If their manipulations are more overt, then look for guidance in the chapters on dominance.

Dependent Manipulations. Dependent children manipulate covertly and usually are not consciously aware of the manipulations. The targets of their manipulations are caring and loving people who find it difficult to deny the children's requests because refusal would make them feel guilty or unkind. Even when the manipulations are explained, kind parents and solicitous teachers find it extremely difficult not to respond in ways that they instinctively feel are right. Adults who respond in this way pride themselves on their sensitivity and concern. It is difficult to convince loving adults that they should not prevent their children's struggles. Particularly in subtle cases, parents and teachers may believe that our approach is "mean" and places too much pressure on the children. You, as parents and teachers, must assure yourselves that these children will build self-confidence and competence *only* through effort and perseverance, and that it is indeed a true kindness to permit these children to experience some stress.

The main manipulations of dependent children will each be described so that parents and teachers may tune into them. An important precaution, of course, is that one should not ignore these same requests when they are genuine.

Help Me. Children who request help *continuously,* whether it is related to chores at home or schoolwork, are probably getting more assistance than is appropriate. In order to determine if they are truly needy, you should compare them to children of similar age, intelligence and developmental stage. Developmental child care books can assist you in determining if your children should be dressing and bathing themselves, riding their bicycles or helping with chores. Let them do as much as they can do capably. Individual intelligence testing will tell you whether they are capable of reading instructions, completing assignments and interpreting math problems.

Children's calls for help at home are directed toward parents, older siblings or other relatives. In school they are directed toward teachers, aides and peers. Sometimes they are in the form of verbal requests and hand raising. However, with time dependent children become expert at "help me" body language. A few tears, facial expressions of stress, nail biting, staring out the window, dropping or playing with pencils, shuffling papers helplessly or working very slowly become the more subtle requests for assistance. Sensitive parents and teachers often pride themselves on recognizing their children's needs, but they must cautiously ask if the needs are real or if they are signals for attention in a pattern of helplessness. There is only a fine line between sensitivity and overprotection, but recognizing and respecting that line will help you to avoid encouraging the "help me" manipulation.

Nag Me. Dependent children move slowly. If they are not working efficiently they can count on being reminded by their caring parents and teachers. If you call it "reminding" now, you can count on their calling it "nagging" eventually. They will blame that nagging on the adults in their lives, particularly their mothers or fathers. Spare yourselves. Don't fall into their trap. Although your children don't seem to mind your constant reminders, and you truly believe that you are encouraging faster speed, you are actually slowing them down. Do you know of anyone who became more efficient through nagging? Therefore, you can't even label your nagging activity as kind. Recognize nagging as a reinforcement of dependency. You are preventing your children from learning to organize their own time by your attempts to nurse them through their activities and responsibilities.

Protect Me. Dependent children use this manipulation to avoid new experiences. Meeting new friends, going to new places, or trying new academic challenges can be avoided by children who tell their parents that they are afraid. Adolescents sometimes label this fear as embarrassment. Whining, crying and tantrums accent the proclamations of fear and make them difficult to ignore. Parents who offer protection are again rewarding avoidance behaviors. Sheltering children from irrational fears is another way of telling them that there is good reason to be afraid, or why else would wise adults protect them?

Feel Sorry For Me. Children who have genuine problems, for example, difficult financial circumstances, divorce, parent illness, physical or mental abuse, or personal health or handicapping conditions, easily move into this dependency pattern. They find out, often by accident, that adults in their environment are willing to center much attention on their problem. It becomes enjoyable for them to receive so much caring.

This pattern is more difficult for adults to deal with than any of the others because these are not totally imagined ills. The children are feeling real pain and have undergone true suffering. It is truly difficult to identify the place where illnesses end and manipulations begin. Are absences from school due to stomachaches or to the avoidance of incomplete homework confrontations? Are asthma attacks real or due to the stress of math tests? Are sore throats the result of an infectious condition or a stressful examination schedule? Do you insist that children carry through their anxiety producing responsibilities, or do you ease their burden and excuse them from assignments? The "feel sorry for" manipulation is difficult to detect and equally challenging to correct. Physical problems and pain may accidentally serve to provide an escape from dealing with reasonable home and school stresses. Parents, teachers and pediatricians must work closely to discern real medical risks, and they must encourage as much independence as is healthfully possible.

Love Me. Hug me, kiss me, cuddle me and reassure me of your love. These are manipulations which tear at the heartstrings of affectionate parents and teachers and appear at first to be harmless requests for affection. They are not at all harmless if tied to children's avoiding difficult tasks or unpleasant but necessary experiences. When Danny, a first grader, would run away from his classroom because the teacher insisted he sit at his desk and complete his written assignments, his mother snuggled him and reminded him of her love before she dutifully walked him back to school. On difficult days, mom also provided special hugs of comfort to help him deal with his stress. The snuggles, hugs and assurances reminded him that he was loved regardless of his school misbehavior. They also served to remove from him any responsibility for changing that behavior. Why change from something easy to something hard, especially when one is assured comfort for the easy task, but outcomes are uncertain for the more difficult responsibility?

A favorite punctuation request by children who have recently misbehaved is "Mom, do you still love me?" and of course, mom assures him that she does. She may try to separate his "wrong" behavior from himself, but why bother? The child simply requires the assurance that he's loved regardless of his behavior so that he may continue his irresponsibility. Mother wonders at the child's insecurity — but what is apparent insecurity is only very convincing manipulation. In some cases, a sincere sounding note of apology is added to the "love me" statement, and "I'm sorry, forgive me" becomes one more type of manipulation.

There are many opportunities for parents to express love, affection and forgiveness. However, these should not be in response to a child's regular pattern of avoiding responsibility. Frequency of requests for love and their proximity to avoiding effort will guide you in determining if your children's requests are genuine or if they are only one in a series of effective manipulations.

Shelter Me. The ogre rituals discussed in an earlier chapter cause one parent to take the role of shelterer. Thus, whatever the "ogre" parent requests, the child can find shelter with the protective parent. If father has commanded that the lawn be mowed before he comes home, and son has not complied, mother can first remind, then nag and finally help out to protect her boy from dad's impatient temper. If daughter has not completed her homework after school as mean mom has insisted, then dad can spend the evening by her side assisting with that difficult mathematics assignment. The child learns a dependent power pattern to cope with the stresses of meeting even the reasonable requests of one parent. There is no real reason for the child to work if avoiding the work provides a sheltering, loving experience with the other parent. Dependent underachievers almost always are reinforced for their dependency by one sheltering parent.

Dominant Conformers. These students often are not recognized as underachievers, depending on the degree of their problem. They are overtly very competitive and will not make efforts or persevere in domains where they cannot excel. They devalue all interests and skills except those where they excel and achieve status. They may indeed be leaders, but in that leadership they can foster a nonacademic orientation. They "put down" teachers who do not recognize their talent, and they can be powerful influences on their peers. They tend to set unreasonably high goals for themselves — they plan to be professional football players, Olympic athletes, concert pianists, Broadway stars, millionaires and presidents. They demonstrate enormous discipline in the field of their choice, as long as they are dramatically superior. If their status decreases so do their efforts.

Because many of these students are very bright, their grades may be average without much effort. Thus their underachievement may not attract attention, even though they tend to "just get by." If their talent is truly extraordinary, their scholastic underachievement may not cause them future problems. However, since they tend to select highly competitive fields, many will face great disappointment after high school. Their academic underachievement leaves no cushion for them to fall back on or toward which they can redirect their efforts. Many of these underachievers are not identified until after high school graduation. They are the high school extracurricular and social elite who do not achieve the success that their teachers and friends had anticipated.

Dominant Conforming Prototypes. Some of these prototypes will be discussed together since they are so similar. The difference comes only in their area of talent rather than in their behavior.

Social Sally and President Peter. In high school Sally and Peter are attractive, well dressed, tuned in to fads and norms and are POPULAR. They are pleasant, well mannered and usually liked by teachers. They're prominant in student activities and presidents of those in which they participate. They are not interested unless they are in leadership jobs. They consider serious students to be "nerds" and will only enjoy A's if they can get them effortlessly. As a matter of fact, too many A's make them feel uncomfortable and "bookish."

Their families are pleased with their social success. They always did place a high priority on good adjustment. Their message about academics has been, "Of course we expect you to do your work, but it's better to be well-rounded than to be too gifted." *Well-rounded* was explained as "getting along well with other children." Their parents have fostered the social emphasis by much social driving and arranging. They provided interesting and unusual parties and encouraged boyfriend/girlfriend relationships and early dating. "We always wanted our children to be popular and happy," they acknowledge.

Their children are indeed popular and happy. However, they do not enjoy classes or learning or people who like learning. If they are bright enough, A's fall only to B's and B's only to C's, because social life is more important than studying. Since they are in the conforming mode of dominance, they do just enough to get by.

It is when they go to college that the emphasis on social popularity is no longer effective. The goals they formally believed were so important lead to a partying style and a social emphasis that does not fit with academic success. Their frustration with failure combined with a social emphasis may lead to alcohol, drug addiction, and even sexual promiscuity — all in search of their earlier successful popularity. Academically they can no longer "get by." Because they don't tolerate failure experiences well, despite their intelligence, they drop out to find a job instead of a career.

It is difficult for parents to understand what has happened to their happy children, who have found their first struggle in college and who discovered that social priorities are irrelevant beyond high school.

Jock Jack, Dramatic Dick, Musical Marilyn and Drummer Don. Of course there are others as well. These talented children earned recognition and attention for their special areas of expertise from early childhood onward. The athlete in whom parents invest their time in training and spectatorship, their money for equipment, camps and private lessons, and most of all their own personal pride, is the center of admiration and attention by peers, teachers and often the entire community. In like manner, the star of the school musical or the leader of the local Rock Group are admired and applauded by adult and peer audiences. The plaudits are intoxicating. For competitive young people the excitement of achieving center stage in the gymnasium, the auditorium or the dance floor appears to provide a sure career direction. Academics seem inconsequential and dull by comparison. Studying and homework are put aside in favor of practice and rehearsals. They "get by" because they know they must have minimally acceptable grades for athletic scholarships or drama study. For Rock Groups, however, getting by isn't even necessary. They only hope for the "right breaks" to achieve fame and fortune. Grades may drop to failure and alcohol and drugs may be viewed as enhancing their music.

These gifted children on whom adults and peers have centered their attentions become addicted to admiration and exaltation. They are performers who feel in control of their lives only in front of an applauding audience. They have been successful and have learned to persevere, but only as long as they are winners. Minor defeats, a second place, or a less than perfect game or performance are part of their repertoire. They have learned to tolerate that kind of failure experience. However, they have no wish to invest effort in peripheral areas where they see no chance of excellence and admiration.

A very tiny fraction of these "stars" will continue to real stardom. They are sufficiently talented that even beyond high school their talents will be recognized. Those few become the professional athletes, Broadway stars, successful rock musicians and solo violinists. The remaining majority discover that the talent that entertained their high school peers does not meet the highly competitive standards of the outside world. For them, life suddenly seems without purpose and full of failure and disappointment. For the many who ignored academic preparation, they have no adequate fall back position. Traveling Rock Groups and Drama Troups abound and music teaching seems like dismal failure to the soprano who pictured herself a Broadway musical or opera star. These children are not prepared for failure and entrance into young adulthood is traumatic without adequate academic skills or admiring audiences.

Parents and young adults alike remember their glorious days of childhood and adolescence, the peak of their life, with no chance of similar attainments again.

Academic Alice. An intellectually gifted child who achieves outstanding grades and is valedictorian of her high school class hardly appears to be a victim of Underachievement Syndrome. Yet Alice's first year in college leaves her paralyzed by depression. The symptoms typical of underachievement appear later for her than for most students but the underlying problem is the same. Alice cannot deal with placing second best in academic competition. For her the B's represent failure and create anxiety which inhibits her rational ability to deal with her problem. Though she may, in fact, be capable of A's, she no longer can organize herself to do the appropriate studying. Nor can she accept B's as reasonable grades — anything less than A's depresses her. She has rarely dealt with such 'failure" before. She has always felt smart and still does, or is she beginning to doubt that? She no longer knows how to prove her ability to the relevant other people, her professors, who are the conveyors of her rewards.

Since the beginning Alice has been smart — gifted, even brilliant. Awards, honors and scholarships have always been hers. Schoolwork was never a challenge; she was always first in her class. Academic excellence was her pride. Parents, relatives, teachers and friends always noted and praised her accomplishments. She had never been in an environment where she was not superior. In college no one was placing pressure on her to excel, but everyone assumed that she would. It was an anticipated outcome — predicted by both family and friends. It was also what she expected of herself — to be spectacularly successful. How could she not feel terribly and helplessly disappointed?

At home Alice's parents had provided an enriched environment and had been proud of her accomplishments. They had not pressured her nor expected anything beyond her capabilities. They actually made efforts to avoid unnecessary pressure and frequently encouraged her to take time from her study for fun. At school, in her small town, teachers had encouraged Alice's excellence and some teachers had provided additional assignments within her classroom. There were, however, no coordinated efforts to challenge Alice — no gifted programs or acceleration. There were no opportunities for Alice to meet or compete with other gifted children from other schools. There were few chances for Alice to experience being second best, and none for dealing with inadequacies or failures. Real intellectual challenge was completely absent from Alice's school experience, and her habit of always being first provided sufficient motivation to maintain her grades. That difficult adjustment which Alice was forced to make in college could have been eased by modifications in both home and school environments.

Dominant Conforming Manipulations. Although dominant conforming manipulations are learned early in childhood, they are typically unobtrusive at that time. Furthermore these manipulations actually support the development of intelligence and talent. They are only problematic in degree and not in quality. If children almost constantly demand praise and notice and if they become accustomed to expecting too much attention, even though it is positive attention, it will cause a serious problem. Determining exactly how much praise to give is difficult, but crucial to the problem. Children who are gifted and talented develop their abilities in an enriched environment where a loving parent, parents, siblings or grandparents make large time and attention commitments to that enrichment. Dominant conformers have learned to demand too much. They depend on continued exclamations of excellence and admiration.

The admirers of dominant conforming children are initially few — the adults in their early environment. That expands rapidly to include relatives, peers, parents of peers, and persons in the neighborhood, on the street and in shopping centers. School experiences add teachers and more peers to the growing crowds whom these children manipulate positively and unconsciously with their exhibitions of talent and brilliance. The fans vary somewhat depending on the talent, but there is always a big audience.

The main manipulations of dominant conforming children are far fewer than for dependent children, and they also are more positive. Parents and teachers should be alert to them, but only in order to not over respond. Ignoring these children's efforts for attention would be harmful, but diminishing the praise somewhat and positively reinforcing more productive alternative behaviors to add balance to the child's learning experiences will help these children. Since parents feel personally involved and excited about their children's successes it is more difficult to bring balance to the enthusiastic praise than one would expect.

Admire Me, Praise Me, Applaud Me. Dominant conforming children are constantly on stage. They are tuned in to identifying observers who will admire them and applaud them. They perform best in front of an audience and their early childhood smiles tell you that they know you are watching. If you're not, they'll attract you quickly. A "pleasant showing off" is probably the best way to label what they actually do, but it seems too harsh a term to describe the way the two year old charms you by dancing in a circle to family applause or the subtle manner in which the three year old selectively enunciates four syllable terms far beyond those which adults typically use. The audience gives rave reviews including "smart," "brilliant," "graceful," "musical," "talented," "genius," "charming," "bright," "natural athlete" and a long list of other verbal credits for children to internalize and to set as specific goals to achieve. These children continue to improve their performance and internalize the praise as pressure to achieve. Although positive expectations are good, there are too many.

Do Not Criticize Me. "I am wonderful, and if you don't tell me that I am wonderful I will feel hurt. I will cry. I will lose my temper or I will sulk." Since these children are accustomed to accepting only the positive, even the absence of praise is viewed as negative appraisal. The crediting of other children's achievements may be seen as painful personal censure, and correction or a suggestion of change or improvement is the worst form of condemnation. It is difficult to communicate anything but praise and admiration without a defensive response like, "Why do you always criticize me?"

The "do not criticize me" manipulation maintains that there are two groups of audiences. "My friends are those who like my performance all of the time; my enemies are those who dare to tell me that I'm performing poorly." Because dominant conforming underachievers equate performance with self, they see censure of performance as a personal attack on self. They manipulate persons in their environment to avoid such criticism whether or not it is intended as constructive. They do learn to accept the constructive recommendations of a small number of experts in their areas of expertise whom they have learned to respect, admire and trust. The talented children do not attempt to manipulate this elite group because the children recognize the status and expertise of these mentors, do not feel competitive with them, and instead see them as models to emulate. All others beware — the "do not criticize me" manipulation is powerful.

Dominant Nonconformers. The most obvious group of underachievers and the most difficult to cure fit into this category. These young people rarely ask for help and tend to blame their environment — their family and the school for their problems. They actively rebel against "establishment" goals and are determined to live their lives on their own terms with little or no consideration for those who love them. They establish their identity by opposition. They push limits and refuse to accept "no." They claim that teachers don't like them, but what they really mean is that they only like teachers who give them special privileges. The more rebellious they become, the fewer teachers they are able to rally to their support.

They feel out of control and depressed unless they dominate other people in their environment. In their adolescent years they are difficult to help without professional assistance. Therefore, it is helpful to identify these children early to prevent the extreme acting out of their problems. They may rebel for years, but many become effective leaders and achievers after they gain insight into their feelings.

Dominant Nonconforming Prototypes

These children are obvious underachievers. They cause parents and teachers stress. Although some appear "cool" and in charge, they are personally pressured children. They may try to obscure their struggles from adults with defensive words and actions, but be assured that they are suffering, much more in adolescence than in early childhood. Growing up is not easy for these youth who believe they must always lead their own way.

Manipulative Mary (Max) and Rebellious Rebecca (Rob). These girls or boys are children who have been given too much power. They overtly manipulate and are bossy. They almost always derive their extensive power from uniting with one parent against the other. Their relationship with their partner-parent is adultlike, and in that mediating alliance they together dominate the other parent. They expect to be treated as adults and feel as though parents or teachers are "putting them down" if they expect reasonable conformity. They accept no criticism without anger. Manipulations that take place include parents against each other, parents against teachers, teachers against each other and teachers against parents. They also exploit friends. They politic comfortably and at their convenience, with little concern for the truth and little concern for the people they cast as "enemies." For those they assign the role of "friend" they are sensitive and caring. However, friends quickly change to enemies and so no one is safe — least of all their parents whom they 'bad mouth" to their friends, teachers and friends' parents. These children are difficult to live with and sometimes it's even hard to remember that you love them.

When the manipulations aren't effective, they turn to rebellion. The peaceful interims between rebellions are successful manipulation stages. Their self-confidence is based on their successful domineering of home and class and friends and is thus fragile. They oscillate between joyful power, obnoxious rebellion and distraught depression. Parents and teachers may see them differently. They may be obnoxious in school and depressed at home, or vice versa. Their rebellious outlets include underachievement, belligerence, cigarettes, alcohol, drugs, promiscuous sex or all of the above.

Creative Chris. These children have early absorbed the message to "march to the beat of a different drummer." One or both of their parents frequently do. They are highly creative, more typically in the intellectually superior rather than very superior range of ability and are obsessed with nonconformity. Sometimes it feels as if conformity to another person's expectations is self-betrayal. Many of these children are productively creative but cannot transfer that productivity to school achievement. If they are creative writers, they don't get their assignments in on time, although teachers will acknowledge the unique quality of their work. If they are artists, they want to do different forms of art than those that are assigned. And if their creative outlet is mathematics, they find a shorter and more efficient way of arriving at the same answer. They get the right answers, but refuse to show their work so they lose credit. Although parents and teachers acknowledge their originality and talent, the children don't permit themselves to achieve by typical standards. They experience the highs and lows which go with control and feelings of loss of control, respectively. Creative classes, teachers and peers frequently provide them with a creative sanctuary and they temporarily may find that they can be very productive and achieve. However, success for any length of time may feel "too conforming" as they strive for their uniqueness, an illusive quality.

Bully Bob or Temper Tom. These boys, but sometimes girls too, dominate their home and school environments. They have been given power overtly and have controlled mother, father or both with temper tantrums, fighting and disruptive behavior at home and school. They want home and school run their way and they make their demands known. At home they typically are successful in directing family life. At school where they meet more frustration, they react to their inability to control with behavior problems. They may easily talk their parents into believing that the problems are someone else's fault, and bewildered mom and dad may find themselves siding with the already too powerful child against other families or the school. Life becomes much more complicated for Bob as he earns a reputation for aggressiveness which he feels required to live up to. When he does make efforts to improve his behavior, his reputation makes that difficult as teachers and even peers and parents automatically assume he's to blame.

This overtly aggressive behavior problem is amenable to change in the preschool and early elementary years if parents and school cooperate, but is very difficult to alter as the child grows older. In adolescence, changing school environments away from aggressive peer groups is often preferable in order that the youth, with help, can create a new image.

Hyperactive Harry. These high-energy children whose unfocused activity prevents them from attending, learning and organizing are placed on the line between *dependent* and *dominant* because they may manipulate their environments in either way. Their high-energy probably has a biological base but also has been nurtured in a chaotic early milieu. Inconsistent messages between adults and within each adult provide no definite limits to a high-energy child who searches for secure boundaries. This child, who needs clearer limits than most, is surrounded by adults who offer little consistent control. Messages involving complex reasoning are given before they are old enough to understand the abstract logic. The kind, understanding warnings of things *not* to do are interpreted as long, soft sounding speeches which accidentally reinforce and encourage the naughty behavior. Previously patient parents find themselves losing their tempers in irrational ways which they would not have thought possible, including spanking and screaming at their mischievous children. Then they apologize to their children for this loss of temper, which totally confuses them. These children soon accustom themselves to the tempers and scoldings which are followed by kind apologetic voices, and so they continue their accustomed style of doing exactly what they choose to do exactly when they choose to do it, without concern for consequences. They more typically fall into the dominant category since they will hit and push and kick and get out of their class seats at will. Occasionally, even in their high-energy style, they will maneuver with whines, whimpers and requests for help and will then be classified as more dependent.

Dominant Nonconforming Manipulations. Dominant nonconforming manipulations are obvious to parents and teachers, although the children will deny they are intentional. By adolescence, they are more likely to acknowledge their tactics to friends and confidants and may even brag about their successes.

Despite the fact that adults may be aware of the children's actions, the children are often so persuasive and persevering that parents feel worn down by their persistence. The dominant manipulators are expert at sensing parent moods, weak moments and alliances and their repeated successes encourage them in their resourceful machinations. However, their confidence is built precariously on powerful control, and their mood swings, which include tears, tempers and depression, help to persuade parents to give them exactly what they want or face the unpleasant consequences. You will want to be alert to their strategies so that you can outmaneuver them. Here are their manipulations — be prepared to be creative.

Admire Me, Praise Me, Applaud Me. These manipulations are common to both conformers and nonconformers. The major difference between the two groups is that conforming students are more subtle and more successful. Nonconforming youth often find these manipulations unsuccessful although at some earlier time in their development they were effective. In other words, the activities that formerly served to make them the center of attention are no longer effective, and their continued searching for that earlier sense of security based in adult admiration encourages more extreme manipulations.

The origin of the manipulations comes in providing too much attention. However, family circumstances, for example, new siblings, growing up, or insufficient talent, place the children in positions where the extreme admiration or applause is diminished. Children who are very verbal and bright may not receive as much notice for their intelligence when their younger sibling begins using impressive vocabulary. The little girl who was the first female child in three generations becomes less noticed when joined by a younger sister. She feels not as smart, not as pretty, and not as special as she used to feel and thus searches for ways to focus attention on herself; sometimes these ways are manipulative, sometimes creative, and sometimes only rebellious and unpleasant. When admired and praised these children respond well; their rebellion subsides. When ignored, the rebellion increases. They want too much and have learned to struggle too little.

Do Not Criticize Me. This second manipulation is also the same as that of dominant conformers, but it is again more extreme. The failure of others to respond to such manipulations will be followed not only by sulking, temper or tears, but also by retaliatory behaviors. If persons criticize, these children look for ways to "get even." For the more aggressive Bully Bob's it may involve fighting. The less physical children will retaliate for being criticized by talking back, talking about, or employing other strategies intended to hurt the critic in return for their own feelings of pain. These children feel mistreated and untrusting when they have been criticized.

Disagree With Me. A major manipulation for these youth is the power struggle. They want to dominate and win and are determined to prove dominance by making other persons into losers. They challenge persons to disagree only in areas where they feel confident they can win, which builds confidence in their personal power. Criticism, to which they are sensitive and to which they overreact, bothers them because they see it as an accusation of weakness. They are practiced debaters and arguers in their territories of strength, but if they feel they are losing they regress to the defenses used when criticized (above). Parents and teachers are often puzzled by the extremes these children exhibit; first they act like seasoned battlers, then suddenly they are reduced to flailing tears. They have sufficient confidence in their aggressive skills to initiate arguments frequently. A tension pervades the atmosphere. There is a continuous readiness for argument that bewilders parents and teachers alike. They carry the proverbial "chip on the shoulder."

Give Me. "Gimme" is the familiar request, also "I wish," "I want," and "I need, more and more." There seems no apparent end to the wished for material possessions and activities. All must be done instantly, all must be had immediately. No's are met with fury or, as they will explain, justified anger. Sometimes there is a thank you, but more often there are no words of appreciation or even acknowledgment. It is as if these children take for granted all that is given but never attain a level of contentment. The process of buying, selecting, purchasing, and accumulating never ends and is another avenue for expressing their domination and control.

Be Mine. "I want so much to be completely close to someone, to trust them completely, to have them as a very special friend." These seem appropriate expressions of desired relationships for an adolescent or young adult. However, the words underestimate the feelings. These young people want relationships of complete control which smother their friends of either the same or the opposite sex. They want so much power in their relationships that differences of opinion are viewed as treacherous; differences in activity preference as disloyalty; other friendships as unfaithfulness and individuality as opposition. These young people find much reason for distrust because they define trust in an intense and confining way. They invest themselves heavily in others, but their requirements for control are so great that friends resist, reinforcing the sense of disappointment and depression. These are children of extremes and they literally want to own their relationships.

See My Difference. A corollary to the primary manipulation of praise and applause is the dominant nonconforming youth's wish to be viewed as different. They want you to see them as belonging to a different group or to no group at all. They ask you to notice their uniqueness, their unusual characteristics, their artiness and their separateness. They may classify themselves as poets, artists, or radicals as long as the classification includes a sense of being unusual. Since they perceive themselves as different, they would like that confirmed by exceptions for them based upon their unique characteristics: "Move the deadline because my story is very creative." "May I write a longer story since I write so well?" "Can I be exempt from the research paper since I've done my own experiment?" Their requests may not be unreasonable; however, there is a desperate sense of establishing difference by bringing attention to their uniqueness.

How Far Can I Push? For these children pushing limits establishes both dominance and control. They learned early not to accept "no" without negotiation. For some it was the pleasant kind of persuasion which flexible mom or dad saw as appropriate under the circumstances. For others it was more belligerent and angry. In either case it was effective and these children have learned the appropriate "people buttons" to push to get most of what they want. A parent's "no" only meant to try a different route, sometimes the other parent or a grandparent. A typical resource used is "other parents let their children" — they know how to make parents feel guilty. The "pushing" becomes a habit, a way of changing peoples minds that helps them to feel in control. It ties the sense of confidence to control. Thus there is helplessness, depression, and anger when people don't respond to the controller's demands and insistences. They continue to push the limits with parents, teachers and even societal boundaries. For these children there are no *no's,* only "How far can I push?"

Determining The Next Step

As you review your formal and informal assessments of your children, you can decide if you as parent or teacher can hope to cure their Underachievement Syndrome or if you will need professional help. Younger children and less extreme degrees of underachievement are relatively easy to reverse. Also, dependent and conforming underachiever patterns are more manageable by parents and teachers than are dominant and nonconforming ones. You may indeed need the assistance of psychologists or counselors to make a reasonable change in persons in this latter group. Peers, alcohol, drugs and sex can be more powerful motivators than parents and school achievement for these youth. Since many underachievers are concentrated in the less extreme dependent and conforming quadrants, there are many children that you can cure.

You are now ready to move to Step 2, communication to teacher, parent and to the underachieving children.

8

The Next Four Steps: Communication, Expectation, Identification and Correction of Deficiencies

The next four phases of the treatment plan for Underachievement Syndrome stem directly from your findings in the assessment. They can take place approximately simultaneously. Each will be described in this chapter.

Communication

The cure of Underachievement Syndrome proceeds most efficiently when parents, teachers and students work together. The initiator of the effort may be either a teacher, the parents or the student; but the effectiveness of the result is largely contingent on clear communication between them. If parents are initiating the effort to reverse the underachieving pattern, it is obvious that they need the support of teachers. It is less obvious, but equally important, for teachers who are facilitating a change in children to communicate with parents. Although it is possible for teachers to help their students without parent cooperation, it is so much easier to work closely with parents and the reversal process takes place more quickly.

If you are a typical teacher, you are already burdened with a full teaching schedule and many additional responsibilities. When you make the decision to cure Underachievement Syndrome for children in your class, do be realistic in the number and types of underachievers you target, especially at first. Also, your chances for success are greater if you have parents who are willing to cooperate. Since you will probably be able to reverse only two or three children in any one school year, begin with those with whom you are most likely to succeed. Helpful parents increase that likelihood. If you have already communicated with the parents and they have voiced their concern about the problem, that's a very good beginning.

If you are a teacher and a parent too, you can empathize with the parent's feelings related to their children. They are disappointed at their poor achievement. In the process of trying to understand the problem, they feel frustrated and guilty. They feel helpless about changing the school situation and do not know what to do or what to change at home. If you are a parent and not a teacher, you are less able to understand the teacher's sense of frustration. Teachers only work with children for one year, and in the typical junior and senior high school for only a very small part of each day. Although they may see the problem, they cannot understand it's cause and they can only dedicate a small amount of time to coping with it. They also teach between 25 and 150 other children.

When they teach the same children all day, most children are, in fact, learning. It is difficult to know how to deal with bright children who apparently refuse to learn. They are tempted to attribute causes of the problem to others and simply avoid dealing with such a difficult issue. They might blame parents or the children's earlier teachers. Sometimes they simply conclude that the children are lazy. When teachers plan to talk to parents, or vice versa, it is helpful to remember that both environments are reinforcing the underachieving pattern and both should change their approach to responding to these children.

The preparation for a conference should be different for teachers than for parents. Teachers will want to formalize the documentation of the problem as part of their professionalism. Parents, on the other hand, should use an informal approach to avoid appearing threatening to teachers. One would think that parent-teacher conferences could be approached without trepidation; however, as many parents and teachers know, conferences about children with problems are fraught with tension. A guideline to helping you to prepare is, if you are a teacher, speak to a parent as if you were the parent, that is, in a caring way; if you are a parent, speak to a teacher in a way that would make you feel comfortable if you were a teacher.

Teacher Initiated Conference

Meetings should begin with teacher assurance of concern for the child, the recognition that underachievement is a perplexing problem, and a statement about the wish to work with the parent to foster the child's achievement motivation. The formal assessment discussed previously should be presented clearly to the parent. Intelligence and achievement test performance should be explained. Creativity (GIFT) dimensions and underachievement (AIM) scores should be described verbally and interpretation manuals should be given to parents with the scores. Inventory scores may need further description by noting that they are self-reports or parent reports and represent the way children see themselves or the way parents see their children, compared with other children and parents. Although these are highly reliable instruments for large groups, they can be inaccurate for any one individual. For example, with GIFT or GIFFI some children respond in the way they believe is desirable rather than honestly. I find this particularly so in the item relative to perseverance and challenge. The scores may thus be inflated in the direction of higher creativity for those few who are not entirely honest and introspective. In the same way, in completing AIM parents who are extremely optimistic or pessimistic in their descriptions of their children can inflate or deflate the scores. As you describe the dimension scores to parents, you may be able to determine whether or not the parents are realistic in their description. My own clinical experience with AIM shows that it is very effective in explaining basic Underachievement Syndrome patterns. Thus IQ and achievement scores become the vehicle for communicating the extent of underachievement. GIFT or GIFFI scores, but particularly AIM scores, help to succinctly explain the type of underachievement. Because parents have actually been involved in the completion of the AIM inventory, the scores are an especially effective means of emphasizing the child's dependency or dominance. It also is very good to have some specific informal examples of the students classroom behavior to illustrate how the problems show themselves in the classroom.

After you have described your impression of the problem at school, it is then appropriate to ask the parents what problems they are noting at home. If they are unable to describe concerns (this rarely happens) or if they deny problems (this is common) you might give them some examples of typical home situations from this book. As soon as parents acknowledge the dependent or dominant configuration, you have taken your first step toward helping their children. Next you should describe the changes that you are going to make at school and discuss suggestions for modifications that they may be able to make at home. Determine together the behaviors and grade goals that you see as realistic and emphasize the place of *process* and *effort,* rather than immediate outcomes. Grade goals should not be unrealistically high, but initially only slightly above where the children are presently performing. Once motivated, children will choose higher goals themselves. Be sure to explain to the parent that change is not likely to be immediate and that there will be vacillation before children learn to recognize the relationship between effort and outcome. Specify the way in which you plan to continue communication. Daily reports, weekly reports or telephone conferences are alternatives. Examples of report forms appear later in this chapter where they will be explained. Written communication should remain simple. Your own time constraints and the clarity of messages make brevity necessary. For more extensive situations, oral communication is more satisfactory.

Teachers should be cautious about becoming too involved in the personal lives of their students and their families. If it appears that the parents require assistance with more than Underachievement Syndrome, the teacher should recommend an appropriate community or private service. Psychological counseling is not an appropriate role for nor the obligation of teachers.

Conclude the conference with a summary of what you have agreed is taking place and what your mutual goals are for the child. It is good to confirm your pleasure at having developed a working relationship with the parents.

Parent Initiated Conference

When parents initiate a conference they are in a much less powerful position than are teachers. You, as parent, are asking teachers to give you personal time and effort beyond that which they allocate to other children. Also, you are not the "expert" in education that they are, yet it is you who are taking the initiative for recommending a change. There is an uncomfortable feeling or "role reversal" taking place for the teachers, and they may legitimately feel defensive.

You might begin the conversation by asking teachers if they think your child is working up to his or her ability. If they confirm your suspicions, you might examine the difference between test scores and school performance to reach agreement on the extent of that underachievement. If recent IQ scores are lower than earlier ones you might note the decline as an indication of underachievement. Together, you could conclude what might be reasonable grade expectations for your child and the kind of effort and time commitment typical for achieving those grades.

It is at this point in the conversation that you could share with the teacher the fact that you've been doing some reading about Underachievement Syndrome and that you believe that your child fits a particular category of underachievers. You could explain that, as a result of your reading, you or you and your spouse are planning certain changes at home and that you would appreciate the teacher's assistance with these changes. Hopefully, teachers will be happy to cooperate, but it is most important that you suggest some reading material that they may review. You may want to loan your copy of this book with your child's appropriate pattern and treatment underlined or you may want to share your child's AIM scores, the interpretation manual or a reprint of one of the magazine articles included in the reference section. Many teachers will be very open to helping you.

However, if your child is a *dependent* child, be prepared. Very solicitous teachers are likely to believe that you are expecting "too much" and are therefore putting pressure on the child. Refer them to the chapter on how to assess and assist dependent children. If your child is *dominant,* rigid teachers are unlikely to be supportive of them until the child has indicated a willingness to make an effort. They will resist a change in their own teaching style and continue to expect the child to comply. Nevertheless, sharing with these teachers the sections on dominant children may influence them. Also, keep in mind that it is difficult for teachers to change their basic teaching approach since they have found it to be most effective with the majority of their students.

Even if some teachers don't buy into your plan, many will. Particularly if you give them information in writing and some time to read that material, they may be happy to help. It would be reasonable not to expect that the teachers will give you a definite answer until they have read the information you've given. Setting up a second appointment at the teacher's convenience would be prudent. By that time teachers can confer and can put together a plan that they can manage during schooltime. Then you will be able to integrate your home plan with their school strategy.

If some teachers are not cooperative, don't be discouraged. It is possible to make dramatic and immediate changes in your children by changing home patterns. Many times parents and teachers have reported to me striking differences in their children brought about only by changing parenting approaches at home. The most typical immediate change in the child is an increase in self-confidence. Further, achievers typically feel confident that their parents and teachers are directing their educational enterprises appropriately. Your sense of confidence is the first step in communicating to your children that you have clear ideas about improving their school achievement. They no longer need to flounder by manipulations and pushing limits; it is the first step in the reversal of their underachievement.

Student Achievement Communication

The central characteristic which distinguishes achievers from underachievers is an internal locus of control, the sense that children can effectively change their own academic outcomes by effort. The vehicle which helps children to develop this understanding of the relationship between effort and outcomes is a communication form that is completed by teachers. The form is shared and discussed by children and their parents at a regular daily or weekly achievement monitoring conference. If parents are actively involved, children receive communication about their progress twice; once from their teachers who distribute the message and again from their parent or parents who receive the communication. If teachers, without parents, are involved in the underachievement cure, a key teacher or counselor should be the regular receiver of communications about progress. The persons with whom the students review their progress will be termed sponsor.

Three forms which are used at the clinic appear in Figures 8.1, 8.2 and 8.3. These may be modified to deal with specific concerns or behaviors. However, they should remain uncomplicated so that teachers will not feel burdened by the time necessary for completion.

Sponsors should plan achievement meetings with children either daily or weekly. For primary children, a brief daily review of accomplishment and reinforcements is appropriate. As achievement and behaviors improve, sponsor meetings should be set for a regular weekly time. Upper elementary and secondary children should have weekly meetings initially. When effort becomes fairly consistent, meetings should move to bi-weekly and monthly.

The tone of sponsor sessions should be positive and instructive. It provides children with the opportunity to review their gains, to receive encouragement and to deal with both the positive and negative consequences of their new efforts. Sponsor sessions become the means for assessing and reinforcing efforts, setting goals and clarifying consequences. Rewards and punishments which may be used will be discussed in the chapters related to dependent and dominant patterns. Regardless of whether rewards are used, student achievement communications from a teacher to children and their sponsors is an important process in the building of the childrens' internal locus of control and personal self-confidence.

Changing Expectations

Children's habits of underachievement have led family, teachers and peers to expect continuing low levels of achievement. Even children's expectations of themselves do not match what is potentially possible in their school performance. Children's expectations should be changed to match the new achievement that is anticipated.

Figure 8.1

DAILY EVALUATION FORM

Student   Teacher
Name _____   Name _____   Date _____

Assignments Complete: _____ All _____ Most _____ Half _____ Less than Half

Quality of general class work: _____ Excellent _____ Satisfactory

_____ Fair   _____ Unsatisfactory

Behavior: _____ Excellent   _____ Satisfactory _____ Fair

_____ Unsatisfactory

Comments: _____

_____

_____

_____

Thank you very much for your help.

Personal Expectations

In order for children to change their achievement, it will be important that those persons near the child overtly recognize the improvement and to note that the new achievement levels are appropriate for the child. This is very important. Underachieving children have their niche and it is all too easy for those in their environment to just maintain the *status quo*. Inertia operates to keep underachievers in their place, and therefore specific initiatives should be taken to alter both status and expectations. If persons in the children's environment do not accept the changes, his or her achievement will seem hopeless to the child. There will be little movement and, after initial attempts, the children will give up in despair.

Figure 8.2

WEEKLY EVALUATION FORM

Student   Teacher

Name _____ Name _____ Date _____

Subject: _____

Approximate grade for week: _____

Assignments Complete: _____ All _____ Most _____ Half _____ Less than Half

Behavior: _____ Excellent _____ Satisfactory _____ Fair

_____ Unsatisfactory

Comments and missing assignments: _____

_____

_____

_____

Thank you very much for your help.

Those important persons in the underachievers home and school should make strong attempts to recognize even small efforts or they will surely disappear. We all know that change is stressful to the changer. More subtly, however, changes in status alter the balance of power in families and classrooms, and the "victims" of status adjustments will resist. Parents and teachers must be assertive facilitators for altering expectancies.

Self-expectations are the first that should be changed. Underachievers lack an internal locus of control. They believe that the whole business of achievement is related to luck or to generous teachers. Many of them have unrealistically high goals; they think that their luck will suddenly change and they will become the A+ student they dream they should be. They don't believe their efforts will make a difference, and they are quick to point out the lucky times that they did receive good grades effortlessly.

Figure 8.3

WEEKLY EVALUATION FORM

NAME _____ GRADE ___ WEEK OF _____ DATE_____

Subject	Behav'r	Effort	Grade This Week	Grade To Date	Teacher Signature
1.					
2.					
3.					
4.					
5.					
6.					
7.					
8.					
9.					

Teacher Comments —   Missing Assignments

_____

_____

_____

_____

Please use the same rating for effort, behavior, and achievement:
A - Excellent   C - Average   F - Failing
B - Above Average   D - Below Average

Depending on the extent and pattern of underachievement, they either expect a magical solution or they believe that even if they made an effort, nothing will be different. Sometimes they assure you that the intelligence tests used to set expectations for them are too easy to be used as an indication that they have the ability to do such difficult work.

Children must be given a clear road map of what is likely to happen if they decide that they would like to become achievers. They should know what reasonable grade goals are and what amount of time and effort those goals will require. They certainly must have the expressed trust and belief of parents and teachers that they *can* achieve those goals, and the realization that adults in their environment will be patient while they are making new attempts. They must realize that while working they will sometimes feel stressed, impatient and disappointed in themselves, but that all of these feelings are benchmarks for achievement motivation and a true index that they are on the correct route.

Sometimes children have so little confidence in themselves that it is appropriate to share actual test scores to prove inescapably that they do have the ability to achieve. Unrelenting belief that they can achieve at higher levels, paired with a constructive insistence on effort, are extraordinarily important to their achievement. Achieving adults can point out the adults in their own childhood environments who believed in them. They may also be able to name those who did not. However, without the first group they would not have succeeded. Sometimes the believers were parents; other times teachers or friends. Communicating positive expectations to your children is a very high priority for their improved perceptions of themselves.

How do you determine reasonable expectations for your child? IQ scores remain the most reliable guideline. Here are some factors which parents should consider in setting their children's expectations based on IQ. These guidelines should be used for underachievers only, since IQ should never be considered as a ceiling for achieving children. That is, for children who perform well, their actual performance is a much more important indictor that their IQ test score.

1. An IQ score of 100-110 indicates average grade level expectation in an average school district. With reasonable motivation, grades of C could be expected and reading and math should be at grade level.

2. An IQ score of 110-120 (Above Average Range) would predict B grades at grade level work, but elementary grade children in this range who have good study habits can probably achieve some A grades as well, depending on the evenness of their specific abilities.

3. IQ scores above 120 (Superior Range) should predict A and B grades, and IQ becomes less important than study habits in determining grades in this range.

4. IQ's in the 130 and above range (Very Superior) suggest A's and B's in *above* grade level work, but this may also vary with strengths and weaknesses in specific abilities. Some children may have higher verbal than performance scores, while others may have higher performance scores. Thus reading and social studies may be stronger than math and science, or vice versa. It is very important that parents not give gifted children the message to 'be normal" which may be interpreted as "get average grades." These children should certainly be encouraged early to use their abilities to learn and to get good grades.

5. In setting expectations for your own children it is important to modify the expectations based on (a) the approximate average IQ of the general school population and (b) the academic grading system of the school, as well as of specific teachers. For example, the average IQ of a particular school district may be around 120 and the average grade for a particular teacher may be B. Thus the child with 120 ± 5 IQ score may be achieving well when attaining B grades, considering the school standard and the teacher's grading habits. Most school districts will be happy to tell you the average IQ for the school. Teachers are less likely to be aware of the average grade in their class. You should consider the student and the teacher environment in setting expectations.

It is reasonable to set two goals for underachieving children: a short-term and long-term one. The short-term one should be set conservatively, but the long-term one may be set a bit more optimistically. Setting goals too high or too low are equally problematic for underachievers, so parents should be as realistic as possible, It is helpful to observe children's efforts. If the effort is low, then goals can be set higher. If efforts appear genuine and reasonably efficient, then the present goals may be appropriate. However, it is important to identify the efficiency of study. Many underachieving children appear to put time into study, but it is not efficiently used time. They should develop strategies for study as well as the motivation to use those strategies.

When parents have established reasonable expectations, they should share these with their children so that the children can accept "ownership" of similar expectations. Parents should provide some rationale for their expectations and should ask children for input to determine if they consider them fair. Discussion of grade expectations should not be the basis of power struggles but should be arrived at by joint concensus, based on the parents' and children's similar concerns. Parents must avoid making their children feel like losers in battle if they agree to the parents' grade goals. Finally, parent consistency will be very important in the childrens' acceptance of grade goals.

When parents and underachieving children reach agreement, the next step will be informing siblings of the changed expectations. This should be done privately so that each sibling is given support for the expected change in status and has been given a clear message by parents that any discouragement of their sibling, no matter how subtle, will not be tolerated. If this communication is given in private to achieving children, the message is more likely to be taken seriously. Parents should announce their pride in having an achieving family, emphasizing the cooperativeness of the enterprise rather than the competition. Achieving children should be encouraged to be supportive and should be made aware that you, as parents, will be looking for and admiring that support. They should view their sibling's achievements as something in which they can share, and not as a "put down" to their own personal accomplishment. Teaching siblings to admire each other's performance is a valuable counterbalancing technique in dealing with difficult sibling rivalry. If siblings are not part of the expectation plan you may find a "see saw effect." As the underachieving child begins achieving, the balance may shift to cause the achieving child to fall down in performance. This does not necessarily happen, but it is a risk if you ignore other siblings in the changed expectations.

Teacher Expectations

Teacher expectations are of critical importance to changing performance. Teachers tend to pay less attention to test scores and are much more attuned to children's past performance. If there were no changes to be made in the home and school environments, they probably would be accurate since past performance is usually the best predictor of future effectiveness. However, since parents, teachers and children are now in a "change" mode, it is particularly important that teachers personally invest in expecting improvement. They may use IQ scores as a guide, but it would be important to have a school psychologist individually test the child. Group intelligence tests are contaminated by underachievers' lack of motivation. Their group test scores have often decreased regularly, or at best, the scores are inconsistent. Since scores tend to be low, teachers using these scores would set goals for these children that are also low.

In addition to anticipating better performance for underachievers, teachers should inform the children of their higher expectations. When children show success it is important not to overreact, but to display pleasure in their achieving what are now reasonable performances. It is equally important not to overreact to occasional setbacks since these should be anticipated enroute to building a consistent achievement pattern. A written note of confidence and reassurance of expected future success is often effective. Comments on paper become important communicators of encouragement. Private messages feel much more personal than those given orally in front of the class. An important caution: teachers who insist that the child is not making and will not make an effort will find exactly what they expect. Negative teacher expectations can be damaging.

Peer Expectations

The effect of peer expectations on achievement is very different in elementary school than in middle and high school. At all levels, peers do have an impact on the cure of Underachievement Syndrome.

At the elementary level the "dummy" of the class is in an unpopular position. Teachers become the interpreter to the class of who the "dummies" and "troublemakers" are. Much of this can be avoided if teachers can manage to keep most negative comments private, yet make some positive comments public. Obviously, teachers can't be expected to manage that kind of control at all times. However, they will by and large set the peer expectations of student achievement by their comments about each child. Since they are in a powerful position to influence negative peer expectations, they are in an equally strong position to affect positive change in peer expectation. Teachers should be careful to make positive statements gradually and not as if a miracle of transformation is taking place. An overreaction to the underachiever's early success will cause the child to give up if he or she isn't consistently successful. Peers will accept a new image of success if the underachiever is gradually given increasing recognition for achievement, and decreased negative feedback. Positive peer acceptance will follow easily.

Middle and high school are very different matters. Here, teachers are much less effective in influencing peers, although well liked teachers can continue to make a positive difference in peer acceptance. If underachievers are part of a peer group with "pro-school" attitudes, their improved achievement may be viewed by their friends as what might be expected of them, and thus they find encouragement from their friends. However, if the underachiever is part of an anti-school peer group, improved grades may make them unacceptable to their friends. You may want to talk to your children about actually changing friendship groups. It may seem impossible to them to move into a different peer group, even if they wanted to, in light of their reputation and school performance. In some cases, where peers are extremely negative, changing schools is a reasonable alternative. A change should not be made hastily, and certainly not without consideration of the youth's input. However, moves from public to private schools or the reverse, coupled with new achievement efforts may facilitate positive peer acceptance.

Placement into special education classes should always be done with great care. Children who are labeled "emotionally disturbed" or "mentally retarded" often have great difficulty dealing with peer expectations. The value of the educational or emotional support which they receive in the special classroom should be considered in balance with the probable negative expectations which peers will establish. Such placement is always a difficult decision for parents and educators to make, particularly if they are not absolutely certain as to whether the diagnosis is Learning Disabled (LD), Emotionally Disturbed (ED) or underachievement. It does complicate Underachievement Syndrome cure when peers have negative expectations of children. Special education may have the unintended effect of reinforcing an underachievement pattern. For example, dependent underachievers are frequently and mistakenly placed in learning disabled or educably mentally retarded classes since dependency characteristics resemble those of the slow learner or the learning disabled. Learning disability classes often provide the one-to-one and small group help which reinforce the child and teachers perceptions that they can learn only on a one-to-one basis. Dominant underachievers are more frequently placed in Emotionally or Behaviorally Disturbed classes. The students' insistance on controlling the classroom causes behavioral problems. These are not easily solvable in the classroom without outside psychological help for them and their families. ED or LD placement, however, reinforces these children's sense of being different. Peers who are not receiving special help label these children as "unusual," or worse. At the secondary level, special education students are often expected to find friends only among others in special education, thus many of the educational efforts intended by parents and educators to be helpful have a very negative and not easily measured side effect. Negative peer expectations adversely affect personal self-confidence for many years and may deter the reversal of underachievement patterns.

The issue of labeling children with diagnosed disabilities is surely controversial. The misdiagnosing of underachieving children as learning disabled, retarded or emotionally disturbed is a much more serious problem because the label limits expectations by teachers, family and peers. This inappropriate categorizing of these children literally stops the effective cure of Underachievement Syndrome.

Identification

Children learn appropriate behaviors more easily when they have an effective model to imitate. The process by which children select and unconsciously copy family models was described in an earlier chapter and is called *identification*. When underachievers spontaneously reverse patterns of underachievement they frequently cite important persons who were pivotal in their change of direction. These persons were the models with whom they identified and from whom they adopted adjustment patterns, work habits, studying practices, and general life philosophies and career goals. Several persons may serve as models for any one person. However, the people in an individual's immediate environment are especially important in influencing goal oriented decisions. Children and young people frequently refer to some adults around them as people they would like to "grow up" to be like.

Sometimes, models chosen may not be appropriate for achievement motivation. Children may choose "rock stars," sports heroes and multi-millionaires about whom legends of miraculous and magical success are woven. These unrealistic models are imitated in their adolescent dress, music styles and fantasies. "Real" person models seem inadequate by comparison since they're not as prestigious as the stage and sports idols. Underachievers tend to select these stars as models to be copied without any thought to the process by which the person has arrived at the lofty height and without any conception of the many thousands who have fallen by the way in competition. They would rather fantasize in ecstacy and expectation about the miraculous discovery of their own hidden talent than invest in the more mundane efforts which would build their skills toward a realistic goal. Hero fantasy is not harmful in itself, but when it becomes a substitute for effort and for the more realistic emulation of working models it can prevent the necessary learning of skills which would lead to achievement. Fantasy becomes an excuse for avoiding responsibility.

Since imitation of models is so important to the reversing of underachievement, we should focus on the sources of models as well as the processes by which we can encourage identification with appropriate models.

Sources of Models

For most children, family members are the best source of identification models. Fathers and mothers, if they are positive achievement oriented persons, are ideal. It's important that their achievement orientation is visible to their children, since children can only copy what they see. Thus if their positive "work self" is reserved only for the work place and their grouchy, negative self is displayed at home, there is little opportunity for beneficial emulation. Although this seems obvious enough when you think about it, many parents are not sensitive to the selves they present to their children. The achievement orientation which they would like their children to imitate is frequently invisible. Since it is not possible for most children to see their parents in the work place, mothers and fathers should interpret and describe their work process to their children. That interpretation must include enthusiasm, challenge, effort and satisfaction if it is to convey a suitable work message to them.

There is certainly a realistic place for mentioning discouragement, frustration and failure experiences, but if the latter negative characteristics pervade the description of work, there will be no reason for children to be inspired toward effort. They will only see a negative achievement model and will use it as a rationale for either rejecting their parents as models or adopting the negative attitudes. They will convince themselves that they don't want to work hard because they prefer a value system which is much better than that of their parents: a "fun" ethic that avoids drudgery and is based on a happy-go-lucky life-style. Making parents into appropriate role models is the most practical way of teaching achievement motivation. To do this successfully, parents' work must be viewed and interpreted as interesting and fulfilling.

The increase in one, three and four parent families makes it challenging to help the underachieving child view a parent's work favorably. The opposition that may have caused the divorce or the absence of a father increases the problem. Certainly step parents can be appropriate models. However, that becomes difficult if the children's birth parent criticizes and belittles them. Nevertheless, building stepparent relationships with children can certainly be a growth experience, and stepparents can become ideal models for children.

Other relatives, including grandparents, uncles, aunts, and cousins, may certainly be good models for emulation. These models need not be frequently available since parent descriptions of their activities can partly substitute for their actual presence. They should be achievement oriented and should also be able to develop a special rapport with the child. Older siblings also can be important as role models. Younger children typically admire their older siblings and it takes only a small step beyond admiration to build that important identification. However, older siblings will be high risk for identification if they have not yet managed to focus their own lives.

Teachers are especially valuable as models. Children often report the special admiration they feel for a particular teacher. They may spontaneously choose one as a model, and any particular teacher may have dozens of students who aspire to be like him or her. However, it takes very special teachers to both win the admiration of students and to guide the youth who see them as identification figures. Teachers can make a positive difference to literally hundreds of underachieving students during their career, although the day to day routines and responsibilities may prevent them from sensing the impact they are making.

In every reader's life there were important teachers who influenced them in positive directions — some who built their skills and others who built their confidence. For children without appropriate role models, teachers fill an important vacuum. In a society in which the structure of marriage is so precarious, positive and caring teacher models become very critical to children. Generally, society should place a greater value on the role of educator in order that children can view them as persons worthy of emulation. It is equally important that the teachers value their roles as educators. There are some unfortunate examples of disgruntled teachers who use their classroom power to grieve to children about unfair administrative or school board practices.

Others bemoan their choice of career to their students, thus unwittingly preaching an anti-education message. The teaching profession is often not sufficiently honored or rewarded. Nevertheless, students are not the appropriate audience for teachers' complaints. Disenchanted teachers are very bad models for the children in their classrooms and can have major negative impacts on underachieving oppositional youngsters.

Community leaders are another source of models. Adults who invest their time in scouts, 4-H, youth church groups and athletic coaching can make that time commitment more valuable if they understand the important role of identification. As adults take special interest in young persons, they also become effective models. Although communities frequently find a scarcity of volunteers to lead young people, those who accept these volunteer responsibilities may make potentially major contributions for many youths searching for adults to admire. If you serve in the significant role of youth leader, it is important for you to communicate to children the value of academic achievement.

Peer models spontaneously impact on youths who have not selected adult models. Peer imitation may be very problematic when the peer group is anti-school and anti-parents. Of course, positive peer groups provide a pro-academic message and encourage study and learning. Peer models may also serve as models for appropriate social behaviors. Unfortunately, it is difficult to point out to a child another young person for imitation without engendering competition and resentment. Younger children may be guided to model selection and imitation to improve awareness of on task schoolwork, appropriate and enthusiastic hand raising, eye contact, pleasant or friendly body language, good manners and general social skills.

When you suggest that children copy others, it is important to remind them that the imitation should only be of specific skills that will be helpful to them. Asking children to actually copy another child's general actions is an invidious comparison and is likely to decrease their self-confidence. However, pointing out two or three behaviors for imitation is not likely to cause harm and makes the learning process easier.

Fiction, history and biography are rich with descriptive material to inspire youth toward perseverance, education and heroism and can provide effective models for many children.

Identifying similarities between their own lives and those of their heroes, and emphasizing how these persons met failures and overcame them, can introduce young people to the pairing of *struggle* with *success*. Since underachievers tend to expect results instantly and tend to see their smallest attempts as major challenges, the extensive time which their heroes invest in work and practice will serve as a concrete illustration of the enormity of effort required to accomplish serious goals. Identifying with such heroes should help young persons realistically assess their own efforts and talents and can provide positive models for success. Unfortunately, society has many heroes on stage and in sports who provide negative messages in their life-styles, and our children are easily inspired to follow these because of their attractiveness, power and wealth. In guiding our youth in adopting a hero as a model for achievement, we should provide an index of quality which they will hopefully choose to follow.

Process for Encouraging Identification

"When I was your age I remember having some of those very same feelings" may be the sincere statement of fact that ties a child to an adult in an identification relationship. For a child, this makes the grown-up very human and approachable. It also encourages the child to see similarities between him or herself and that adult. You may recall that two of the three variables that lead to unconscious copying of an adult model are *nurturance* and *similarities* between the two. In a statement that couples personal concern and similarity, the adult may be taking a big step in influencing a child to find personal direction. The third variable to enhance identification is power, but all three variables need not be present for imitative learning to take place. In deliberately selecting models for identification similarities between adult and child are helpful, however, it is certainly wiser to look for positive similarities.

Unfortunately, when children are underachieving and have a poor self-concept or are oppositional, they are likely to be attracted to inappropriate models who share the same talents and experiences. Thus young adults who may not have established their own identities, and who may be confused about their own direction, may be readily available negative models for underachieving teenagers. Since they are older and appear more experienced, powerful and exciting, youths who see their own frustrations as similar to those of flashy young adults are ready prey. The young adults may think they can help these youths, with whom they might counteridentify, and the helping process gives them a sense of personal self-importance. However, because neither truly have a sense of realistic direction they may flail and fail together. Young adults who attract high school youth to a rock performance group, a traveling drama troupe, an arts community or an extreme religious sect provide models and inspiration to these youth. Temporarily they provide security, shelter and support for the youth's opposition to parents. These rarely are permanent or positive, and in the process educational opportunity doors may be closed. Sometimes they drop out of school or give up college scholarships. Sometimes they alienate their families beyond repair.

How can you avoid these negative identifications? Protect your child from the vacuum that evolves when potentially appropriate models no longer see anything positive in the adolescent. When parents and teachers continually criticize their children, the children will not select these criticizers as models. Avoid this negative cycle so often generated by rebellious adolescents. Search for the positive in children and they will be more likely to follow your guidance in selecting environments where they will be surrounded by appropriate role models.

Music, art, language, science, computer and drama summer camps, youth travel, camping grounds, and special schools may be effective in channeling the adolescents' choices of models. Visiting a family member out of town or taking a career oriented job are other alternatives in which positive models can have impact on your children. Changing the physical setting can have the effect of preventing the children from following the "path of least resistance" and inspiring them by exposure to people who are positively involved in growth experiences. An environment where youths are surrounded by other motivated young people who share their interests and dedicated teachers who inspire them can be pivotal in giving purpose to an underachieving child. Increasing numbers of such opportunities are being made available by camps, universities and private schools during the summer months. An inspirational summer can make a difference, particularly if participants maintain communication during the school year.

A parent/child one-to-one adventure is an excellent way to encourage identification with a parent model. A negative father/son relationship or stepfather situation can change into a pairing of admirers after the two have shared a week's camping or boating experience. A one-to-one car travel adventure, where two family members are not distracted by parent or sibling rivalry or pressures of the job or school, can provide the bonding which causes two formerly oppositional relations to admire and respect each other. Children may see for the first time reasons to admire and copy qualities of their parents. One spectacular week can provide a strong foundation for positive identification and emulation. It can melt the opposition and provide a solid basis for parents to influence and guide their children.

Correction of Deficiencies

The next step of underachievement cure is the easiest, but it cannot be neglected or the entire plan may fail. Children who underachieve may not have learned basic educational skills which will be necessary to their further success. For very gifted children skills gaps may be minimal, but for most children, depending on the length of time of their problem and on their abilities, there may be major deficits in their skills. The subject areas fall into four basic categories: reading, math, writing and language.

A tutorial system is most expedient for efficiently eliminating skills gaps. However, there are a great many risks in one-to-one instruction. So although it is appropriate for the task, there are some suggestions that tutors should follow to avoid reinforcing Underachievement Syndrome.

1. Avoid fostering dependence. Explain concepts. Have children demonstrate understanding. Insist on independent problem solving and carrying through of assignments. Children absolutely should not have someone sitting by their side as they complete assignments. Encourage them to push their own limits.

2. Provide a goal oriented framework for the students, including time lines and the charting of accomplishment. Tutoring should feel purposeful. Will they be able to test out to a higher reading or math group? Can they learn to write for a school newspaper? When they achieve their goal, may they choose to discontinue tutoring?

3. Move children through material as quickly as they can handle the skills. These are bright children receiving individualized instruction. The sense of rapid progress will encourage their confidence in their achievement and will generalize to their classroom.

4. Tutoring poorly can reinforce the underachieving pattern. Tutoring well can provide a springboard to achieving better in school. Underachieving children can easily trap tutors into their manipulations. Tutors, therefore, should understand the child's pattern to avoid the trap and help them correct the deficiencies as quickly as possible.

The Last Step

The final step of Underachievement Syndrome treatment plan is divided into three sections. Read all three regardless of your children's diagnosis. Then select the modifications at home and at school which are most appropriate for your children.

9

Dependent Children – Modifications

The recommended environmental changes for dependent children will be the same for conformers and nonconformers. You may be tempted to assume that the first group will outgrow their minor problems. That is unlikely without modifications in the responses of important persons at home and school. Parents and teachers who are willing to interpret the problems and react to these children in a new way will alter the habits that have maintained their Underachievement Syndrome.

Parenting Modifications

Understanding the causes and characteristics of your children's patterns is the first important component of your change. However, as kind and sympathetic parents you may have difficulty finding the courage to replace many of the reinforcements that you accidentally provide to your children. As you modify your usual responses to your children, you may fear that you are not being sufficiently sympathetic or supportive. You might feel guilty about your parenting and even think of yourself as unkind or inadequate. You may worry that these differences will cause your children to suffer further or fail. You may sense so much internal pressure about your fear of their failure that you may experience it as if it were your own personal failure. Since any or all of this is likely to happen to you, read the following words of encouragement several times before you begin.

1. If you do not permit your children to work independently now, they will surely fail later and accurately blame you for that failure.

2. If you overprotect and do too much for your children, they will resent your stealing away their independence.

3. Your children cannot learn independently when you keep them enslaved in dependence.

4. Your children's dependence on you makes you the thief of their self-confidence.

5. If your children use tears, whining, complaints, physical ailments or noneating as manipulations, you are being *unkind* to respond to them as if they were real problems.

These precautions should help you through the difficult days ahead. If you have the courage to weather this change, let me assure you that you will feel more confidence as a parent, and after your childrens' initial struggles are accomplished, you will enjoy with delight their rapid growth in competence and confidence.

Vote of Confidence

Do not do for children those things of which they are capable of doing and should do for themselves. Any child development book will let you know what typical children of their age are doing. Dressing, washing, doing chores and, most important, doing homework should have very little if any of your intervention. If your children are accustomed to reminders, nagging, sympathy and assistance, they have learned to focus your attention on dependence. You should learn to refocus that valued attention on the completed task. Remove yourself physically from the scene of attention-getting dependence, but be available and complimentary when the job is complete. A comparison of a dependent versus independent morning routine will serve as an example. If your child is dependent, he or she probably fits Inset 9.1; try the instructions on Inset 9.2 to strengthen their morning independence without nagging.

The ingredients of the early morning vote of confidence include (1) encouraging and insisting on the child's independence, (2) withdrawing your nagging attention from dependence, and (3) relocating that positive attention and reinforcement to the completion of the independent task. There is a negative

---

INSET 9.1 DEPENDENT MORNING ROUTINE

Mom: Bobby, are you up?

Bobby: (No answer)

Mom: Bobby, it's time to get up!

Bobby: Um - awfully tired - a few more minutes.

Mom: Bobby, you better get up, you'll miss the bus! (Repeated with increasing volume 3 to 10 times)

That's only the beginning. Admonitions to wash face, brush teeth, eat breakfast, hurry, wear different clothes, remember lunch money, school books, notes and finally warnings about the soon-to-arrive school bus or parent pickup add to the unrelinquishing din. Arguments between siblings on bathroom use, clothes exchange and breakfast choices punctuate the distressing beginning of the day. If two parents are awake, interparent debate about the degree of nagging reinforce the hassled start of each new morning.

---

consequence that takes place if the child does not complete the task — for example, no breakfast. The negative consequence is rarely used but should absolutely be enforced if necessary. The positive should be emphasized, and do try to voice confidence in your children that you initially may not feel.

The same basic ingredients can be applied in reversing any dependent pattern. It fits well with bedtime routine, chores, trying new experiences, mealtime and of course, homework, but homework will be given special attention later.

1. Encourage your child briefly and if necessary insist.

2. Move your attention from an incomplete task to the completed task.

3. End the child's task with a pleasant consequence.

4. Emphasize positive accomplishment, not potential negative consequence.

The Place of Shelter

Protection is certainly appropriate for children who are being physically or sexually abused by a parent. Sometimes shelter from verbal abuse is also necessary. However, a multitude of parents

---

INSET 9.2 "HOW TO" - FRESH MORNING START!

Step 1: Announce to your children the guidelines for the new beginning. From this day forth they will be responsible for getting themselves ready for school. Your job will be to await them at the breakfast table for a pleasant morning chat.

Step 2: Night before preparations include the laying out of their clothes, getting their books ready in their book bag and setting the alarm early enough to allow plenty of morning time. They will feel just as tired at 7 a.m. as they will at 6:30, but the earlier start will prevent their usual rush.

Step 3: They wake themselves up (absolutely no calls from others), wash, dress and pick up their room. Breakfast comes only when they are ready for school. Absolutely no nagging!

Step 4: A pleasant family breakfast and conversation about the day ahead! Parent *waits* at the breakfast table and is not anywhere around them prior to their meal together.

Question: What happens if they don't dress in time for breakfast?

Answer: No breakfast. (That will only happen two or three times for children who like to eat.)

Question: What happens if my children don't like to eat breakfast?

Answer: Fifteen minutes of cartoons after breakfast, when they're ready for school will probably be effective.

Question: What happens if they don't get up?

Answer: They miss school and stay in their room all day. That will happen no more than once.

Question: What happens if they don't have enough time in the morning?

Answer: They go to bed 30 minutes earlier and set the alarm 30 minutes earlier until they find the right amount of time necessary for independent mornings.

Question: Does this routine work?

Answer: Absolutely, with elementary aged children. Sometimes with high school students.

---

shelter their children from a harsh voice, an appropriate spanking or a reasonable requirement for responsibility. Mothers, especially, have a tendency to recoil from a husband's occasional scolding of their child and they seem to fear permanent damage to that child. Typically, these same mother's will scold and lose their tempers without a similar concern for any negative impact on the children. The logical conclusion here is that mothers often hear their own voices as being quieter than their husbands'. Children are resilient enough to deal with a loving parent's angry voice and need no cushion from the other parent.

If parents lose their tempers frequently, it is an indication that they lack control of their children — these children are not listening, respecting or obeying. The parent who provides a shelter or protection for the child being scolded is thereby encouraging the child to further disobey and show disrespect. If the scolding parent is demanding reasonable effort and discipline, the sheltering parent is reinforcing *reduction* of effort and *avoidance* of responsibility. Yet mothers and fathers often do this to each other. By undermining each other's requests and demands they again steal children's self-confidence. The sheltering parenting is teaching avoidance manipulations instead of helping to develop competence and confidence. The protected child learns that when tasks are difficult, uncomfortable or high risk, it is appropriate to escape and search for protection rather than cope with the stressful challenge.

If you and your spouse have differing perspectives on child-rearing and discipline, make some compromises. There is no one right way, except the one that the two parents agree to. It is better to be too strict or too lenient than to teach children to manipulate their parents to avoid responsibilities. The sheltering parent may feel loved and like a "good parent" at the time he or she provides shelter. As children grow more discerning they are likely to label that parent as *weak*. The parent who views the shelter as kindness later will have difficulty interpreting the child's lack of respect stemming from the parent's weakness. Furthermore, both parents may get disgusted with their child as they watch that child's expertise in avoiding, making excuses, giving up and complaining.

Of course, there is a place for shelter. If one parent does abuse, the other parent must assertively take a stand to protect the child. That is a different form of protection and is not related to the dependency issue.

Encourage Same Sex Identification For Boys

The importance of modeling was discussed previously but it must be reemphasized. It is very important for male self-confidence and achievement for boys to have a male identification figure. Mother-dependent and mother-identifying boys frequently have underachievement problems. There are two main reasons: first, they tend to achieve only when they receive more than the typical amount of attention and assistance that they are accustomed to in a too close one-to-one relationship with mother; second, they tend to have social problems based on our society's continued hostility toward boys that do not appear to fit the male stereotype during the late elementary school years.

For the mother who has a close one-to-one relationship with the verbally bright, delightful son that she adores, and in whom she has tremendously invested herself, this request may seem like an impossible and unfair demand. Furthermore, since it isn't necessary to make a similar demand of fathers, this suggestion may be viewed as a "call to arms" to women's equity groups. The only way I can redeem myself is to remind the reader that I believe that the close one-to-one relationship of mother and child did undoubtedly provide the child with his or her enhanced verbal ability and better intelligence. However, the child must grow from dependence to independence. For a boy in our society, at least at this time, that growth seems much more difficult without identification with a male role model. This is not a recommendation to mothers to sever relationships with their sons, only to loosen the ties to permit growth and freedom. The mother-son relationship is an important basis for the son's relationship to other women and finally to his wife. It should not be cultivated as a dependent relationship.

In an intact first or later marriage, the easiest way to encourage male identification with father or stepfather is to permit the two some time together, including work and play activities that both enjoy. Building a garage, hiking Grand Canyon, fishing a quiet stream, etc., are relationship builders that seem effortless. Time constraints are a major problem. Men may not have long vacation times and may put a priority on spending time with the whole family or in the company of other adult males. Wives may not wish to be alone with the remainder of the family or give up valued time with their husbands. That special one-to-one time may involve sacrifices and may be minimal in amount. Nevertheless the potential for quality relationship building is so good that I strongly recommend reasonable sacrifices to make it possible. It can provide the basis for a close identification which can serve as an inspiration for independence for young men.

There are substitute activities for father absent homes or for situations where fathers may not be appropriate models. Wilderness trips, work experiences and other situations which bring boys together in an intense living/working alliance encourage boys to deal with the challenge of independence and the discovery of appropriate male models and behaviors.

If you happen to be a fortunate woman who loves and respects her husband and you make that known to your son, you may be able to stand back and give them space for closeness. The necessary identification will follow spontaneously and you will enjoy the child's confidence that comes with the change.

Expressing Feelings

All of us would agree that it is good for children to be in touch with their feelings, to understand and communicate their sadness, anger or frustration. Certainly it is not good to harbor thoughts without expressing them since often they become exaggerated. After they build up within us, we may become irrationally angry and no longer can identify the reason. It is better to teach children to talk things out productively. However, Poor Polly's, Perfectionist Pearl's, Tormented Terrence's and Depressed Donna's may find that talking about sad feelings can be a passive dependent way to control an adult. Hypersensitivity and feeling sorry for oneself can become a manipulative pattern for avoiding more productive problem solving techniques. The kind parent attention may serve unintentionally to teach children to overreact to criticism or peer teasing and to feel sorry for themselves. Expressions of self-pity may also serve as manipulations that maneuver one parent against the other, as in "ogre" rituals where children tell one parent how terrible the other parent is making them feel.

How do you as caring parent determine if your talk sessions are productive or if they are mainly manipulative sympathy sessions? The fine line that divides appropriate empathy from a "feel sorry for me" ritual is not always clear, and changing a manipulation pattern is always temporarily painful for parent and children. It engenders guilt in the parent and frustration for the children, so be prepared for both. Here are some helpful guidelines:

1. Frequency of sympathy sessions are an important clue to manipulation. Children who need to express their sadness continuously are over-reacting or overexpressing. Shorten the sessions and direct children to more productive activities. If it appears to be their way of cornering your attention, be sure to focus your attention on more positive and independent activities.

2. Examine the facts. If children use sympathy sessions as a way to dramatize their nonacceptance by peers, check out that information with teachers, coaches or even scout leaders. These children already may be well accepted, but would prefer greater popularity or power. Perhaps they have only discovered your oversensitivity.

   There is no value in your feeling sorry for them. There is value in determining the facts and encouraging better problem solving techniques. They may have to settle for your advice to not evaluate themselves based on whether other people like them of not. It may be that your encouragement of independence will help them through the adolescent developmental stage where popularity is revered.

   Attending to their expressions of feelings makes sense; but dwelling on their sadness only encourages it in a nonproductive way. They may act a lot sadder around you than they do around the rest of their world, only because you provide so much solace for their sad feelings. That sadness may not be based on the genuineness of those feelings. Check out other information and keep sympathy sessions short and helpful to your children.

3. Manipulations are taking place if children's sympathy sessions always include a villain. If the focus of their constant complaint is your spouse or a sibling or a teacher, they are learning a style of becoming close to you based on having a common enemy. This is especially problematic in an oppositional marriage or a predivorce situation. Too many children trap their parents into unwarranted sympathy when a spouse makes reasonable requests for responsible behavior. The kind of sympathy that shelters your child and alienates your spouse is bad for the marriage but even worse for the child. It teaches the child a style of controlling the persons they love by "putting down" the competition for that love.

Children may do this in obvious ways if parents are willing partners, as in already troubled marriages. They do it in more subtle ways if that is the only way the parent will tolerate it, e.g., "isn't it too bad that Scott (his younger brother) isn't nice to my friends?" That is the older brother's subtle way of making Scott look bad. If dependent children are using manipulative sympathy sessions, each session will be directed at blaming others for their own problems. Your tip off will be that the sessions are always person centered, with your child gaining your sympathy based on an alliance with you against another person.

The underlying consideration of parents of dependent children should be that they provide an opportunity for children to talk to them about concerns, but these talks should lead to productive growth, rather than reinforcing avoidance of challenge. Children's successes should be punctuated with loving talk sessions, so they learn that growth also fosters intimacy, not just failure.

Teaching Competition

Dependent children avoid competition. They don't like sports because they don't want to lose. They don't get angry or throw the bat. Instead, they avoid the entire process. They will say they don't like the activity or don't feel like participating. That expression of their wish not to participate then attracts parent attention and persuasion.

Family game playing is a good exercise in learning to compete. Also humor helps children to deal with losing. Don't give a lot of attention to poor losers. Label it "poor sportsmanship," ignore the loser, and go on with the fun of the game. If it sounds to the dependent children that they're missing fun by withdrawing, they'll soon rejoin you. Permit them to do that without a lot of attention or explanation and they'll soon forget their sadness. Absolutely don't persuade; that makes it difficult for children to rejoin without losing face. Game playing should always be designed as fair competition. That may mean you should give children a handicap, but don't ever just let them win. That takes away their sense of control and teaches them to depend on winning for fun. Learning the balance between winning and losing is the key factor. Anytime winning is fixed before the game is played, it invalidates the purpose of teaching competition.

Competition against oneself encourages dependent children to learn to enjoy the process. Setting records for basketball throws, speed or accuracy of math facts, or number of books read sets in motion ideas about the fun of personal competition. The Guinness Book of World Records (1985) may be used to initiate and inspire the concept at home or school.

Too much competition appears to cause children problems at home, which typically happens when winners and losers are fixed. Siblings will feel more pressure if the winner feels forced to keep first place and the loser sees no chance of changing that outcome. Structuring games where the outcomes are not assured helps children to express the sibling rivalry in acceptable and fun ways and aids in the dissipation of negative feelings about competition. The hilarity and laughter which accompanies game playing relaxes tension, encourages all to do their best to win and gives dependent children the openings to take the risk of playing. However, if the game playing gets too serious, it only encourages the existing competitive pressure and will deter the child who feels sure of losing.

Modeling intrinsically interesting activities helps dependent children's motivation. Since they often fear competition, they have learned to escape to noncompetitive activities, to television, computers and even books. Don't hesitate about limiting escape activity, particularly television watching. Although they may learn a great deal in their escape modality, the process is usually passive and does not encourage personal investment of self. Instead, share or develop interests or hobbies which are satisfying and active. Although there is no competitive goal, modeling active pursuits may provide the first steps in building children's confidence and independence.

Obviously activities which provide personal satisfaction without competition are appropriate throughout life, but for dependent children they play a special role. There is little risk. Potential gains include increased activity, planning and goal direction, as well as opportunities for sharing interests with peers and adults. For Loner Larry it provides the basis for developing friendships. For Sick Sam there is the possibility of focusing attention on productive activity. Perfectionist Pearl will have the opportunity to work without the pressure of excellence, and Passive Paul and Depressed Donna will find that such activities initiate self-confidence and personal control. Interests in plants, animals, science, stamps, dolls or coin collecting are only a few of a long list of activities that are not competitive but broaden children's interests. A small gift may initiate the activity and one absorption may attract children to two or three others. With added confidence, children may rapidly expand their curiosity and involve themselves in more than you expected. If you do have problems getting children started, include them in your own activities and model the excitement and enthusiasm that can grow from noncompetitive involvement.

In conclusion, since dependent children have learned to avoid competition due to fear of failure, you can encourage their risk taking by providing a safe environment in which they can compete with family members, by teaching competition with self, and by encouraging productive activities in noncompetitive ways. All three will help these children build confidence. The absolutely "do nots" are:

1. Don't just let them win.

2. Don't feel sorry for them or overreact when they lose.

3. Don't pay a lot of attention to their being afraid to try.

4. Don't let their avoiding of competition keep the rest of the family from having fun.

Teaching Deferred Judgment

Dependent children are often afraid to contribute creative ideas. They are highly critical of themselves. They fear they must produce "perfect" or "correct" ideas and they evaluate so frequently that they may be unable to think of almost anything at all. For some dependent children, it is difficult to encourage them to volunteer any but shallow or brief information, while others may contribute very rarely but the quality is extremely creative. Their idea production is disrupted by their continued negative self-evaluation. Teaching children to defer or postpone judgments of ideas thus enhances their creative problem solving skills, their thought production, their risk taking and their self-confidence.

There are quantities of specific strategies for developing creative thinking, many of which are described in *Education of the Gifted and Talented* (Davis and Rimm, 1985; Davis, 1986). Underlying all of these strategies is the basic concept of postponing the evaluation of ideas until the individual or group has an opportunity to stretch the imagination and accumulate an extensive list of thoughts. Highly creative persons are fluent and express many ideas, although only a small fraction of the total may be original and practical. Children will be enabled to produce more ideas if pressure for high quality is removed. They must be given a safe environment in which "bad" or "dumb" ideas are also accepted. The concept of *deferred judgment* means that during a period of time allocated for idea production, no one, not even the children themselves, will be permitted to criticize, either positively or negatively, the ideas which are produced.

This strategy for idea production can be conducted on an individual or group basis. Brainstorming (Osborn, 1963) is the title given to the popular group process for creative idea production. Alex Osborn coined four simple rules to govern the process:

1. *Criticism is ruled out.* This is deferred judgment, which contributes to the creative atmosphere so essential for uninhibited imaginations.

2. *Freewheeling is welcome.* The wilder the idea the better. Seemingly preposterous ideas sometimes lead to imaginative yet workable solutions.

3. *Quantity is wanted.* This principle reflects the purpose of the session: to produce a long list of ideas, thus increasing the likelihood of finding good problem solutions.

4. *Combination and improvement are sought.* This lengthens the idea list. Actually, during the session students will spontaneously 'hitch-hike" on each other's ideas, with one idea inspiring the next.

It is an extremely effective method for persons in groups to originate ideas that they are not likely to think of under evaluative pressures. Children can be taught to individually find ideas for problems using a similar model. For example, suppose your child needs to come up with an idea for a science fair project. Dependent children often come to their parents for suggestions, since they have little confidence in their own abilities to initiate good projects. Parents typically respond, first, by suggesting they think of their own idea. However, after a few minutes (or days or weeks) of dependent manipulations, parents who care about their children and don't recognize the dependency trap will sit with their children and make suggestions for possible projects. Together they may review books or former winning ideas until the parent finally recommends something that appeals to the child. The child may resist trying anything, and thus cause the parent to spend even more time assuring the child of the parent's willingness to assist.

Although the child and parent feel that the cooperation is good, the entire project and relationship is one of dependency and provides "the vote of no confidence" from parent to child that maintains the fear of risk taking and the paucity of idea production. The deferred judgment approach should be used instead. It will encourage idea production and independence. Here's the script. You need to practice your part as parent only a few times to feel comfortable and encourage your child's independence.

Mom: Billy, your teacher sent a note and it says the science fair project ideas are due by next Friday. That's only a few days away. Do you have your project planned yet?

Billy: Naw, mom. I don't think I'll enter this year. I just can't think of any good ideas — unless mom, you have any suggestions?

Mom: Billy, I learned this good way of thinking of ideas and after I show you how, I just know you'll be able to develop your own project plan.

Billy: I don't think so. I'm not good at science ideas.

Mom: You don't have to be good at this plan. Anyone can do it. (Sits down with Billy and together they write out steps for plan.)

1. Gather up science books around the house and your school science books. Take these up to your room at your desk.

2. Get pencils and pad.

3. Leaf through books and daydream a bit about ideas you see.

4. Write down any possible project ideas.

   a. They can be silly.

   b. They can be hard.

   c. They can be impossible.

   d. They can seem dumb.

5. Don't criticize any of your ideas; just keep writing.

6. You can put some ideas together.

7. You can borrow ideas from books or pictures or other kids.

8. Remember, don't criticize any ideas.

9. If you run out of ideas from books, look around the room; you may see some more. Look out the window to find more ideas. Anything can be on your list.

10. Try to write down at least 30 ideas down before you stop.

11. Now go back and look over your list.

12. Cross out the ones that don't interest you or seem truly impossible.

13. Leave four or five in your list that look pretty good.

14. Think through your plans for those four or five.

15. Bring your plans for those and you can have a little meeting with dad and me and we can hear all about your plans and can help you if you should need a little bit of help. I know you'll be able to find ideas this way because I've tried it and it really works.

Children who are taught techniques for idea production begin to incorporate these approaches into their general thinking and develop the confidence that dissipates passivity and perfectionism. Encourage these techniques by teaching them and by personally modeling them by incorporating them into your own problem solving approaches. Some books which can be used to learn creative problem solving techniques are included in the references.

Independent Homework

Dependent children typically establish ways to avoid doing homework alone. Sometimes they manipulate parents to sit with them at the kitchen or dining room table; sometimes having a parent in the same room to nag them or answer their questions suffices. Some children ask only for occasional help; others expect parents to take turns answering questions ('You do this one; I'll do the next'); and some very dependent children manage to persuade their parents to do most of the work ('If you don't help me get it done tonight, I'm afraid I'll fail'). The frequent comment of parents is that their children will not work unless they, the parents, are sitting at their side. This "help me" pattern frequently begins with the recommendation of a teacher because the child seemed to require more than the typical amount of assistance in school. Threats and worries about failure maintain the habit for the child and prevent children from building the self-confidence which comes from working independently.

Parents who want to change this pattern, and you must if you hope to transform your child into an achiever, should plan to prepare for an initial struggle. A new desk or the cleaning of a thoroughly buried work surface sets the stage for the new independence. The desk or table should be in a separate room away from the family traffic. No parents or siblings should interrupt the homework flow, and radios, stereos and TVs are definitely taboo in the initial stage of establishing independence. For the teenagers who insist they cannot work without music, you can point out that they have already established that they are not very effective working with music. However, you can assure them that when teachers communicate to you that homework and study have improved, they can certainly add music to their study time on an experimental basis. Be firm, but positive. They really are more likely to concentrate better in silence initially, although children who are established good studiers may have their choice of study environments; they have earned it. Dependent children have not yet proven themselves.

Children who are accustomed to getting help with homework will creatively uncover dozens of reasons why they cannot work without you, or they will suffer aloud so you can hear their moans and complaints. Sometimes they will daydream and produce nothing to prove their point and to establish to you that doing their assignments alone is an impossible feat.

In order to encourage independence you must be absolutely firm. To make it fun and to focus attention from help to completing the task alone, token reinforcements as well as reinforcement by attention initially may be necessary. Explain that in order to help them make the change it's possible to make their homework completion into a game and they will be able to earn activities, prizes, or money based on their accomplishments (see inset 9.3).

INSET 9.3 ENCOURAGING INDEPENDENT HOMEWORK

Dad: Troy, I've talked to your teacher and he assures me that you have very good ability. Now that I know that I want you to get in the habit of doing your schoolwork on your own.

Troy: Gee, dad, I just need mom's help. Can't she just help me a little bit? (A few tears) I just can't do it without her.

Dad: No, neither mom nor I can help you because we really want you to prove to yourself that you can do it, but we have some good ideas that will make it fun.

Troy: (Sad face, but listening)

Dad: We'll start by moving grandpop's old desk up to your room so you can have your own study space.

Troy: (Faint smile of interest)

Dad: Then we'll set up a study time. Your teacher suggested that one hour a day for a sixth grader would be about right. So we'll start with that. Of course, that's only for five days. You get two days free of homework. If your work seems to be very good and you don't need that much we can cut that time down. Of course, if you don't finish your work in an hour, you will have to work longer than that. That study time will be in your room, at your new desk, before watching any TV and with no radio or stereo on.

Troy: Dad, that definitely won't work. I have to watch cartoons when I get home to relax and unwind after school.

Dad: Son, that cartoon watching will have to wait. I like to watch TV to relax too, but when I sit down to TV, it's really hard to get up to do any work. So I wait to watch TV until after I've finished my work. You'll have to do the same thing. I don't mind if you have a snack or sit around or go outside for 15 minutes, but by 4:15 I expect you in your room working and absolutely no TV until you're done and I've checked your work. That way you'll be all done with your study time before dinner and we can shoot some baskets after dinner and watch TV when it gets dark.

Troy: I know this just won't work. My cartoons aren't on at night. I think I should watch TV for half an hour before homework.

Dad: Troy, part of this new homework plan is that you are going to earn some fun things for doing your homework on your own. It's not that we're really paying you for homework, but we thought it might help you to make a game out of it. Now you'll need to think of something you might want to save up for.

Troy: (Full smile) Gee, dad, that sounds neat. What kinds of things can I save for and how do I get the prizes?

Children do well with daily or weekend activities or small prizes as reinforcers. Adolescents typically prefer money or larger gifts. The activity chart in Figure 9.1 may be copied or modified for use. In selecting a menu for rewards, you'll want to consider your own budget and the quantity of material possessions and privileges to which your child is accustomed. Don't give too much away or there will be little left with which to motivate your child. For the child who already has too many material possessions and experiences, it is sometimes difficult to find a reinforcer. A guiding rule is to use as little as possible, but just enough to be effective. The child must see the reward as worth working for and you must view it as a reasonable commitment that is consistent with both your budget and your value system. Don't offer or suggest anything that you do not want your children to have.

Dad can now explain a reward system which he has selected as sampled in Insets 9.4, 9.5 and 9.6.

A most preferred reward for all dependent children is personal, one-to-one attention. Since they are attention addicted children, moving the focus of your attention from dependency during homework to the successful completion of that homework is critical. A game of chess or checkers or some time working together on airplane models is very effective. A special snack, e.g., banana split or ice cream soda with parent company, also is excellent for families not worried about weight control, but should be modified to something less caloric for those with potential eating problems.

Figure 9.1

ACTIVITY CHART

Activity	Day	Weekly Total	Day	Weekly Total

INSET 9.4 POINT SYSTEM FOR TYPICAL HOMEWORK
SCHEDULE
(GRADES 5-8) (ONE HOUR)

1 point for every page read
2 points for every page written (e.g. workbooks, social studies or science questions, or copied writing)
5 points for every page of math
5 points for every page of creative writing
5 points for every page studied (read and outlined)
Expected earnings 20-25 points within one hour

INSET 9.5 SUGGESTED REWARDS FOR POINT SYSTEMS

Daily Minimum. Days with a minimum of 20 points may be counted up. Thirty to 50 days could earn a family excursion, night baseball game with dad, a fishing trip or a pizza party. A special game or toy is also effective. For younger children this may seem too long-term and weekly goals should be established, for example, five days a week with 20 points could earn bowling with dad or special meal out or having a friend overnight.

Daily minimum schedules work especially well with slow workers.

Cumulative Points. Points can be accumulated toward short or long-term goals. Very long-term goals are rarely effective at first, but as the children accumulate points they often gain momentum. Cumulative points work better with children above fourth grade level and can be saved toward toys, cameras, boom boxes, bicycles and even computers. Points are equated to money (3 to 5 cents a point may be effective). A record of earnings are charted and maintained until enough has been earned to redeem the earnings for the reward. Some adolescents enjoy using the point system to earn spending money, and if parents have no objection to "paying" children for homework it is effective, if they have no other source of income. Cumulative systems work well for motivating children to do extra work.

INSET 9.6 POINT SYSTEM FOR YOUNGER CHILD
(GRADE 1-4) (15 TO 30 MINUTES)

1 point - reading a story
1 point - reading work book page
1 point - practicing flashcards (ten cards three times)
1 point - one math or writing page
Set 3 point minimum for daily sticker or baseball card; extra sticker or card for each 3 points; extra points may be added to next day's total.

A specific framework should be set up for study time initially, although exceptions may be made for scouts or music lessons on some days. Creating regular study times and places provides the basis for habits of study and removes the responsibility from parents to children.

A guiding time framework which we use for clinic children follows.

Grades 1-2 — 15 minutes
Grades 3-4 — 30 minutes
Grades 5-6 — 45 minutes
Grades 7-8 — 1 to 1 1/2 hours
Grades 9-12 — 1 1/2 to 2 hours

These are minimum times and we use them only initially. They may vary somewhat with the requirements of the school and the ability of the child. Time is increased if assignments are not completed and is decreased if achievement is very good. When Underachievement Syndrome is cured, children may set their own time requirements.

Scheduling homework time for before dinner works with many families and leaves the evening free for family fun or television viewing. Awarding extra points for initiating study and setting oven timers as a signal to begin studying are helpful in changing from dependence on mother's naggings. Of course, mothers will have to use maximum self-discipline to refrain from the typical reminder they are accustomed to using. Establish the initiative on the child's part right at the beginning of discussing the reward system.

What do you do if you are concerned about the quality of your child's work? A parent should be checking work each night at work completion time. A thorough check is unnecessary but a brief perusal should indicate if children have made reasonable effort. If the work is carelessly done, the parent should send the child back to the desk to redo the assignment carefully. Don't go through and correct each example and don't lose your temper and scold. A few direct sentences and the insistence on quality should be sufficient to inform the child that you expect good quality. A sample statement is:

"That work is not as good as you can do. Go back to your room and do it over well. As soon as you're finished I'll be waiting to work on your model with you."

Extra points may be added to the chart for especially good quality, but failing performance should never be accepted by the parent.

What happens if your child does not understand the work and you are not sure whether it is honest nonunderstanding or manipulation? Tell children to try to understand it on their own at least three times before coming for help. If they can't do the lesson after that, they may come to you for an explanation. Describe the concept slowly and permit them to try one example or question in front of you. Then insist they go back to their room to finish the rest. A word of praise to your spouse on their new independence, within their hearing range (referential speaking), will serve to send them to their room wearing their pride in independence as a badge of honor.

Who should be the prime monitor of charting and homework? For girls it may be mothers or fathers, but for boys, if at all possible, it should be fathers. Mothers and female teachers are frequently the main communicators of educational tasks. From a boys' perspective learning may appear to be "women's work." Conscientious mothers often are hesitant about passing the responsibility to their spouses, particularly if fathers or stepfathers do not appear to show interest. However, interested, persistent and positive fathers are extremely effective in communicating a serious schoolwork message to dependent boys. Although fathers may be less persnickety about the quality of the actual schoolwork, boys seem more willing to accept the responsibility and challenge of handling the homework independently, if the homework message comes from a male.

A persevering father giving calm and determined supervision is extraordinarily effective in communicating to a boy the importance of doing his homework. If you don't have the luxury of a father at home each night, mothers will have to supervise. They too can be effective, although they have the disadvantage of not being a same sexed model.

When parents and children have decided together on their study plan and reinforcement schedule, it's best that they write an agreement or contract agreed to by all. Children and parents, and even the teacher should sign the contract and it should be taped in an appropriately visible location to remind children and parents of their commitments. An example of such a contract is included in Inset 9.7.

INSET 9.7 SAMPLE STUDY PLAN CONTRACT

Troy, his mom, dad and Mrs. Norbert agree that Troy will spend at least one hour each day, five days a week, studying and doing his homework independently at his desk in his room. He will do this before he watches TV and there will be no radio, stereo or TV on in his room during study time. After his work is complete his dad will review his materials and together award him points which Troy will save up toward the purchase of a bicycle. Troy's mom and dad will not remind him to study and he will take the initiative independently. This agreement may be changed only by mutual agreement of the undersigned.

Troy

Mom

Dad

Teacher

Incomplete Schoolwork or Homework

The first signs of underachevement frequently are incomplete work at school or not handing in the required assignments.

Dependent children frequently do not finish their schoolwork in school because it may seem simpler to bring work home where they know they will receive help and attention from parents. An appropriate message to parents from teachers will help to encourage work completion of elementary children, especially if it is reinforced at home either by charting points or by a daily reward activity. An example of a form used daily for elementary children is shown in Chapter 8 (see Figure 8.1). For dependent children, behavior and work quality need not both be included in the chart. Only reinforce the target behavior you want to change, specifically, work completion. You may want to provide special attention or treats on days that work is complete and a study schedule may not be necessary. If you use a point system, be certain to give many more points for work completed at school than for work done at home so that children do not decide that it is better to do schoolwork at home where they can earn points for their efforts.

Daily feedback reports are not appropriate for most children beyond fifth or sixth grade. By this grade level the incomplete work has shifted from classwork to homework and the problem is displayed by students not handing in assigned homework. The weekly forms (see Figures 8.2 and 8.3) are appropriate for communication where there are many subjects and teachers. This form may be circulated and collected by the guidance counselor or carried from class to class by the student. Adolescents may hate to carry the form initially, but as weekly feedback improves they come to enjoy the positive teacher encouragement. If teachers are cooperative and supportive, it encourages the students to be responsible. The weekly form documents incomplete work and helps students to "catch up" before they are so far behind in their work that they give up.

Incomplete homework and inadequate study are the main cause of poor grades for underachievers, and so school/home communication of regular effort is an important key to reversing underachievement. Daily and weekly reports enable the student to establish the relationship between effort and outcome. An internal locus of control and scholastic self-confidence result directly from integrating a process-product orientation. It requires perseverance and effort on the part of teachers to cooperate in the enterprise, and parents who ask teachers to help should certainly let them know how much this extra effort is appreciated.

The school/home communications should continue until students are working consistently and have learned by experience that one failure experience will not be terminal; they can recover and continue to make efforts to maintain good grades. They should also be able to realistically and honestly evaluate their own progress before the daily or weekly communications are discontinued. When you feel confident that the student's own self-report matches what the teacher would be sharing with you, you can move from dependence on written communications to the student's personal reports. Do this cautiously, since it is common for dependent children to return to a pattern of defensive lying and regress to old habits if they have not yet confidently established new ones.

There are some precautions of which parents should be aware. First, some teachers simply will not participate in daily or weekly communications. Fortunately, they are definitely in the minority, but if your children happen to be in their classes don't "spin your wheels." They may agree to cooperate but they will soon sabotage your efforts. Instead, ask them for their preferred form of communication. They may have an alternative suggestion worth trying. Second, elementary children are likely to avoid carrying notes home. They may start, but not follow through. You may need to attach both a positive and negative consequence to bringing home the communications. The consequences should not be large. They can vary with the children's value system and their cooperation. The most effective reward for good behavior, including delivering the communication, and work completion that I have found was 15 minutes of father/son alone time each night. Negative consequences should only be used if children do not bring the communication home. No watching TV or a loss of outdoor playtime will keep the communications coming.

Most critical to the system is teacher and parent consistency. This means that despite busy after school times, parents must review the communications faithfully and must positively encourage progress. Weekly communications for junior and senior high school students may be mailed home. If they are to be brought home on Fridays, weekend social life can be curtailed based on noncompliance. Be absolutely firm and consistent if you expect your student to take the responsibility seriously.

Inset 9.8 describes a grading reward system which can be used with weekly reports. For most children it would be better to start with the process reward system described earlier, where actual schoolwork is rewarded rather than grades. But for some older children or for students who have shown good initial progress with the first system, moving to this weekly grade system will encourage a sense of change and growth. It is critical to reward effort in the same way that you reward actual grades, and for some children you may want to reward effort more than grades. An underlying assumption is that if children make the effort and have reasonable ability, then acceptable outcomes will follow with time

---

INSET 9.8 SUGGESTED REWARDS FOR GRADE SYSTEMS

Rewards for report card grades are not effective motivators for dependent children because they are too long-term. Children will typically begin the quarter enthusiastically but will give up with the first poor grade. Monetary reward systems, geared to saving up for something special, can be very effective if based on weekly grade reports. Both effort and weekly grades, but not the cumulative grades, should be counted. An example of such a system follows, but should vary based on reasonable grade goals for your child and on the number of weekly grades:

A = 50 cents
B = 30 cents
C = 10 cents
D = minus 30 cents
F = minus 50 cents

Bonuses for exams and report cards may be offered as end of semesters approach but they are only effective if outcomes seem clearly within reach. A banana split or an ice cream sundae at a special ice cream shop are a favorite bonus for some students with whom I've worked.

Monitor reward systems regularly and pay children or record amounts as agreed to. Do not take away earnings or alter agreed upon arrangement based on displeasure with or punishment for unrelated activities.

---

and children will continue to achieve as long as they sense that relationship between effort and outcomes.

Once you have set up positive and negative consequences, avoid overreaction. That is, don't tell your children they are doing superb work when their efforts have improved only slightly. Most important, don't give up, get angry or lose control when failures come after initial successes. You are helping them to learn to deal constructively with failure. They should view that failure as a learning experience to determine the extent of effort necessary to reach their goals. Your overreaction confirms their suspicions that they cannot really be as successful as the tests indicate. If your dependent children are already in senior high school, and only a few years remain in which to prevent their closing doors on a college education, your inner feelings of tension may be so extreme that you do indeed feel like you will explode each time they fail.

Calmly remind yourself that if you persevere with both positive and negative consequences and your vote of confidence, you are modeling the most important characteristic which they must learn — persistence in a difficult task.

Compensatory Skills and Extra Work

Dependent children who are underachieving but who have good abilities will fall behind in basic skills with continuing nonachievement. The most typical skill problems for dependent children seem to come in writing and math. Their verbal skills are often very good and many of them read well, but the written work which accompanies the reading lags behind the reading skill. Since they are not competent in the associated reading skills they may be placed in lower reading groups. Math is also a problem for dependent boys for reasons discussed earlier in this book.

Goal directed tutoring, as discussed earlier, is certainly appropriate for closing skills gaps, but charting and rewarding the practice process should be used as the basis for encouraging the development of additional skills. Depending on the skill deficiency, extra credit reading, writing or math should be added to the study chart. This additional work should be encouraged so that children can take pride in the quantity of reading they have accomplished or the math practice workbook they've completed. Keeping the extra credit work goal directed, or determining ways that children can earn extra credit in school, will help them gain a sense of success and confidence relative to their academic performance. However, be sure not to reward extra reading on the chart if the child is already using reading as an escape from homework.

Many dependent children write slowly. It is impossible to determine the chicken/egg relationship here, whether slow writing encourages parental attention to dependency or dependent children write slower because they are less confident. Nevertheless, increasing writing speed is a goal worth pursuing. This can be accomplished using a personal self-completion model and can be applied to copying verbal written material or to doing math facts. The necessary materials include a digital watch and multiple sheets of the same math facts or written material to copy. Children copy the first material and set a baseline time which can be recorded on an old calendar. The next day they again write the same material and mark their time. For each time they beat their earlier time and write the material in fewer minutes or seconds, they earn five points on their chart; otherwise they receive only the two points they normally would receive. Writing the same material every day may get boring, but they will soon find that they can write much faster. The selections they choose for writing should be shorter or longer depending on their age and can be varied every week or two.

The same approach can be used for speeding math fact knowledge. Begin with easier facts and do the same page for a whole week. Many dependent children become very tense during classroom timed tests. They will become much more relaxed about timed tests if timing themselves becomes a daily habit.

As children get in the habit of doing more than expected and parents take pride in the additional work their children learn to do, the habit of doing only enough to get by will change to one of always accomplishing a little bit more than is expected. Doing extra is characteristic of achieving persons and giving recognition to the extra efforts your children make will help them to change their negative self-image. It will be helpful if teachers also reinforce their students' new image of doing more instead of less than is expected.

Avoiding Dependent School Placement

Staff meetings about dependent children often conclude that these children work well on a one-to-one basis but not within the larger class. That should never be used as a reason for labeling the child as having a learning disability. Dependent underachievers often exhibit many of the characteristics of the learning disabled, but dependency is not reason enough to separate these children from the mainstream.

Parents often believe that their children will be getting something extra by being placed in a Learning Disabled (LD) class. Actually, unless your children have true neurological disabilities, it would be better not to label them and give them and their teachers an escape from dealing with the real tasks at hand. The LD label can be misused as a convenient excuse for not taking full responsibility for assignments and for getting more help from teachers and adults than is truly necessary. It is extremely important to remember that dependent children manipulate adults in their environment by requesting more help than they actually should have. However, they believe that they require the additional assistance and, paradoxically, adults who do too much for them prevent them from discovering their real abilities. It is a cycle of kindness which encourages helplessness. Children convince parents of their inadequacies and parents and teachers reinforce their lack of competence and confidence. School placement into LD or other special education classes are an institutionalized way of convincing children, teachers and parents that the children lack abilities, when actually their weak abilities come primarily from a dependent achievement pattern. There certainly are children who have specific disabilities, but funding allocated for these children should be reserved for their very real needs. The section for teachers on learning disabilities will help parents discern the difference between disability and dependency in their own children.

Teaching Modifications

Many of the changes to take place at school are similar to the modifications at home, since the child usually interacts with adults in similar styles in both environments. Teachers should be sure to read the parent recommendations, and vice versa, to see the applications of the same processes. The modifications at school directly complement home changes. If parents will not cooperate, it is nevertheless possible for teachers to reverse underachievement in school although it probably will be more difficult. In order to apply some of the home strategies to the school environment it will be helpful to enlist the help of a counselor or school psychologist. Thus the communication between parent and teacher would transfer to an alliance of counselor and teacher, with the counselor providing one-to-one attention, reinforcement and support for the child's independent accomplishments in the classroom.

Vote of Confidence

Most children and parents like a kind solicitous teacher. Certainly, highest on my list for teacher credentials would be a sensitive person who genuinely cares about children. It is sometimes difficult to set limits to empathy, yet an effective teacher must be able to identify what the symptoms of pressure are actually communicating in order to avoid inappropriate sympathy. The confusion comes because *deprivation and excess frequently exhibit the same symptoms.* That is, children who show signs of pressure, e.g., nail biting, ready tears, sad body language or shyness, may be telling you that parents are expecting too much from them; but they may just as likely be letting you know that they are overprotected and that parents are not expecting enough of them.

If children's intelligence and other diagnostic tests indicate average, above average or superior abilities and you, as teacher, are expecting them to produce only grade level performance, those indications of "pressure" are much more likely to mean that parents are not expecting enough of their children. However, particularly in a younger child, teachers worry that they may be placing too much pressure on the child. If they communicate to parents their concern about too much pressure, they compound the problem further. It is at this point that teachers must tell themselves to be strong and firm. The message to the pressured children should be that they are hard workers and therefore *can* complete the required tasks. Assure them that hard workers don't give up and that once they are good at hard work, it becomes easier. If you pretend not to see those little tears and comment on the children's perseverance and problem solving skills, the tears will disappear to be replaced by confidence.

Sensitivity is a good quality to develop in children. Hypersensitivity is destructive of self-confidence and should not be encouraged. Ignoring it is the best way to extinguish the symptoms of hypersensitive helplessness which seem to accompany the slightest effort for these children. If ignoring children's tears makes you feel guilty, tell yourself each time that you are truly being kind to them by not noticing their signs of helplessness and that you are enabling them to develop a better self-concept. I know that I am imposing a great deal of stress on some teachers with these recommendations; however, you will soon see that the recommendations produce favorable outcomes in those children and your own personal pressure will subside.

Sometimes children do not have the ability to understand concepts in instructions. They may truly need your help. In this case, the teacher should take the extra time to explain and help. Inset 9.9 suggests ways to discriminate between dependent manipulations and true disabilities.

INSET 9.9 WAYS TO DISCRIMINATE BETWEEN DEPENDENCE AND DISABILITY

Dependence	Disability
1. Child asks for explanations regularly despite differences in subject matter.	Child asks for explanations in particular subjects which are difficult.
2. Child asks for explanation of instructions regardless of style used, either auditory or visual.	Child asks for explanations of instructions only when given in one instruction style, either auditory or visual, but not both.
3. Child's questions are not specific to material but appear to be mainly to gain adult attention.	Child's questions are specific to material and once process is explained child works efficiently.
4. Child is disorganized or slow in assignments but becomes much more efficient when a meaningful reward is presented as motivation.	Child's disorganization or slow pace continues despite motivating rewards.
5. Child works only when an adult is nearby at school and/or at home.	Child works independently once process is clearly explained.
6. Individually administered measures of ability indicate that the child is capable of learning the material. Individual tests improve with testor encouragement and support. Group measures may not indicate good abilities or skills.	Both individual and group measures indicate lack of specific abilities of skills. Testor encouragement has no significant effect on scores.
7. Child exhibits "poor me" body language (tears, helplessness, pouting, copying) regularly when new work is presented. Teacher or adult attention serves to ease the symptoms.	Child exhibits "poor me" body language only with instructions or assignments in specific disability areas and accepts challenges in areas of strength.

8. Parents report whining, complaining, attention getting, temper tantrums and poor sportsmanship at home.	Although parents may find similar symptoms at home, they tend to be more sporadic than regular, particularly the whining and complaining.
9. Child's "poor me" behavior appears only with one parent and not with the other; only with some teachers and not with others. With some teachers or with the other parent the child functions fairly well independently.	Although the child's "poor me" behaviors may only appear with one parent or with solicitous teachers, performance is not adequate even when behavior is acceptable.
10. Child learns only when given one-to-one instruction but will not learn in groups even when instructional mode is varied.	Although child may learn more quickly in a one-to- one setting he/she will also learn efficiently in a group setting provided the child's disability is taken into consideration when instructions are given.

It is critical to realize that some children who are truly disabled have also become dependent. The key to distinguishing between disability and dependence is the child's response to adult support. If the child performs only with adult support when new material is presented he/she is too dependent, whether or not there is also a disability.

Completing Classwork and Homework

Most dependent children do not complete classwork in school or do not finish their homework. It is even more frustrating to find that some will do the assignments and not hand them into you. The communication and home reinforcement described earlier in this chapter for parents works ideally to eliminate these bad habits. If you, as a teacher, can encourage effective parent cooperation, you will be likely to be successful in changing the pattern quickly. The length of time expected for change will vary with the strength of the pattern, age of the child and the follow through of the parent/teacher pair. If you can persuade the child's same sexed parent to cooperate, that will enhance your chances of success. The forms included in this book are effective, but you may want to design your own to direct them toward special problems that the child exhibits. However, it is critical not to incorporate too many behaviors into the form. You will find that the use of the form becomes ineffective if it is too complicated. Concentrate on a few areas at a time.

There are many underachieving children whose parents may not be willing or able to cooperate effectively. That does not prevent you, as classroom teacher, from reversing the pattern. However, it may take a bit longer and it will certainly involve more of your personal time and commitment. You may take responsibility for providing the daily or weekly reinforcers. Of course, they will have to be inexpensive. Since attention is the most potent reinforcer, your personal time spent with a child can make a tremendous difference. That time is a scarce commodity, so don't attempt more than is reasonable. There are other school resource people to assist you, guidance counselors, school psychologists, speech therapists, learning disabilities teachers, gifted class teachers and subject teachers may be happy to help. At one elementary school a classroom teacher and a learning disabilities teacher made a most successful team for encouraging work completion, independence and positive behavior in a very dependent third grader. They effectively reversed the underachievement pattern in school prior to changes that were made at home.

The underlying principle that will help you design your approach to changing these children's achievement pattern is to redirect your attention from dependency and inadequacy to effort and accomplishment. Your personal interest in the child and the communication of your confidence, paired with a feedback system which emphasizes effort and patience, will provide the critical modification of reinforcements.

Focusing Attention

Dependent children are the daydreamers. The apparent inability to focus attention and concentrate are directly related to their nonabsorption of information taught in the classroom and their poor study skills. Their staring out the window, looking off in space and restlessly moving hands and feet are annoyances to both parents and teachers. If they are engrossed in an activity, they do show complete task absorption, and although this may happen infrequently it does provide indisputable evidence of their concentration capability.

Focusing attention is likely to increase as global motivation and goal direction improve. Involvement in intrinsically rewarding activities also enhance children's concentration. However, teachers and parents may want to devise some special signals for assisting children in attention control.

A discussion of the importance of eye contact for communicating is one effective means of encouraging children's concentration on teacher's verbal presentations and instructions. Teachers also may arrange a quiet signal to assist children in looking directly at them while the teacher is speaking. For example, if the teacher arranges to touch her own eye or eye glasses or tap the desk with a ruler, that signal may assist the willing child who is attempting to improve concentration. A reward system in which the teacher awards a token for eye contact may be used for a younger child.

Adolescents who are attempting to teach themselves to concentrate at school and at home should monitor their own focussed attention by setting their stopwatch for 15 minute intervals to estimate the percentage of that time period they were actively tuned in to their task. By charting their on-task thinking, they can gradually learn to improve those percentages and can gain a sense of control over their productive study. These tasks require willing learners; initial motivation must proceed these last important steps of improving school performance.

Other devices which assist children in concentrating at home include actively reciting or writing material, studying while standing or pacing, using mnemonic memory techniques and forcing meaning into rote memorization tasks. Adolescents may create their own inventions for helping themselves to attend to the teacher's presentations. Encourage them to do so.

When children do not attend in school it is helpful to know what they are thinking about. Most children whom I've questioned indicate that their thoughts are mainly mundane, e.g., yesterday's baseball game or what one student said to another. A few may be creatively engrossed, and some may be troubled by school or home worries. For this latter group, some time for discussion of their concerns is appropriate, and for the imaginers, some safe place to direct their creative thinking may be helpful.

However, for most children who are "spaced out" in your classroom, boredom, noncomprehension of information or ordinary daydreaming are the time wasters that prevent them from learning.

Teaching Goal Setting

Dependent children rarely set realistic goals for themselves. In their day-to-day school world they mainly set no goals at all. Their distant future goals are either nonexistent, romanticized or illogical. Living self-sufficiently and independently alone in the mountains of Colorado or becoming a great baseball announcer or player are typical plans, but even more frequent is "I don't know." They will require teacher assistance in setting short-term realistic goals so that they can experience some sense of internal locus of control and some confidence that they can accomplish something. Often, when a teacher or parent suggests goals the children initially show no interest. That is mainly because they have had so few success experiences that they fear another failure, or else they don't see the goal as sufficiently lofty to reward them with the recognition they would like to have. You will have to persuade these children that they are capable of achieving these goals, and that once they have attained them they will feel good about that success. The children will require a step-by-step description of the process they can follow to goal attainment, the strategy they must use, and the markers by which they can measure their success. Any conversation with the child relative to goal setting should be a private and individual experience. Parents may be included after the initial meeting with the child.

Appropriate goals for bright underachieving children are movement into a higher reading or math group, inclusion in a gifted program, inclusion in a special class or performing group, participation in a specific enrichment experience, removal from a special education class or, for a few very gifted underachievers, it could mean skipping a whole grade. A higher reading or math group is typically an appropriate goal for many elementary children, and a special enrichment or accelerated class is an attractive opportunity for a junior or senior high school student. Insets 9.10 and 9.11 present two sample goal setting conversations between a teacher and student intended to guide teachers in the persuasion process. It is very important in selecting an "upwardly mobile" goal for underachieving children that it is truly achievable and, further, that school policy will permit upward movement for them if they show appropriate skills. It is thus important that school policy makers set reasonably flexible guidelines for vertical movement by children into higher skill groups. Last, but also critical, are the children's personal commitments to making a real attempt to achieve the higher status.

INSET 9.10 CONTRACTUAL CONVERSATION FOR HELPING AN ELEMENTARY STUDENT MOVE TO A HIGHER READING GROUP

Mr. Reed: You know, Mark, that since the school psychologist tested you and since you've been completing more of your reading workbook pages, I've realized that you have the ability to move up to the high reading group. You really are a very good reader and I would like to see you challenged.

Mark: (smiling) Mr. Reed, I think I could read with the "Blue Birds" but they have too much work to do and I don't think I could finish it all.

Mr. Reed: Well, the tests tell me that you could, with a little practice and a little catching up. You know you're quite a bit smarter than you think and you can really do hard work well. All the reading you do at home has been a big help.

Mark: (still smiling) You mean I could just read with the other group right away?

Mr. Reed: No, not exactly, but let me show you what you would have to do. (Demonstrate with textbook and workbook.) Here's where your group is. There are 20 stories that I would want you to read. There are 40 workbook pages that come between where you are and the next group, but I've picked out 20 of the most important ones. I've written each story name and each workbook page number that you need to do on this chart. If you come see me for a few minutes after school every day I can teach you some new words and make sure you understand the instructions for the work page. Then all you should do is read one story a day and do one workbook page a day at home. You can tell your mom and dad about the story, bring the workbook page in to me and mark what you've done on the chart. If you read a story a day and do a workbook page too, in 20 days you'd be ready to take your reading test. I feel almost sure you could pass it and then I know you'd be ready for the challenge of that high group.

Mark: (hesitatingly) Do you really think I could do all that?

Mr. Reed: Absolutely. It won't seem so hard because you do just a little at a time.

Mark: I guess I'll try. I'd really like to be up there with my friend, Alan.

Mr. Reed: Well, that's where you belong, so let's write a little agreement. I bet your mom and dad will be proud of you too.

INSET 9.11 CONTRACTUAL CONVERSATION FOR HELPING A HIGH SCHOOL STUDENT ESTABLISH ELIGIBILITY FOR AN ADVANCED BIOLOGY COURSE

Mrs. James: Scott, do you have any idea of a career direction you'll be taking? I mean, now that you're taking initiative you can see that you have some real talents.

Scott: Mrs. James, teachers have been telling me since I was a little kid that I'm smart and not working up to my ability. I think they're wrong. The tests the psychologists give are just easy, but the schoolwork is really hard for me. Even now that I've been doing my homework, I'm just getting B's and C's. So what's so smart about that? It doesn't even seem worth the effort.

Mrs. James: Scott, the tests really aren't wrong and they only seem easy to you because you really are so capable. Actually, your scores are in the top 1% of students your age and that really does mean you're capable. I know you're doing your homework now, but you've really just started doing that and it takes a little while to bring your grades up to A's and B's where they belong.

Scott: It's hard for me to stay motivated. The work seems so routine and boring. Even in science, my favorite subject, the work just seems dull.

Mrs. James: Scott, what about if we try an experiment? You know you really have the ability to be in the accelerated science class and you would probably find that more stimulating. You have just one more quarter of the school year left — not enough to bring up your whole year average, but it is enough to demonstrate that you can really accept a challenge in science. If you could do just three things for me, I believe you could prove to yourself and to the science teacher that you could handle the accelerated program.

Scott: Well, I'm not sure I want to be with all those smart kids. All they do is study.

Mrs. James: Well, what about just trying my experiment and if you don't want to move up you won't have to. It's just a way to let you see what you really can accomplish with just a little more effort. I think you'll like the feeling.

Scott: Maybe. What do yo want me to do?

Mrs. James: First, Scott, I'd like you to add 15 minutes a day to your science study after you've done your homework. I'll meet with you a couple times to show you how to use that 15 minutes. Second, I'd like you to read two or three autobiographies of famous scientists so you can understand the excitement and challenge they feel. And last, I'd like you to work on an independent science project of your choice between now and the end of the year. I'll be glad to help you plan it. If you do all that and only if you want to, I'm sure you'll be ready for the gifted science class. Scott, I really know you have the ability, and our country needs good scientists. It takes a lot of work to reach a career in science, but it can be really satisfying. You ought to at least find out what you can accomplish.

Scott: I don't think it'll work out but I do like science so I'll try it. How do I start?

Mrs. James: Well, let's write down our agreement first. Then we'll set up a weekly meeting during your study hall so I can help you with the details. I know this is a big decision for you Scott, but I have a lot of confidence in you and I know you won't disappoint me.

The successful accomplishment of the students' initial goal adds a great deal to their self-confidence and makes a perceptable change in their motivation. They feel a sense of control and confidence. However, in setting their second goal they easily fall back into a pattern of setting goals too high, thus increasing the risk of failure. You will need to remind them that they need to exercise patience. A's may certainly be within their ability, but B's or perhaps C's are more reasonable at first since they have just moved into an accelerated group. More modest goals will help to build the confidence that will eventually lead them to the excitement of excellent achievement.

Becoming one of the smart students, rather than the smartest student, should be established as satisfying. Being 'first" should be described as fleeting and unrealistic since, in adult terms, few ever achieve such stardom and children must become accustomed to the mere glory of high quality accomplishment. As these children accomplish more and more of their achievement goals they should be reminded that they are opening doors to personal growth opportunities; during their underachievement period they were continually closing those doors and limiting their future. Remind them that they can't always expect to succeed at everything; no one does. The balance of success and failure is now shifting and you should help them to identify their positive accomplishments. Plan a ten minute meeting with these children weekly to review their successes and to encourage their personal goal setting. The ten minutes may be reduced to five as they become more successful, but don't lose the weekly opportunity to reward their progress. Prior to your modifying their reinforcements, you were spending much more time attending to their inadequacies and dependencies. Now they've learned to attract your attention more positively, but their performance and confidence may not be secure for a long time, and so your investment in positive attention may remain critical to them for quite a while.

As a teacher, you'll want to reward yourself frequently, too. Remind yourself that you are truly important to these underachieving students. If you become the pivotal person in their lives, the one who changes their achievement direction, they will remember you throughout their adults lives as the person who made the difference. Changing that underachiever may take major effort and a good deal of persistence, so don't hesitate to give yourself credit for your quality teaching. You deserve it.

Teaching Organizational Strategies

Dependent children are sometimes very organized, for example, Perfectionist Pearl, and sometimes completely disorganized, as with Passive Paul. They tend to choose one extreme or the other and their organizational failings may relate to time, materials and/or information. It is easier to discourage rigid organization than to deal with poor organization. Children who depend on rigid structure should respond favorably to creative problem solving exercises. Teaching organizational strategies can best take place by modeling good organization and by allowing time in the school day for children to gather materials, file papers, clean desks and lockers, and write assignments in assignment notebooks (see Inset 9.12). Demonstrating personal organization approaches and encouraging students to share exemplary and creative organization strategies with their classmates will help them to value order in their school lives.

There is a fallacy that equates creativity with chaos. While it is true that many creative persons appear from the outside to live in disordered environments, it is in a sense an illusion. Creative persons do not depend on rigidity and do tolerate ambiguity well, but they have a real skill in organizing chaos and they frequently are very detail oriented. Their work space may appear to be a mess, but they can typically find exactly what they want when they want it. Dependent underachievers take no responsibility for ordering their time and materials. Modeling organizational strategies and allowing time for organizational tasks will be helpful.

Organizing information for study is such a critical skill for all children that achievers and underachievers alike should get practice. Too many young people arrive at college without an understanding of the study process. Study skills appropriate to content areas should be taught and exercised in every classroom. Of course, many teachers do teach children to study for their subject, but many would prefer to delegate learning to study to a special course. So many children hesitantly admit to me that they don't know how to study that I feel convinced that many teachers believe that someone else is teaching them. Just in case your underachievers have not learned, I recommend you teach and permit them to rehearse those content appropriate study skills.

Repetition in learning content oriented study skills can only help all children.

INSET 9.12 ASSIGNMENT NOTEBOOKS

Underachieving children almost always lose assignment notebooks. Sometimes achieving children do also. Here are some effective assignment reminder alternatives.

1. Assignment notebooks can be full-size spiral notebooks. Each day's assignments should be on a fresh page. The page is torn out when all assignments are complete. The advantages are: 1) the notebook is less likely to be lost because of size, 2) the child derives satisfaction from tearing out completed pages and showing them to parents or teacher, 3) the new assignments are always on the top page. One disadvantage is that it is somewhat wasteful of paper.
2. Assignments can be written down in each subject notebook. All subject notebooks should be carried home each day.
3. Teacher can prepare a special assignment form for children to be placed in loose leaf notebook. Time at the end of day can be used to permit children to copy assignments in the appropriate place and gather necessary books.
4. Children can be permitted to create their own assignment reminder strategies. Some children are very inventive, and once they invest in their own devices they remain committed.

Tests and Grading

Underachievers must learn to earn grades. That is, if they see their test grades as random events which are unrelated to effort they cannot build that personal sense of locus of control. Often students tell me that they can't even guess whether they did well on an exam. They see their quantity and quality of study as unrelated to their grades. Of course, sometimes this is only a defense for Underachievement Syndrome children. However, in many situations it is directly related to teacher-made tests and grading systems. Children should be able to feel that if they study they will perform better on tests than if they don't. That builds that important sense of personal control. Underachievers and achievers alike feel frustration and a sense of helplessness if they continually increase their study only to find that their grade never changes. Furthermore, after they have found increased study to yield no gains for them, they decide to experiment with decreased effort. If teachers do not have a rational test and grading process, these children may indeed find that the lesser effort has no marked grading effect. They are reinforced for reducing their effort. If tests and grading continue to appear irrational to the students, achievers easily fall into underachiever patterns as they lose locus of control. Underachievers who have made initial effort at reversing their patterns give up and justify their old effortless style.

How does this happen? It may happen if teachers set their grading standards too high or too low. In the case of standards which are too high, children have to increase their effort too much to improve their grade and reasonable improvement in study does not result in identifiable gains. If standards are too low, rewarding grades come so easily that students who make small or no increased efforts see improved grades as unrelated to real investment of self. The first causes more frustration and harm to children than the latter and is much more common in classrooms.

Irrational grading also takes place more frequently with subjective testing than objective testing. Thus essay questions, term papers, compositions and speeches are harder to evaluate consistently than mathematics problems or true-false questions. Grading fairly becomes even more difficult when teachers must establish criteria for either very small or very large classes. The first is a problem because differences may not be great enough to vary the grading, but the teacher feels commited to use a range of scores. The last is difficult because it is an enormous task to use consistent criteria through hundreds of term papers or essay questions.

The third reason for unreasonable grading is related to habit or stereotype. Teachers may think of particular students as A performers and others as C performers and may use this unconscious grade expectation in rating their papers. So the A student may indeed find an A on her essay because of an A reputation although he or she made little effort compared to past assignments and the C student may feel despair at a repeated average evaluation although he or she is certain that there is considerable improvement in both effort and the resulting work.

Teachers can help dependent children and all students to gain a better sense of control if they clearly explain the rules of the examination game. They should indicate before tests the content and skills to be mastered, the type of questions to be used and the criteria which will be established for grading. If grading standards are neither too easy nor too hard and if teachers are careful not to prejudice their grades by past performances, there will be a much greater likelihood that underachievers will be able to regain their sense of personal control over test results and will thus be encouraged to increase perseverance.

Social Rewards

Social acceptance by peers is important regardless of children's ages. For some it feels more consequential than for others, and it takes on its greatest urgency during adolescence. Dependent children are frequently well liked by adults and some are accepted by peers as well. However, if their dependency receives a considerable amount of negative attention from teachers, they may become known to peers as "dummies," "mentals," "babies," or one of the many other hurtful labels that exclude them from the youth culture.

In changing children's self-images and peer perceptions, it will be important to heighten their awareness of how their dependent behaviors have caused them to be alienated from friendship groups. Don't give them the impression that "being popular" is a first priority, but earning the respect of peers is a worthwhile goal. Of course, in schools where the peer group is anti-achievement, this is not an effective technique. However, in almost all elementary programs and in many secondary schools, students continue to value reasonable achievement, and children who attract attention to their helplessness and to their irresponsibility are not accepted as effective persons. It will be helpful for teachers to point out that reasonable class performance will actually help them to be accepted by other students. Your underachievers will not be convinced easily, but if you can give some student examples it will help. Peer respect should not be suggested as a primary goal, but as school performance improves, underachievers do tend to gain respect among classmates and are less likely to be victims of teasing and jokes. As they develop confidence they also are less vulnerable. It will be worthwhile for teachers to tell the child that changes are visible since they may evolve gradually without the child's awareness.

As teacher, you may also facilitate social acceptance for dependent children. For example, you can appoint partnerships for projects. Pairing dependent children with other students who are accepted by the class will foster peer support, providing the partner is not so dominant that the dependent child becomes overwhelmed. Because the dependent partner may easily fail to accept responsibility, team members each should be required to list his or her tasks as part of the total project. Task groups of three are not nearly as effective as pairings in assuring inclusion of dependent children. Larger groups of four to eight children will only be helpful if the division of responsibility can be clearly designated and monitored. However, if each child can be made to feel like an integral part of a project, then grouping will be effective in encouraging dependent children's cooperation, confidence and group acceptance.

Competition of the total group with another class or school group will encourage cohesiveness and inclusion of the dependent children. Dependent underachievers may benefit by some hints on how to be effective group members. Their self-esteem will grow as members of the peer group voice their support and as they, too, learn to encourage the efforts of their peers. Becoming a good team member is almost always worth discussing in class. Also, crediting a few students with exemplary teamwork, particularly if dependent underachievers can be included with socially accepted high achievers, is an effective strategy for changing their peer image. Most adults can look back to their own school days and remember how a teacher changed the peer image of the "dummy" of the class. Teachers who are well liked by most students can be amazingly effective in influencing peer acceptance.

Punishment

Some common teacher punishments should be re-examined before use with dependent children. Keeping children in for recess to complete school assignments typically is not appropriate for these children. They may prefer the alone time with their teacher to the peer group recess relationships which they actually may find quite uncomfortable. Thus the threat of a lost recess either may serve no appropriate purpose or may even reinforce their noncompletion of assignments.

Writing names on the board for unfinished work is equally inappropriate. It highlights dependent children's inadequacies to the class and serves only to confirm the children's suspicions that they do not measure up to typical student performance. For most children, whose names may appear only occasionally, it does no harm and may serve as a reminder to stay on task. Dependent children will see their names on the board daily. How can they hope to escape their dilemma?

Withdrawal of privileges based on incomplete work can be used sparingly, but frequent use will only prevent these children from participating in the important and rewarding activities. Dependent children give up so easily that you will soon find they miss most of the privileges you hope to use for motivation.

As classroom teacher, you will find yourself in a dilemma similar to the one the parents of these dependent children are in. Punishments aren't very effective in motivating them. They don't seem to care, and very soon there is little left to take away. Your use of punishment has had no effect on improving their performance. You will soon conclude, as their parents did, that punishment is not a helpful motivator for dependent children.

Why do so many teachers use punishment for dependent children even though it usually is not effective? Teachers also need to have an internal locus of control. It is important for you, the teacher, to feel that you are accomplishing something with your students. When typical teaching methods are not effective, it seems logical that taking away privileges may be a productive alternative. However, although it seems rational and logical, it is only effective if children personally feel they can do something to change their consequences. Unfortunately, they feel doomed to failure, depressed, sad and helpless. You wish you could shake them out of their lethargy, but though you scold, lecture, reason, explain, threaten, punish and intimidate, they show no signs of the energetic application you know they are capable of. Save yourself the frustration. Only personal attention, inspiration, individual interest, persuasion, creativity and short-term activity reinforcements will be effective. Teachers, prepare for patience. These children will depend on your support and encouragement, but will be weaned only gradually from that dependence as instrinsic interest, achievement, good grades and positive attention replace past dependencies.

Creative Problem Solving

Deferred judgement and brainstorming were discussed in the parent section of this chapter. Creative problem solving approaches should be built into the curriculum of every classroom for all children. They are as basic to school learning as the three R's. Although they are essential for all children, there are some specific ways creative thinking serves the special needs of dependent children. These passive children, who tend to think they are not very good at originating ideas, will discover that they can depend on some specific strategies for making creative classroom contributions. For the perfectionists who prefer the structure of right and wrong answers, creative processes may feel uncomfortable and will not be their preferred style of learning. With practice and opportunity, they will be much more willing to risk the idenfiniteness inherent in novel ideas, and they will expand their educational risk taking. Their initial discomfort will change to enjoyment of idea production as the satisfaction of being "right" expands to the fulfullment which comes with the creative process.

Creative thinking strategies are a high priority for the Passive Pauls and Perfectionist Pearls. They will be helpful to these dependent children in deciding on projects, stories and reports and can be used to deal with peer relationships and other personal dilemma. A few strategies which adapt easily to the classroom will be described in Insets 9.13 and 9.14. Others can be found in Davis and Rimm (1985, Chapter 11 and Davis, 1986).

One fifth grade teacher planned a daily creative thinking time — just five to ten minutes each morning — for a fun activity which encouraged children to expand their thinking and defer judgment. She fostered a truly creative atmosphere which generalized to all school learning. The activity was appropriate to achievers and underachievers, the gifted, average and below average children. Creative thinking is a basic skill and teaching children to postpone their evaluations frees them to build confidence in personal idea production. Quality will improve as quantity increases. Encouraging quantity removes personal pressure from the students who believe they must always produce high quality creative ideas.

INSET 9.13 ATTRIBUTE LISTING

The student lists the main characteristics or attributes of the problem and then lists the various ways each can be changed or modified (Crawford, 1978; Davis and Rimm, 1985).

An example of using attribute modifying for designing a science project based on the experimental method or in a sample experiment would include the following basic attributes:

> Statement of the problem
> Materials and Equipment
> Methodology
> Conclusions
> Applications

Modifying each step of the experiment would force the child to creatively examine the impact on the next step. As an example of using attribute listing for creative writing for a child who has difficulty finding ideas for a story, the child can begin with another story but modify some or all of the listed attributes:

> Title
> Characters
> Setting
> Beginning
> Climax
> Ending

They will not only learn a great deal about the structure of stories, but will find that their modifications have resulted in an entirely new and creative story — which they previously thought themselves incapable of writing.

INSET 9.14 MORPHOLOGICAL SYNTHESIS

Morphological synthesis provides a structured method which basically extends the attribute listing technique described by Allen (1962). Children who may be convinced they are not very creative will find this a risk-free way of discovering that they can find many ideas by combining attributes in unusual ways. They may list variations of attributes along the axes of a matrix and can easily combine two, three or even four of these to inspire ideas. For example, a student who may be looking for an idea for a social studies project could use a three dimensional morphological synthesis to include Modality, Country, and Topics. The topic list and the countries can be taken directly from their textbooks. Lots of ideas will present themselves and certainly selection from so many ideas will be fun and will build confidence.

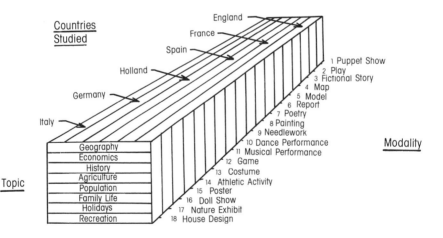

Teaching Competitive Skills in the Classroom

Children usually know the rules of good sportsmanship, but they rarely know how to deal with feelings related to winning and losing. Since dependent children are poor competitors they cope with competition by denying their competitive feelings. They say they "don't care" or they're "not interested," when they mean that they don't think they'll do very well. They tend not to like children who are successful because by comparison, they feel so inadequate. Since classrooms are basically competitive, helping children to identify and be in touch with feelings related to competition is the first step in showing tham how to compete well.

Discussing competition in a value laden way will feel threatening, and students will be likely to deny any feelings other than those which they know are socially appropriate. They will verbalize all the attitudes about sportsmanship which they've heard from their teachers and parents, but saying the suitable words will probably not assist them in acting in appropriate ways. Creative thinking strategies discussed earlier can be helpful to discussions about competition. Inset 9.15 provides an attribute listing (Crawford, 1978) approach to identifying feelings and exploring creative ways to function productively in competition.

Individual classroom competition should be minimized, even though achievers will thrive on it. Underachievers and even average students fall victims in a highly competitive environment. Small group or team competition will teach children competitive coping strategies while avoiding the risks that dependent children, always losers in competition, will suffer.

Personal competition with oneself is an excellent strategy at school as well as at home. This may be more difficult to conduct in crowded classrooms, but can be very effective for helping a dependent child build confidence. The timed tests by which children learn their math facts lend themselves nicely to personal competition standards. The teacher could recognize each day those children who beat their previous record. This approach leaves fewer children discouraged, and enhances the speed of everyone's multiplication skills. A special category for those children who manage to maintain their very fast speed, but not exceed it, would eliminate the problem of accidentally penalizing the experts. For example, the teacher could ask for the hands of all children who performed the tests in less than five minutes or who did better than last time. Winning becomes possible for all, but not without real effort. There will continue to be losers in the contest, but all children will see winning as within their reach.

INSET 9.15 COPING WITH COMPETITION

Classroom Discussion on Competition

Step 1: Let's begin by making a long list of places where children feel competition

Ex.   Sports, board games, schoolwork, with sisters, brothers, cousins, music, art, dress, popularity, etc.

Step 2: Now, let's think of lots of different possible outcomes when we compete in all those areas.

Ex.   Be first, be second or third, tie for winning, come out in the middle, lose, not join in because afraid to lose, be in last place, quit in the middle.

Step 3: What kinds of feelings may people have if they win, tie, lose or quit?

Ex.   Excited, happy, sad, depressed, mad, smart, dumb, rejected, hate someone, etc.

Step 4: What kind of things do kids do when they have feelings?

Ex.   Shout, clap, jump up and down, throw the bat, curse, lose their temper, blame other people, cry, quit, run away, never play again, say bad things about the winner, start a fight, practice more next time, quit, etc.

Step 5: Which things work best for helping you to be better at competition?

Step 6: How can you teach yourself to cope with the bad feelings and do some of the better things?

Step 7: What ways can you improve your competitive coping?

Steps 1 through 4 involve deferring judgment. Step 5 and 6 involve evaluation. Step 7 requires application. Discussion level will vary with age and sophistication of children. The first three steps could take the form of a challenging written assignment for older children.

10

Dominant Conforming Children - Modifications

Dominant conforming underachievers are difficult to identify because the extent of their underachievement tends to be much less extreme. They rarely fail courses, doing just enough "to get by." Their underachieving pattern often is not recognized at all by their families. During the elementary and high school years they may not be viewed as having a school problem. As a matter of fact, these children usually function precisely in the style preferred by their parents. They are more similar to achievers than to other underachieving children, and it isn't until after high school graduation that their earlier underachievement becomes apparent. Dominant conforming children will move into nonconforming patterns, either dominant or dependent, if the competition in their area of expertise becomes too intense. This is less likely to happen in high school, but when it does occur they may become manipulative, rebellious, anorexic or depressed. It is more likely to present itself in college when they are confronted with a profusion of talent and must make the adjustment to comparatively lower levels of success.

Dominant conforming children are frequently multi-talented. Their good intellectual capability, paired with such additional talents as social leadership, dramatic or musical talent, excellent physical coordination and attractive appearance, provides them with the raw materials for success. Their home environment fosters success in positively motivating ways. These children receive much attention for their superior skills in their areas of expertise. They excel from the start and are able to maintain their excellence, despite competition in sports or music or drama or schoolwork or social life. It appears that they are good competitors because they work hard and exhibit excellent perseverance in their chosen areas of dominance. However, they manage to avoid learning to deal with failure by not getting involved in areas where they are not first or extraordinary.

Parents and teachers may observe this in their children, but since they seem happy and successful they decide it best not to overreact to the B's which should be A's or the sudden disinterest in basketball in favor of swim team. When their son who was former class president announces that he's no longer interested in school government or their daughter decides to drop out of the play because she only got a small part, they assume that these symptoms are a normal part of growing up or of adolescent decision making. Those parents may be correct. Adolescents should certainly have the right to change interests and decide for themselves where they want to invest their time and energies. However, a pattern in which children only perform well when they can be recognized for excellence portends more serious problems later.

These children do manipulate home and school environments to maintain this problem. It eventually may cause dramatic underachievement and often some related emotional problems. Parents and teachers can prevent the problems if they are alert to them. However, parents often have so strongly counteridentified with their children's successes that they are blinded to the potential problems. Modifications of reinforcers in school and home are not complex, but it is difficult to convince parents and teachers to change their reinforcers. This will become clear as we describe the necessary changes.

The root of the dominant conforming pattern comes from children receiving too much attention for excellence. Although the attention has enhanced the talent, the children have internalized a pressure for continued attention. They become addicted to this attention and are willing to maintain high performance only in areas that elicit the attention. They will not function well if they are not assured of that audience.

Parenting Modifications

Changing reinforcements when you don't see a problem, but are only told that there might be one some day, may seem like an unreasonable action. Why should you do anything different if your child seems contented and successful? Of course, you don't need to change — unless you see some of the symptoms of Underachievement Syndrome. If those signs appear, they are the 'tip of the iceberg" and it makes no sense to avoid dealing with the problems that lie beneath. The changes will seem logical and not at all drastic once you become comfortable with them. Making small changes can be a genuine long-range kindness to your child.

Monitoring Counteridentification

Gifted achievers frequently have one or both parents who share a similar interest or talent with these children. Bloom's (1981) research certainly supports the crucial role of parent interest, enthusiasm and shared abilities in enhancing the achiever's accomplishments. However, that same intense interest can cause problems. If you are a competitive, achievement oriented adult you feel extreme excitement when your children are successful and intense disappointment when they fail. It's very difficult not to feel these experiences as if they were your own very personal wins or losses. Your children seem like extensions of yourself. The more similar their expertise or experiences are to those of your own childhood, the more genuine and personal the victories and defeats feel to you. It is difficult to separate yourself from those children in whom you've invested so much of yourself. If you are an artist, your children's art talent may represent the fulfillment of your own dreams. You are sure that the academic achievement which excited you and rewarded you should provide similar excitement to your children, and you personally share the thrill of the praise they receive from their teachers. Socially, if you were well liked and popular, or if, in contrast you felt unaccepted, you can identify with the awe of your daughter's first date or your son's early phone calls from girls. Certainly, if you were an athlete and received the glories of senior high trophies and peer adulation, or if you didn't quite qualify for awards, you can imagine how your son will feel as the crowds cheer and marvel at his football successes.

Why must you separate yourself out from your child? Why is it so critical for you to be enthusiastic without being overwhelming? Or disappointed without being depressed? The intensity of your feelings conveys to your children such strong emotional messages that there becomes an urgency to their victories and a distress to their defeats that go far beyond the impact of the actual events. Of course, they should enjoy the thrill of winning and deal with the disappointments of losing, but when parents overreact winning becomes so important they dare not participate in activities where there is a risk of losing. It is certainly irrational to expect your children to be continually victorious and you truly don't expect that, but your emotional intensity is conveying this impossible message to them. You should ask yourself whether it really is important to your children to be the most popular person, best athlete, star in the play or valedictorian or whether these are your emotional pressures that you are unintentionally conveying to them. Certainly you want them to compete and to make their best effort, but those are different messages than you are communicating emotionally. Celebrate your children's excellent performance and empathize with their struggles, but permit them to feel their own experiences without burdening them with adult personal pressures.

Competition

You will note that competition is included in all three chapters on modifications. It is basic to the underachievement problem regardless of the underachievement style. There is no reason to repeat the recommendations already presented in the dependent section for teaching competition at home, but there are some issues that should be added here.

Dominant children usually live in highly competitive families. Dominant conforming youngsters have found areas of activity where they can be winners. They only need to put winning in perspective. They can value excellence as long as they don't tie their valuing of persons to that excellence. The message that we like children who "win," who are "the smartest," and who "excel," should be changed to "we like our children who try, who are responsible, and who make positive and sincere effort." If it feels to children that they have to perform "best" to earn your love and attention, they will only select areas of participation where they are convinced that they can excel. As parents, you should model getting involved in some activities where you do not always win.

You will want to voice respect for the talent and skill of your competitors so that your children can hear that admiration process. However, the admiration shouldn't mean that you hope or expect that your children will attain those great heights. For example, if you and your son play tennis and you're watching the Wimbleton tennis championships, explain to him how to observe the players and learn from their skills, but please don't suggest, as so many parents do, that if he practices regularly he may be playing tennis at Wimbleton some day. You are building unlikely dreams and unreasonable competitiveness. There will be time enough for such lofty goals if he displays extraordinary talent. At this early date, competition with his friends is a reasonable standard to set for both fun and glory.

Parents frequently tell their children "that they can do anything if they're willing to work hard enough." While it's true enough that practice enhances skill, your children, despite all efforts may not make it to Olympic sports, the Metropolitan Opera, Harvard Medical School, the Broadway stage, the National Ballet or the Green Bay Packers. While these expectations usually are delivered in jest to children, children are likely to take them seriously. Dominant conforming children may begin their efforts immediately and may assume that if they're stars of the sixth grade basketball team, they're on the way to professional basketball. They practice basketball earnestly but schoolwork seems undeserving of a similar commitment. Learning to work in arenas where they are not stars is an essential component of learning to function effectively in a competitive society.

Intrinsic Motivation

In addition to learning to function in competitive environments, competitive children should develop interests that are intrinsically enjoyable, and activities that are not competitive nor rewarded by outsiders. They often don't do this because they are so invested in their area of expertise. The urgency of winning is so strong that they can hardly imagine spending time on an activity that produces no external reward. Gifted adolescents have shared with me their sudden realization that they have developed very few interests other than those in their specialty areas. There seems no purpose to participation if there is no contest and no recognition for their success. This narrows experiences for young persons who should be exploring their world.

Modeling interests that are intrinsically rewarding has already been suggested as a priority way to develop involvement. That is, a parent's sharing of noncompetitive activities with children will broaden enthusiasm and encourage participation. Membership in peer groups which are interest centered or participation in specialized summer camp experiences will encourage children to broaden their involvement. There are, for example, science, language, computer, drama, music, basketball and art camps, to mention a few. If the children's special talent is drama, and they are already a star, a drama camp would only increase their experiences in competition while a language camp would introduce them to a new area of interest. If sports is their field, but they should be expanding into noncompetitive activities, then drama camp will lure them to the excitement and fun of the stage. Specialty programs present varying values for children. They can be used to teach and encourage competition and challenge, or in this latter example, they can open up new and broadening experiences for highly competitive children outside of their typical talent area.

Learning to enjoy noncompetitive interests is important for all children, but seems especially important for dominant conformers who focus only on winning.

Parent Messages

Communications from parents in the form of verbal statements and actions are amazingly effective in guiding dominant conforming children. Early messages are much more important than those given in the teenage years when these highly competitive children have already discovered their strengths. The most important message relative to school achievement is that academic learning is central while all other school related activities are of lesser importance or peripheral. Thus band, chorus, sports and drama are important in that they provide a full and enriched life for children and adults alike. Certainly, developing interests and even competitive activities in these areas is appropriate and should be encouraged, but schoolwork and study should have first priority. If that message is clearly stated when children are younger, they will know by high school that geometry homework is to be completed even though play rehearsals last until 9:30, and that a heavy basketball schedule is not an excuse for skipping a class because homework is not complete. Actually, there are many parents who inadvertently give the opposite message. For example, one parent informed me that she told her gifted, academically unchallenged child that the most important part of school was her extracurricular activities. She gave a clear message to her child of the secondary importance of school learning.

Parents who take children out of school for shopping trips and sports events are sending a message that "schoolwork is unimportant." When children are excused from school, there should be a clearly educational or medical reason for that excuse. Field trips or family trips which provide unique learning experiences obviously qualify. If other family events should make it necessary to take children out of school, then the message of school importance can be given by requiring the child to collect and complete all school assignments. This will provide reasonable flexibility for families while continuing to communicate the parent valuing of academic responsibility.

The central versus peripheral message is especially important to dominant conforming children because their field of expertise, or showmanship, is so much more enticing than the more mundane activities of the classroom. As the child demonstrates unusual competence in a talent area, parents and schools should certainly make allowances for children's special training and practice needs. It may be that such gifted children should have a lightened number of academic requirements. However, they should be cautioned to maintain the minimum number to permit them to have alternate career options should they not qualify in their highly competitive first talent area. Quality standards also should be expected in subjects which may be important to alternative careers. For example, the aspiring dramatic actress eventually may need to compromise and teach Drama and English. Although that may seem an unlikely outcome to the star of the high school production of *Carousel* or *Fiddler on the Roof,* he or she certainly will have to learn math and science to continue for that college degree. Many youth from first grade through college have declared to me their rationalizations for not studying or doing homework in subjects they are certain are irrelevant to their future. I have become convinced that many folks are telling their children that educators don't know anything about education. There truly is a basic core of skills that educated citizens should master by adulthood. Parents should communicate to their children that they are expected to learn to read, write and do math even if they "hate" any one of those subjects.

This suggested modification in the home environment should never be interpreted as nonsupport for music, art, drama or athletics. To the contrary, all of these forms of creative enrichment are extremely important, but for most children they should be viewed as supplementary to the core of good academic learning and thinking.

Sensitivity

Dominant conforming children, except for the specifically academic type, usually are well liked by peers. Their elementary and secondary school days are typically productive and active. They view themselves as winners by virtue of the fact that they have only selected activities in which they are successful. Since they usually are happy peer oriented youngsters, they rarely take the time nor have the wish to develop sensitivity to the feeling of others who may be less successful. A quotation by Daddy Warbucks from the popular musical play *Annie* (Meehan, 1977) reads, "You don't have to be nice to the people you meet on the way up if you're not coming back down again." This summarizes succinctly the confident air of success that surrounds the popular high school sports, drama and music stars. These youngsters are little prepared for the reality that often follows their peak teenage years. They do come back down again, and the effect of seeing less successful peers surpassing them as they descend is cause for depression for these youth who are accustomed to thinking of themselves as center stage and superior.

When they face their initial defeats and failure experiences they will be young adults in college or in the work world, sometimes far from family supportive members. How can you as parents best prepare them for the real world of potential disappointments — to which they have not become accustomed? These children who often brag enthusiastically about their accomplishments and boast with bravado of their victories should be sensitized early to the feelings of the majority of persons, who have multiple failure experiences. By encouraging empathy and support for others, they may vicariously learn coping strategies that will help them adjust to the balance of failures and successes, which is part of virtually every adult life. Parents can encourage empathy by asking questions and making comments which direct their children's attention to the feelings of others. However, since your children will be counting on parent applause for their performance, suggestions of sensitivity to losers must be made in a way that does not take credit from their own successes. If they feel you are giving more attention to the losers than to those who are victorious, they may reasonably complain about your lack of support. Some appropriate sample statements and questions that may be helpful to you are presented in Inset 10.1.

Note that in each statement the parent does comment to the children on the successes of their performances before suggesting consideration of how others could use their support. If parents don't do that it becomes so much of a "root for the underdog" philosophy that the winning children feel deflated by the nonappreciation of their own efforts. Children will not always follow through on parent's suggestions of sensitivity, but your bringing it to their attention even at the time of such victory will help them form a habit of empathy. As they share with their friends those experiences of defeat which must sometimes come to all, they can vicariously share and learn strategies for coping with defeat.

Teaching admiration, mentioned earlier, is another means of developing sensitivity which can assist the high school star in the real world beyond high school. Even while your children are winning they can learn to notice, admire and communicate their admiration to other performers. Since they are in the habit of competing, they tend to feel inadequate each time someone performs better than they do. When they do meet real competition, even when it is on the other team, the gracious "good sport" should develop skill at admiring and respecting, rather than deprecating, the talent of their rivals. Although it is truly a difficult skill for highly competitive children to develop, it gives them a mentally healthy way to deal with being second best, which they tend to deny by habit. For dominant conforming children

INSET 10.1 SAMPLE STATEMENTS TO ENCOURAGE EMPATHY

Johnny, that was a really great game. You truly were a sports hero and your dad and I were impressed. I think your friend, Troy, had a really bad game. I never saw him play so poorly. Do you think he could use some of your encouragement?

Mark, your brother Jeff is really in a bad mood. He did terribly at the track meet. Do you have any ideas on how you could make him feel better about trying again in the future?

(During a party, mom calls Stacy into kitchen and privately shares this conversation.)

Your friend Jean keeps coming in to talk to me. I don't mind her coming in here but I think she feels left out. You're so popular; do you have any ideas on how you could help her to feel included?

Two standing ovations! I don't think I ever saw such an enthusiastic audience. You are really a star. Wouldn't it be neat if on the last night the cast could figure out a way to get the backstage people to come out and take a bow so they could share that applause?

who are accustomed to winning, to congratulate more skilled players is an act of courage which will prepare them for the realistic appraisal of their own skills in later adult competition.

Teaching winners to be sensitive to the feelings of others without dampening their own enthusiasm is more difficult than it may appear. They feel more confident and comfortable in the bravado of victory than in thoughtfulness or the admiration of competitors.

Academically talented children also must develop coping skills for the world after high school to avoid underachieving patterns in response to greater intellectual competition. They too must be reminded to avoid boastfulness. In academic rivalry they may not realize that their enthusiastic exaltation of victory can have the effect of discouraging others who are losers by comparison. Sensitive enthusiasm, recognition of future competition, and admiration for other scholars will help them prepare for the more challenging intellectual population they will meet in college.

Acceptance of Criticism

Dominant children prefer to do things their own way. They feel good about themselves only when they are fully in control of their activities. Criticism of their performance causes them to feel out of control. Their defensive reaction to criticism is a symptom of their problem. Obviously, it is irrational for them to believe that they are perfect at their skill, yet they invest considerable effort on avoiding performances where they might not be praised.

For example, musically talented children may manipulate you into persuading them to perform on the pretense that they are shy. They are thus avoiding any risk of criticism since they know that your response to their reticent performance can only be applause. You would certainly withhold any negative comments since you assume it might injure the child's already precarious self-confidence. Don't bother persuading them. Go on with the show. They love to perform and will soon volunteer if you don't make it into a power struggle.

As another example, children may prepare a class report or story which they feel certain is excellent and they are positive that their teacher will admire it. However, they don't want to show it to their parents until it is graded. Parents may recommend that they make a few minor changes which would undoubtedly improve the grammar or the story. However, any such criticism would be intolerable because then the story would not be completely theirs. They don't want to change a sentence; it takes their control away. After they've received their A, they'll be happy to show it to you, but any criticism will be met with 'well, I got an A so I guess it's fine." Anything that produces less than an A may not make it into your hands for review, unless you request it.

If children are truly going to develop their potential talents and not become underachievers, they must learn to cope with criticism. Don't permit them to manipulate you into backing off. Teach them to be analytical especially in their talent areas. If they become accustomed to constructive criticism, both positive and negative, they will take it in stride. Children who receive only praise do not tolerate negative criticism well. Evaluate in writing.

Make it an analysis of strengths and weaknesses and permit them to decide whether or not to act on your suggestions. In that way they become accustomed to evaluation and will not feel that they are in a power struggle which they must "win" or "lose."

If your children are already defensive about criticism, begin the process in a new area of learning first. They will not need to be so protective of their reputation in an area where they are not experts. Also, analyzing other persons' performances together in a positive way will help the dominant conforming child to recognize it as a contructive and invaluable activity. Little tears should be ignored in initial assessment stages. They indicate hypersensitivity which is not conducive to accepting challenge. You will want to tread carefully at first, but persevere. Learning to deal with criticism constructively will be helpful to your children throughout their lives.

There are times to postpone evaluation or avoid it altogether. The emotional times that accompany victory or defeat are not good times to evaluate. Objectivity is not possible and overreactions are certainly likely to occur, especially in the case of the defeated. Time pressured situations also do not invite criticism. Children will not welcome appraisals when they are completing the typing of their composition in the morning just before catching the bus. Of course, they may have deliberately arranged that time pressure situation to avoid evaluation. Nevertheless, it is better to say nothing than to precipitate a crisis which will certainly not accomplish your purpose. Times of initial idea production are also not good for evaluation. Deferring judgment until children have had plenty of time to play with ideas encourages creativity. You should consciously state the rules for deferring judgment as a reminder that you will definitely not evaluate at this time. Finally, don't get in the habit of criticizing or evaluating everything. Children should have areas of freedom where they can count on minimal or no evaluation. If parents literally criticize everything, children have justifiable complaints.

Teaching Modifications

The modifications at school will again match the changes recommended for parents at home. However, some teachers are in dramatically powerful positions to make impacts on dominant conforming children. Coaches, music teachers, drama advisors and specialists in the youth's talent areas are viewed as models. They may be much more influential than parents, particularly by early adolescence. The underlying communication to these children involves helping them put their talent area in competitive perspective for future planning. They should participate in their field of excellence but combine that with an appropriate education to avoid closing the doors to careers and lifestyles which may turn out to be more realistic.

Central and Peripheral Messages

The basketball coach or the music or drama teacher may be very enthusiastic about the most talented children they work with. They may counteridentify with these students much as parents do. They may see within them the talents, ambitions, wishes and disappointment that they felt as adolescents. Influenced by their own unfulfilled wishes, they may inadvertently direct these youths toward a path that concentrates too heavily on their specialty field. Their own enthusiasm for and commitment to the field, mixed with the belief that they have discovered unusual talent, can cause them to emphasize the talent area at the expense of other learning. Since these youth tend to have excellent rapport with their coaches and mentors, they may literally accept every communication as gospel truth. These coaches are in a superb position to alert talented children about realistic competition and about the central importance of broad academic preparation. The specialty teachers probably are not as excited about math as drama, nor as good at writing compositions as at playing tennis. Nonetheless, they should familiarize themselves with the total child they are educating in order to avoid influencing these youth to invest so much time and energy in their specialty that they neglect less glamorous areas of talent.

Other faculty, who observe these children's disinterest or underachievement, should ask the specialty coaches to make appropriate compromises which allow children to participate and develop their special talents, but permit them to maintain achievement in academic areas. Certainly both are possible, and the drama or football coaches are in excellent positions to give messages to children about central and peripheral activities. Excellent academic preparation is central, but obviously not sufficient for these children. Keeping extra curricular activities "extra" will permit children to enjoy the special challenge of these talents, but continue to participate where they do not excel, that is, in other course work.

Challenge and Competition

Teachers who discover children in their classes who are continually first in either an academic or nonacademic talent area should be aware that, despite curriculum adjustments, these students can best experience the sense of challenge in the company of other students with similar excellent abilities. Certainly, wrestling with complex curriculum provides one kind of challenge, but realizing that there are peers who are equally capable provides an opportunity for competition and stimulation that these children seldom experience in their own school environments. Directing them to an activity where they can share their talents, but may not be "first," provides good experience in functioning without an admiring audience. If children become accustomed to this kind of challenging environment, they are not as likely to be devastated when they emerge from their more sheltered high school surroundings. They will be more realistically readied for adulthood.

There are a great many enriched cultural, academic and athletic environments where children can be directed for interaction with equally talented students, for example, the summer camps mentioned earlier. Even brief experiences can be helpful to these talented children. During the school year, depending on your location, there may be high-level city youth orchestras, bands, choruses, math, debate and forensic meets and many, many sports opportunities. There are fewer clubs and camps for potential writers, photographers, artists, actors and actresses, vocalists or academically talented children than for athletes or musical instrumentalists, but specialty teachers usually know about opportunities that do exist. Students who plan to participate in high-level learning experiences that may be competitive, will benefit by teachers warning them of the excellence they will encounter. For some dominant conforming children, confronting competition for the first time, even in a summer camp, can be a disappointing experience to which it will be difficult to adjust.

Criticism

Underachieving students will be more willing to accept criticism from favorite coaches and teachers in their specialty area than from other classroom teachers or their parents. If English teachers or math teachers criticize the basketball stars or rock band singers, the response will typically be that "the teacher just doesn't like me" or "I can't do math." Remember, dominant children are show people, and the lack of praise is seen as criticism. It is difficult for adults to give them enough assurance, but here are some suggestions.

Don't criticize these children in front of their peers. They "lose face" easily and you may become a permanent enemy. Sarcasm and humor are also likely to be viewed as unfair, unreasonable and insulting. They don't laugh at themselves easily. Reserve humor and light sarcasm until they've accepted you as a friend. Then handling humor and sarcasm will be good exercises for them.

At first, you will want to begin most every criticism with a compliment. For example, "I really think you're trying, but your paragraph included too many subjects." This approach may sound a bit awkward and indirect, but teachers should pair honest observations of effort with the criticisms, at least some of the time. The key is for these children to see you as an ally. They tend to dichotomize persons into either friends or enemies. It takes a special effort for teachers to evaluate in a supportive way, but it will facilitate these youths' acceptance of criticism. When they securely identify you as a supportive person, you'll find you can be a bit more direct. However, don't be manipulated into backing away from the evaluation process. Students become less defensive and more comfortable with criticism when they become accustomed to recognizing the constructive part it plays in their learning.

Dominant children often compete with teachers in power struggles, and may choose unpredictable class times to establish their superior power. The intellectually and socially dominant are particularly adept at attempting to show their peers how smart and powerful they are by proving their teacher wrong. Furthermore, the dominant conformers who tend not to be "trouble making" students will frequently find allies in peers and parents, and you may discover that what you thought was a simple deserved criticism of a child's work or behavior becomes a major social battle with formidable opponents. These children are seasoned battlers and they like to win. If you take them on in contests, don't expect them to be fair. You are likely to hear things about yourself that they've told to students, other teachers or their parents that you can't even remotely identify with. They will manipulate to win, and since they have a strong reputation based on their excellence, their audiences believe them. Avoid confrontations; if you remain their ally, you can help and even criticize them. If they cast you as their enemy you will feel frustrated and helpless and cannot assist them in change.

Sometimes you may find yourself in confrontation with these children even though you cannot recall the origin of the problem. When you sense this has happened, your most likely chance of success will be to have a personal conference with them. In discussing the situation with the child your role should be one of strength and fairness: neither rigid nor too weak. The conference should be problem oriented with no winner or loser. If you are punitive the confrontation will go on. If you appear ineffective, the child may apologize but continue to "bad mouth" you and try to dominate you in peer situations. You should maintain respect by your own power and by recognizing his or her strength. Dominant children can be unkind to those they view as weak and whom they have cast as rivals.

Intrinsic Motivation

Engaging in an activity without an audience seems boring to dominant children. They expect continuous praise, feedback and admiration. They tend not to get involved in intrinsically motivating activities since it is not the process but the outcome which interests them. Teachers can use this dependence on feedback as a bridge to introduce them to new interest areas which are noncompetitive and have no external rewards. Students should develop interests and activities where personal growth and satisfaction are motivators. Some examples of classroom assignments that stimulate children to work for intrinsic satisfactions appear in Inset 10.2. These can be interspersed among the more typical graded lessons for variety and to purposefully teach children to do work without external reward.

The last item on the list, extra credit projects, may appear to be an extrinsically motivated assignment. Of course, it is the actual awarding of credit which motivates the child to begin the independent effort. However, once involved in an activity where they are more or less assured of credit, children will develop the personal sense of accomplishment that we call intrinsic reinforcement. Extra credit projects are an excellent way to tempt dominant children into the world of self-directed exploration of interests.

INSET 10.2 SUGGESTED ASSIGNMENT TO ENCOURAGE INTRINSIC MOTIVATION

1. Projects graded by Pass/Fail
2. Self-graded assignments
3. Individually selected projects
4. Special interest trips and speakers
5. Discussion sessions on personal interests and hobbies
6. Small group projects
7. Total class cooperative projects, e.g., murals, plays (these have audiences but are cooperative ventures without class stars)
8. Community member interviews
9. Surveys and questionnaire analysis
10. Scientific experiments
11. Extra credit projects

Many teachers withdraw the opportunity for earning extra credit from those who are doing poorly on regular assignments, with the message to invest their time in studying instead. For dominant underachievers, who don't expect to get good grades when they conform to the teachers rules and who prefer directing their own study, they will be much more willing to do productive work if you encourage them with extra credit to engage in some personally selected learning experiences. You should, of course, guide them to truly challenging and worthwhile activities in order to assure that they are learning relevant material in their individual way.

11

Dominant Nonconforming Children - Modifications

Modifying the reinforcements of dominant nonconforming children is the most difficult challenge. They are the most resistant to change, especially during the high school years. Their behaviors make them unpleasant to live with. They may be belligerent, rebellious and even hostile. Yet beneath the protective shield there is often a bright, sensitive child who is easily hurt. These dominant children feel confident only when they are in control. Unlike dominant conforming children, they do not find acceptable areas of expertise where they perform well and receive attention. They are often "has beens," youths who remember their earlier childhood as a more satisfying time when they were adored or when they were "perfect" or when they earned all A's or when they were "daddy's little girl." These are young people whose position as "center stage" has been removed, and their manipulative and rebellious behaviors are efforts to return to the glorious period of their life when they were so admired.

These children will struggle and resist acknowledging their problems as their own. They are the children who, by adolescence, parents and teachers will be unlikely to change but only to help. Many will require psychological help to assist them through high school and college years, and all will struggle through adolescence and young adulthood until they come to terms with becoming less then they hoped to be. Their goals were set impossibly high; they wanted to do something spectacular or reach stardom. They feel like failures as they perceive their peers surpassing them in accomplishments. They flip flop from the highs of dominance to the lows of failures with little of the patience and perseverance needed to direct their high-energy toward productiveness.

Parents and teachers have a difficult chore in affecting change in these youth. If your children are preschool age, the job is relatively easy. In elementary grades and junior high school it is a bit more difficult. The senior high years are the most challenging. However, after high school if they are on their own and motivated toward change, they actually are more likely to reverse their underachievement than earlier. Be prepared for patience, and expect many failures. However, if you can persevere with these children's problems, you can expect them to become successful adults. They are basically very achievement oriented and motivated.

Parent Modifications

You will have no doubt at all that changes must be made for your dominant nonconforming children. You also will feel helpless and out of control, not sure when or how to intervene in their lives. If you ask advice of any two persons, you will get two different responses. You will feel confused, disappointed, guilty, very disgusted with parenting, and not at all sure where to turn. Despite the fact that it seems that your children control you, it is important to realize that they don't feel secure at all. To the contrary, as long as their life is a struggle for power over others, you can be sure that they are suffering and feeling unsure of their own personal direction.

In modifying their reinforcements at home, it will be important to see the world from their perspective, but not necessarily to act toward them in ways that will gratify their immediate wants. As parents you must take the long range view; as children, they can't. It is your role to direct them according to their needs, but not necessarily according to their present wishes. If your child is difficult to live with and unhappy too, you surely know that something more must be done, even if you are convinced that you've tried your best. The recommendations which follow come from practices that we've used in our clinic and that have been effective, but not easy. If you can't make a difference, keep in mind that these children are in the most extreme quadrant of our underachievers. You may need professional help and positive results may not be immediate.

Early Childhood Dominance

Some children seem to seek dominance from birth. It seems that by instinct they sense that their parents don't know how to control them and although they are fed, watered and loved, they are not contented. By age three, some parents tell me that their children are controlling them and that they find themselves yelling, screaming and acting in irrational ways that they never projected for motherhood. "I ask him to sit in the corner and he won't;" "I put her in her room and she comes out;" "I tell him he must eat his vegetables. He eats them and throws them up right at the table." These parents can hardly believe they've given birth to such misbehaving "monsters." These children have somehow discovered they are in charge of their caretakers; they have an early and very severe case of nonconforming dominance. However, there is great hope when discovered early. *You can take charge and you must.*

In those preschool years there does appear to be a magic wand solution to regaining control of your children that is 100% effective to date. It is also effective with many children up to age eight. Beyond that it works with some, but not with others. It is not intended for adolescents. If you follow the cookbook recipe for "time-out" explained in Inset 11.1, your children will become much calmer, will actually obey your requests and will not behave as obnoxious little brats. You will be in control of your children, and you will be a much more confident parent. As long as you maintain that positive control and don't regress to the powerless level of screaming and impossible threats, your children will not return to the insecurities of continuously pushing limits. The change will be dramatic.

I know you don't believe me while you're reading this — parents don't believe me in my office either. However, they come to their next visit smiling, convinced, and ready for the next guildelines. The dramatic reversal takes place because you have changed your role from follower to leader. Prior to that your children were in command and didn't know how to cope with excessive power. You have just given them positive direction and they feel so much more secure. You're bigger and in charge, and they are now content to follow your secure lead.

260

INSET 11.1 RECIPE FOR SUCCESSFUL TIME-OUTS
(FOLLOW EXACTLY)

1. All adults and older siblings must follow all rules.
2. One adult tells the child briefly (2 sentences or less) that the consequence for specific enumerated naughty behaviors will be to stay in his/her room for ten minutes of quiet with the door closed.
3. The naughty behaviors should be specified. Don't select all, just the worst, e.g., hitting, temper tantrums, talking back to parents.
4. If the child is likely to open the door when it is closed, arrange it so the door can be locked from the outside. Door handles may be reversed or a latch can be used.
5. For the first and all times the child misbehaves in the stated way, the child should be sent or escorted to the room without the parent losing his/her temper and without giving any further explanation beyond one sentence, e.g., "You will stay in your room for ten quiet minutes."
6. If the child slams the door, loses his or her temper, bangs on walls, throws toys, screams, shouts, or talks, there is to be absolutely no response from anyone. Expect the first few times to be terrible. Remember, absolutely NO response from anyone.
7. Set timer when child is quiet.
8. After ten minutes, open the door to permit the child to leave. There should be no further explanation or apology or warning or discussion of love. Act as if nothing unusual has happened.
9. Repeat as necessary.
10. After one week, only a warning of the closed door will be necessary to prevent undesirable behavior.
11. Child will become much calmer and appear more secure.
12. If you use "time-out" for warning purposes, ALWAYS follow through if the child disobeys. Remain CALM.

Now some readers will feel that Inset 11.1 describes cruel and unusual punishment that you would not inflict on your children. You will want to modify it by explaining to your child afterward how much you love him or her. If you do, you will cancel the effect of the time-out by giving your child a double message. This time-out is effective because it completely withdraws attention. If it is punctuated by your words of love, the child continues to control you. If you're reading this book, your children know that you love them. It certainly is appropriate to remind them of your love, but not at times when they've behaved poorly, and certainly not immediately following their punishment. Dominant children are show persons. They like to function with an audience.

Withdrawing their audience tells them that their act is ineffective, and they should select more appropriate showmanship. As long as parents deal consistently with children's incorrigible actions by completely removing the audience, the children will search for more praiseworthy behaviors. However, this is a strong habit you are changing, so expect them to make every effort to upstage you in their last scenes.

Even in early childhood children should be given opportunities to make choices and participate in decision making. However, these choices should always be limited by adults. They can choose from a defined range of activities, behaviors and material possessions. As they get older you may broaden the range available to them, but throughout childhood and adolescence parents should control those limits. If you progressively extend their freedom as they make responsible choices they will feel independent, trusted and within reasonable control of their lives. Ironically, if children are given too much freedom early, they feel out of control and search for a sense of control. They take freedom from adults and trample adults' rights by requiring continuous surveillance. By providing them structure, and flexibility within that structure, children and adults can live together comfortably.

Wish, Work, Wait

Parents who struggled through their own childhood and are now successful are anxious to reward their children with the material possessions and rewarding experiences of which they were deprived. Parents who as children had unlimited material possessions also may be tempted to shower costly things and activities upon their children. Children who find that all their requests — and later their demands — are immediately responded to grow accustomed to that habit and expect it to continue. Parents who give so much so easily are at the same time taking away from their children their sense of efficacy and confidence that comes when "wishes and wants" are followed by "work and waits." That sense of instantaneous delivery by someone else gives children the power and audacity to ask continuously for things, gifts, and activities.

When children generalize that habit of immediacy to education and schooling, they find themselves unprepared for reality. They have only learned to wish and want, not to work or wait. They want to be instantly smart, immediately successful and to easily complete their tasks. They want to wave a magic wand to be declared bright, talented, and creative, and they interpret intelligence according to a criterion of immediacy. They assume other good students learn instantly, get good grades with quick study, and so they deny themselves the satisfaction that comes with effort.

Teach your children to work and to wait. Despite the material possessions and experiences they have, they should be learning a process of effort and patience. They can learn that from planning, working and saving with you for events which will be meaningful. You also can help them to generalize those concepts to education, where planning, effort and patience will reward them with deserved success. No matter how much you wanted all those possessions and experiences that you were denied, don't give them effortlessly to your children. Don't steal their work or their wait!

Avoiding Confrontations

Dominant nonconforming children have built their confidence based on winning power struggles. Since it is a tenuous basis of self-esteem, they must continually manipulate persons in their environments to reinforce that sense of power which comes only from winning and being right. In order for them to feel good about themselves, they must make others feel bad. They continuously compete against almost everyone. When comparison and competition are not part of a relationship, they invent methods of causing invidious comparison. Of course, one method is to brag or "put a person down." An equally frequent habit is instigating an argument or confrontation which they know they will win.

This custom of arguing about everything with everyone can make home and school life quite unpleasant. Bright children will insist that they are being reasonable, and will cleverly chastize their parents about being dictatorial rather than rational. They obviously enjoy the process of debate; however, if you observe carefully you will notice that they rarely settle for reasonable solutions. They continue in the arguments until they win or until they have pushed their parents beyond self-control. When parents or teachers have lost their tempers, children automatically consider themselves "right" or "winners" since their adversary's loss of self-control is viewed as weakness or failure.

Dominant children enjoy the sense of victory over their parents or peers because it makes them feel successful and powerful and gives them fuel for seeing their opposition as inadequate. They search for ways to prove their power by initiating struggles in which they are assured of success. This habit begins when parents feel they should explain reasons for all that they require of their children. Parents are persuaded to ease these responsibilities by their children's apparently convincing logic. As these children find themselves victorious more and more frequently, they are reinforced for their ritual arguing. That habitual struggle for power actually has little to do with reason or logic but is based on competition for control. Some children capture authority from their parents very early. By adolescence children who are accustomed to the power struggle rituals feel depressed and angry unless they are victorious.

As parents you should reprogram interactions with your children to avoid this style of interchange so that their discussions and debates are based on rationally evaluating ideas and are not initiated only for the purpose of winning power. The underlying rule which you may use to guide your relationship with your children is:

Avoid confrontations unless you can win.

Your role is to stay in control of your children. That is not intended to be dictatorial. Certainly, with increasing age and maturity they should earn increasing freedom and decision making. However, you are to be their guide and leader, and if you relinquish parent power before they are mature enough to find their own direction, they wander aimlessly searching for someone's guidance. There is a vacuum where there should be parent guidance, and peers and assorted adults move in to fill the void before the children have developed a value system with which to judge those who influence them.

In order to win a confrontation you must have the power to follow through to insure that your children obey your requests. Thus, sending young children to their room for time-out is effective. It asserts your power and is enforceable. Sending rebellious teenagers to their room is usually ineffective. They will delight in proving you powerless by climbing out the window or cleverly engineering some other way to escape or flaunt you. Don't try it. It only assures them that they can still outmaneuver you. It is a great challenge for parents and teachers of nonconforming powerful children to outperform and outthink them. As children get older there are fewer controls that parents can assert. By high school, there is money (sometimes), a driver's license, the car, or perhaps some other special material possession that you can regulate. Sometimes even these are hard to enforce.

Again, if you can't win, don't confront. Persuade, inspire, excite, influence, model by example — but don't argue. Every power struggle you lose reinforces your children's habits of domination and puts you into a weaker and weaker position. As you increase your vocal volume to motivate your child, you decrease their respect for you. The increased loudness represents decreased control. As you lose power, they become further addicted to owning control.

Families are not intended to be adversarial relationships. You build respect with quiet control. Choose your confrontations carefully so that you don't develop an atmosphere of battle. If 7/8 of your family time is spent disputing differences of opinion or arguing for control, there is little remaining time in which to develop an atmosphere of positive growth. Since the initial purpose of your inviting your children to discuss issues and express their opinions was to encourage democratic involvement and individual and family growth, you can see that you have overshot your mark. Now you must show authority where you still have power to control, and defer all other power struggles to less confrontational strategies, e.g., inspiration, persuasion, suggestion, demonstration, fun activities, etc. These latter approaches give children choices within limits that you can regulate, yet still keep the home atmosphere sufficiently positive that hopefully they will want to please you instead of spite you. Use caution; dominant nonconforming children are habitual fighters. They automatically manipulate for confrontation and victory. Adjusting to a less confrontational atmosphere will seem strange for everyone, but it does leave more time and space for mutual growth and trust.

Emotional Ups And Downs

Victory in competition, control of others and a sense of power provide emotional highs for dominant nonconforming children. As they approach victory, and they feel confident of winning, they also become enthusiastic. However, an absence of goals or losses of power cause these children to feel lethargic and depressed. Of course, it will not be surprising to parents to find their children disappointed or depressed in response to an obvious "loss" because they can recognize the cause of the problem. If a child performs poorly in a tennis match or breaks up with a boyfriend, there's good reason for sadness. However, it often is much more difficult to uncover other reasons for depression. Extreme mood swings are very common and will worry parents. It is important to identify the cause of depression so that you can modify the reinforcements which maintain the ineffective problem solving pattern.

Dominant nonconforming children become depressed when adults say "no" to something they want very much. If you, as parents, have definitely refused permission to see a girlfriend, participate in an activity, or buy a new outfit they have selected, these children will use depression as a manipulation to influence you to change your decision. They may cease communication with the family, close themselves up in their rooms, not come to meals, and ignore your questions which indicate you are worried about their sad mood. Depending on how determined they are, and how successful they've been before, they eventually will lure you into getting their original request, or else into doing them some alternative favor which will make them feel they have won the power contest. Their depression will then completely dissipate and they will swing into a "high" mood again, and you will be left wondering at the amazing change in their temperament. If you've given in to their wishes, despite the fact that you resolved not too, you will feel helpless, out of control, and not sure of how you arrived at that point. The recommended changes for handling this problem will depend largely on how extreme the problem has become.

If you have a small child who shows sadness, tears or depression when events do not go her way, begin early to ignore the sadness or tears or to respond to them simply. For example, you might say, "I know you're disappointed that you can't go to

Angie's party, but you must go to grandmom's house for her birthday dinner. There just isn't any sense in crying about it." A pat on the head or a hug will be comfort enough for her suffering, but don't overreact to the sadness and certainly don't permit her to convince you that this week's friend is more important than her grandmother. If she continues to pout at grandmother's, ask other family members to ignore the sad face, take her aside and privately voice your disappointment at her behavior and go on with the party. If she is not an extreme case she will rejoin the family fun within half an hour. If she is already an expert mood manipulator, she may act despondent all weekend. Since you know the cause of her depression and since you do not want to allow further manipulation, persevere in your nonresponse. You are actively breaking a very difficult behavior habit which can get very much out of control in later years.

The most important skill you must teach these small children is the habit of accepting "no" graciously. Permit them to suffer a bit. Don't feel so sorry for them in those minor disappointments that each sadness is met with a too comforting release from their sorrow or a compensating favor. Permit them to work through these minor disappointments to prepare them for tolerating larger difficulties ahead.

If you have adolescent children who habitually manipulate you with depression, and you have identified clearly that the reasons for their depressions are the "no's" that you give, they are already in a precariously powerful and dangerous position. The most critical change you should make is to think carefully about your responses to their requests before giving them. Avoid saying "no" unless you are absolutely sure that you *can* and *will* be able to defend and maintain that position. An alternative to saying "no" which helps them to break the habit of always expecting to get what they want is the *want, work, wait* position described earlier. This moves responsibility from you to them and focuses their attention from manipulating you to their own personal effort. Here's an example:

Thirteen year old Andrea is determined to get contact lenses instead of glasses, which she sees as no longer fashionable. You're tempted to say "no" since her glasses are only one year old. Contact lenses are expensive and you're not sure Andrea will handle them responsibly. If you say "no," be prepared for depression and manipulation until she makes you change your mind. Don't confront unless you can win. You can't win this one because her manipulative depressions are already extensive. Instead, the conversation should sound like this:

"Andrea, I can understand why you'd like contact lenses and I think it's a good idea to get them as long as you understand the additional risks and responsibilities that go with them. I think it is fair for you to help pay for them since we did buy glasses recently and contacts are an expensive investment. If you save your babysitting money for half the cost of the contacts, we'll put in the other half of the money you need."

This response avoids a power struggle and allies you on your daughter's side. It permits her to *work* and *wait* for her request instead of expecting it immediately; furthermore, it permits her a graceful way out of a power struggle. Should she decide that the contact lenses aren't worth saving her money for, she can simply forget the whole issue or let you know she has decided to direct her funds to a different want. This is a far superior substitute for the more typical "No, we can't afford it" or "No, you can't have everything you want," which would be followed by days or weeks of depression manipulations and the final decision by parents to purchase the contacts. Obviously, not all requests can be met with so easy an alternative response. However, if your dominant nonconforming children are accustomed to manipulating you with depression you should make every effort to change the habit by not rewarding it. There are two main ways to prevent the manipulation:

1. Do not give children what they want or a substitute alternative in response to their sadness and depression.

2. Direct their demands to opportunities where they can earn privileges and earn the confidence that comes with personal control based on effort rather than manipulations.

Threats of suicide are the most powerful manipulation that dominant nonconforming adolescents can use. These threats, even though you feel sure they are manipulations, should always be taken seriously. Young people who threaten to kill themselves should receive professional help, whether or not they think they need it. Suicide attempts are more potent as maniplations than are threats, and professionals can usually help to avoid children's actual attempts. Obviously, the act of suicide is final. It can result from feeling powerless, which comes when children who have become accustomed to a great amount of control find themselves unable to control multiple factors in their lives. Of course, adolescent suicides do *not* all stem from a history of reinforcing depressive frustration.

The moping and depression of dominant children, either conforming or nonconforming, is not always related to depressive manipulations. There is a less serious form of the problem which takes place frequently and causes parents to worry unnecessarily about their children's sadness. It also causes parents to annoyingly probe adolescents with questions which these young people probably don't know how to answer. It takes parent observation to determine the cause of the problem, and mainly patience to permit adolescents to resolve it themselves. There are also some preventative measures that can be planned.

Dominant children are actively competitive and usually very social. They tend to be active and since they gain their confidence from involving themselves with persons, they name as 'boredom" any lull in activity which adults would see as relaxation. It is a feeling of lack of direction, or as they would say "nothing to do." It is especially acute immediately after an intense activity or after a very successful goal directed activity. The contrast between a highly social summer or a championship tennis season and the inactivity of no immediate goals or social life feels dull by comparison and dominant children experience an emptiness that they don't quite understand. If the adolescents are dominant conforming types, the contrasting letdown that comes after an exciting football season will dissipate in some new social or extra curricular activity and parents need do nothing but observe and understand the transition. However, in the case of dominant nonconforming children, the boredom and sadness are more likely to erupt into some unforeseeable display of power. It is almost as if the lack of other goals causes the youth to invent a battle and a power struggle. It will be better to prevent than punish afterward, so look for the symptoms and creatively distract the opposition to a cooperative adventure. Here's an example:

> Todd's parents had sent him to a private military school against his wishes and in response to underachievement and general irresponsibility at home and with peers. Todd, a dominant nonconforming child, was determined to win the power struggle directed mainly toward his father. He failed his classes in the military school in defiance of all the school's efforts at control. He contrived stories about the school and his parents, and finally wrote letters home which included vague threats of suicide. The parents were heavily involved in a confrontation which they couldn't win and decided to permit Todd to return home and continue school in the local community. With the glorious power of victory over his parents, Todd returned to spend a quiet summer before the school year began. His parents felt safe and confident about the summer. They lived in a country home on a lake. Neither Todd nor his peers drove yet, but with fishing, swimming and boating activity to keep Todd busy, his parents felt that although summer might be tense, it would at least be uncomplicated. The early part of the summer found Todd sad and uncommunicative. When given the opportunity to invite friends to the lake or to visit selected peers, he was uninterested. Family activity was not sufficiently appealing either. Todd fished or watched television and had little positive conversation with family or friends. There were occasional small arguments with his dad as if Todd were attempting to let the family know that his father remained the enemy.

> About six weeks after Todd's return, Todd got drunk at home alone when his parents were out for the evening. He then drove the family "Blazer" into town in his inebriated condition, stopped briefly to talk to a few friends, went for a further drive during which he managed to drive the vehicle into a ditch. He survived the accident with no injuries to himself or others, although the car repair bill approached $1,000. When asked for his reasons for the sudden alcohol binge and the illegal and irresponsible driving, Todd could only say that he was bored and didn't really know why he had taken the apparently impulsive action. He claimed he had no prior plan. However, he had been storing one beer at a time from the refrigerator for a period of time in order to accumulate the eight beers he consumed during his night of boredom.

If there is no apparent frustration, the quiet depression of a dominant nonconformer may signify a sense of lack of purpose. These are energetic youth. They do not enjoy inactivity or relaxation. Life is boring if it is not busy. The out-of-control depression that they experience must be diverted to positive planning or it will result in senseless destructive actions whose only purpose is to provide excitement and opposition. Although Todd could verbalize that he was bored and that he was angry at his parents for having sent him to military school, the reason for his anger no longer existed. That is, he had won that battle and felt the excitement and power of that victory. With nowhere to direct his energies plus a habit of opposition to his dad, the drinking and driving allowed him to assert his power in a new father/son duel.

How could this have been avoided? A want, work, wait regimen may have served some diversion. Of course, finding the right combination is not always easy. However, within one week of arrival at home, a regular work project, in which Todd could earn money toward something he wanted, should have begun. A job alone would not be sufficient, since there must be an important goal direction for Todd's work, for example, saving up for a guitar or a bicycle to have before school. Planning an adventure trip with his father for later in the summer would have helped heal the wounds and cement a more positive relationship. Redecorating his bedroom or remodeling the boathouse into a clubhouse for parties would help give integration to his returning home and social life. It might also provide him with the courage to again initiate peer relationships. For Todd's and Chris's and Mary's and Bob's, the dominant nonconforming children, you will have to subtly inspire a positive cause, or support their own creative projects, in order to avoid their being distracted to negative nonconforming activities which only maintain family combat. If these youngsters are engaged in positive activities, they can direct those dominant energies and can earn confidence. However, we must recall that their drive is toward nonconformity, so it is unusual and different activities which will appeal to them — an unusual trip with a parent, remodeling the barn into a social hall, sewing a different wardrobe for fall, writing a drama to be produced by peers, or preparing for an art exhibit or other special contest. These children are driven by a wish to be different, so try to help them to make their difference positive and productive.

I strongly suggest that you enforce some alone time for very young children during which they learn to invent ways to keep themselves busy. If children have learned early to initiate their own activity and to derive satisfaction from nonoppositional involvement, they are not likely to suffer from boredom based depression. Therefore, if you are reading this book when your children are elementary school aged or below, there is still time to insist that "I don't know what to do's" be met with enforced time and activity of their own by themselves, instead of with the continuous flow of activities parents feel they must provide for their children. Paradoxically, the way to prevent boredom depression for young children is to insist they use their own time to discover their potential for inventing activities. For adolescents, it typically is too late for this approach. You may have to take the first steps in directing them to constructive activities in which they can get involved in order to avoid more negative options.

Responding to depressions of these children without reinforcing them is difficult. Reacting to their successes is much easier and more fun, and more important than it may seem. Celebrate with them and praise their efforts. Emphasize their perseverance and their victories. Of course, you must also sensitize them to the feelings of the vanquished, but not so much that you take away from the pleasure in their accomplishment that you enjoy together.

Some parents feel that because these children exhibit mood swings, they should try to calm them down in victory. However, reminders of immodesty, conceit or other criticisms of their performance at the time of celebration will make these children feel that you wish they had not done so well and that you begrudge them their success. This will encourage oppositional feelings which are just below the surface anyway. Your joining them in their joy, spontaneously and without overreaction, will feel good to them and assure them of your support. Later, when the emotional high is over, you may make comments on bragging or other sensitive issues if necessary. However, if criticism is appropriate be sure to begin the conversation with your delight at their success. These are oppositional children who, if not reminded of your support for them, will feel as if they are being criticized. Prevent their reaction of defense by providing them the psychological safety of your alliance.

Maintaining The Positive

How does one manage to remain positive when dominant nonconforming children are determined to push parents and teachers beyond their limits? How do you manage avoiding overreactions in the form of severe punishments which, after you think them through, you decide are too extreme and should be modified? Dominant nonconforming children have developed antennae which tune into your every mood. They know your weak moments and the appropriate "people buttons" to push. They are practiced at manipulation and well rehearsed in litigiousness. They are established, persevering persuaders, and the brighter they are, the more expert they are at convincing you of their points of view. If they have established power as children, they will not give it away. If you talked to them as adults at age six, don't plan to treat them as children at age twelve. In their own words, such treatment feels like a "put down" and it angers them because it seems so irrational. Persons who have freedom feel controlled when it is taken away. Thus if you wrench your children's freedom away once it is given, you can expect them to feel punished and resentful. They will become defiant and you will find yourself in a continuous power struggle which you and your children feel helpless to avoid.

In order to elude the endless negative environment of punishments and put downs, negotiate with these children. You will first have to invent a negotiation inventory. Include four components in your stock taking: strengths, weaknesses, controls and rewards. The first includes talent areas and positive qualities your children have managed to retain. The second, weaknesses, includes all those personality qualities that your children exhibit which you despise. The third, controls, include those areas of adult power which you have not given away. The last, rewards, are those tangible and intangible reinforcements which will continue to motivate your children. See Inset 11.2 for a sample inventory for one adolescent girl. Tack your inventory in an unobtrusive spot so that you and your spouse may review it or add to it each night, preferably out of view of your youngsters. The list provides you with your negotiating options.

Make an effort to notice and mention a strength at least once a day, and try to extinguish as many weaknesses as possible by not responding to them. Obviously, there will be some problem areas for which you must take a much firmer position. Pick the one or two problems which are highest in priority to you and select your negotiating tools from your controls and potential rewards. Select the least potent control and the smallest reward which you believe will be effective in controlling your most pressing issue. Present this alternative to your child in a positive and persuasive manner.

INSET 11.2 SAMPLE NEGOTIATION INVENTORY FOR ADOLESCENT GIRL

Strengths	Weaknesses	Controls	Rewards
Creativity	Disrespect for Parents and Teachers	Spending Allowance	Additional Monies for Clothes or Special Events
Sensitivity to Others	Argumentiveness	Clothing Allowance	Special Trips
Kindness	Overeating	Drivers License	Invitations to Friends to Join Family Events
Intelligence	Procrastination with Schoolwork	Specific Social Events	
Attractiveness	Poor Study Habits	General Weekend Social Activity	Concerts, Ballet, and Drama Productions
Creative Writing		Concerts, Ballet, or Drama Productions	
Cooking Ability			
Good Taste in Clothing			
Musical Talent			

See Inset 11.3 for an example. Maintain this contingency as long as it is effective. If it is ineffective you may wish to select a more potent control or a more powerful reinforcer, but be absolutely certain not to use up your controls or rewards prematurely; the long list of negative behaviors to be changed will remind you that you should hold on to all the power you have. Be very sure not to use punishments that are not on your list, since you have not thought them through and you may not be able to follow through on those. Be absolutely certain that you don't unintentionally follow a negative behavior with a reward, despite your children's efforts to coerce you to do this. Finally, make every effort to notice and mention those strengths privately to your child as well as referentially to your spouse or relatives. Don't hesitate to occasionally, but not all the time, follow positive behavior with one of the sample rewards — intermittent rewards are more powerful than are regular ones.

INSET 11.3 SAMPLE NEGOTIATIONS CONVERSATION WITH ADOLESCENT USING NEGOTIATION INVENTORY

Parent: Jane, we would really like to help you get out of your school procrastination habit. You are intelligent and you are creative, but your grades reflect neither because you put off doing your homework and studying. It would be good if teachers could appreciate what you can do when you make the effort.

Jane: The schoolwork is not creative and not challenging, and I just don't see why I should do it. The teachers give more and more busy work.

Parent: I'm sure that is true for some assignments, but I can't believe all the work is busy work, and I know that all the assignments are part of a plan for your learning. What about if you agree to an experiment with doing your work on time?

Jane: Yuk! Do I have to? Seems dumb.

Parent: Your dad and I have agreed that you do have to, but we're hoping you'll do it willingly and positively, and we're willing to pay you for your efforts as part of the experiment.

Jane: Pay? Now that sounds interesting. I've spent all my allowance and I was hoping to get some new clothes for school.

Parent: Well, that would be great to save toward. Here's our plan. We've arranged with your counselor to give us a weekly report from your teachers every Friday. Here's the report form. (See form in Chapter 9.) There is a space for missing assignments. For every week there are no missing assignments you get $5.00. For every grade of B or above you get an extra dollar. That would mean $10.00 a week for just doing your work.

Jane: Not bad - wouldn't take too long to get those jeans I want.

Parent: Now here's the part you won't like. If there are any missing assignments on Friday, then you have to bring your books home and complete the assignment before you go out on Friday nights.

Jane: Ha! Then I won't do it. I just won't bring my report back. Then how will you know?

Parent: I guess we'll just have to assume that you haven't done you're assignment so you'll just miss the Friday nights at the football games. But Jane, we wish you wouldn't do that. We really don't want to punish you at all, and if you just keep up with your homework and never get behind, we'll never have to punish you and you can make some extra money. And Jane, the real bonus is that you'll accidentally find out what a good student you can be. Jane, will you give it a try?

Jane: I guess I don't have much choice. Okay, I'll try it!

Teach yourself to be flexible in your rules, but rigid in delivering the consequences. For example, children may select the time of day to work on their long-term assignment and their style of work. Deadlines may even be moved slightly if intense effort is shown. However, if they do not complete their long-term assignment and are not even close to finishing, then they do not go to the weekend party you agreed to as their negative consequence regardless of all their persuading. They will try to convince you that they will take their punishment next week and that this is the party of their very best friend, but you must be absolutely rigid and unbending if you expect them to take your threats seriously. In your initial negotiations leave room for their choices and control, but do not change the consequences once they have been definitely set.

Don't overreact and "double the punishment" or expand the negative consequences because they don't seem to mind. That "not minding" is part of their way of telling you that you haven't won the contest. They do care. Don't add to their resentment by irrational threats and punishments that you can't truly control. Using your list as a guide will help you to plan carefully and fairly and will prevent that series of negative actions and reactions which are typical for dominant nonconformers. Notice in the conversation in Inset 11.3 how many opportunities the parents used to remind Jane of her strengths and their alliance with her. However, they were firm without overreacting. The withdrawal of social privileges is effective only if parents are confidently definite and continue to emphasize the positive.

Parenting Together

Team parenting of dominant nonconforming children is the greatest challenge. You will feel all extremes of emotion from despair at their frequent stubborn opposition to the exhilaration and pride that go with their successes. It is difficult to co-parent as you watch your children struggle and as they manipulate one of you against the other or both of you against the school. You will repeatedly resolve not to become engulfed in their manipulations, then suddenly find that somehow you are misunderstood or misquoted and right in the center of a confusing muddle of miscommunication. More than once you will try to remove yourself from the entire morass of parenting these children only to find that your guilt and your love have not permitted your escape and you will resolve to make one last effort. You and your spouse will find that these children are the continuing center of your conversation and your attention despite all your efforts to back away from their overwhelming problems. However, that talk will not merely be discussion but debate, disagreement and continuous argument about the best way to deal with these difficult youth. It is not surprising that parenting together is most difficult. It may even be the most difficult test of your marriage.

How can you manage to parent as a team without isolating these children whose self-concept is dependent on their succeeding against opposition? Here are some precautions.

1. BE CERTAIN NOT TO SAY ANYTHING NEGATIVE ABOUT YOUR SPOUSE IN ONE-TO-ONE CONVERSATION WITH YOUR CHILD, EVEN IF YOU DISAGREE WITH YOUR SPOUSE'S BEHAVIOR. Dominant nonconforming children manipulate parents against each other because they feel secure and mature in an alliance with one adult against another. It is not unlike an alliance between nations which have a common enemy. These children search and even compete for such powerful relationships, and they will manipulate and misquote you when they change positions and attempt to build a partnership with your spouse. If you disagree with your spouse's

approach, then you should talk that through and make your compromises. That may be difficult, and in cases of divorce almost impossible, but it is the only way to avoid the difficult manipulations.

2. IF YOUR CHILD IS MISQUOTING YOU TO YOUR SPOUSE OR OTHERS USE ONE OF SEVERAL ALTERNATIVES. Write down your agreements and sign them; include both parents in your discussions with your children, and be sure the children explain to you in your presence their understanding of any agreements.

3. USE CONVERSATIONS WITH YOUR CHILDREN TO POINT OUT THE EXCELLENT QUALITITES OF YOUR SPOUSE. They will respect that parent only if you give them a clear message of high regard. If you teach children to oppose one parent, they are also learning to oppose other adults, including yourself. They should build their feelings of confidence based on accomplishment, not opposition.

4. REASSURE YOUR OPPOSITIONAL CHILDREN FREQUENTLY OF THEIR PARENTS' MUTUAL SUPPORT FOR THEM. However, be positively firm in not permitting them to manipulate either of you. They will be quick to see spouse support of each other as a betrayal of them and will feel hurt and depressed. Since they are in a habit of seeing relationships between others as a betrayal of commitments to them, you should assure them frequently that spouses can respect each other while both still love their children. This is a difficult reality for these youths to cope with, and they may feel emotionally isolated unless they are reassured frequently. One of the parents (the "good" one) will be placed in the position of mediator by these children, in order to persuade the other, unless the parent absolutely refuses to play that role.

Although it may be tempting to one parent to use that mediator position in the hope of being better able to support the child, in reality this mediator role does not succeed. It is an effort by the child to maintain an alliance with one adult in order to feel more powerful than the rival parent. If you take the child's position against his/her other parent, you may feel like the "good" parent. However, you are relegating the position of "bad" or "dumb" parent to your spouse — which leaves no alternative for your child but rebellion and underachievement. Stay together and reassure the child that you are both supportive. Since you are taking power away from the child, they will need continued assurance of your mutual support coupled with firm limits.

If your children are dominant nonconformers, you already know how difficult parenting can be. You have found yourselves trapped in their manipulations often, and have wondered just how all those miscommunications could have taken place. Your present attempt at change will initially be greeted by further anger, rebellion and depression. But if you parent together and continue to cultivate the positive in these children, they eventually will feel more secure in a family where both parents clearly love them but also discipline them appropriately.

Communicating About Achievement

Internally pressured children who fit in the dominant nonconforming quadrant typically blame the pressure they feel on others, usually their parents or their teachers. Although you may have never even suggested that you expect them to get straight A's, unless they are excellent achievers, they will say that you are pressuring them toward impossible goals. They will communicate that message to other persons, for example, their counselor, teachers, their mediator parent, and sometimes a convenient grandparent, aunt or uncle. These people may easily be fooled into believing that the children's difficult behavior is caused by the pressure they are feeling to achieve. They believe the children instead of realizing that this is a defensive manipulation. You, as parent, are put in a most difficult position. If you expect less of them their manipulations will have been successful and they can avoid achieving responsibly. If you set realistic achievement expectations which are beyond their present performance and require that they put forth reasonable effort, you will soon hear from aunts, grandparents and teachers about your ineffective parenting. Since your children are having problems, this will reinforce your guilt and you will be tempted to ease the expectations. It will indeed feel like a "no win" situation.

There are some appropriate yet safe messages to give to these children. You can say that you expect them to put forth effort and you can quantify that effort in terms of reasonable time expectations. You should probably confirm those with teachers. You also can set logical grade goals for underachieving students which fit with their ability and their strong and weak subjects. One step above where they presently are can't be too much pressure for chidren who have been making little effort. Don't worry about not setting goals high enough for them. If they are complaining to you or others about the pressure that you are placing on them, it may be accurate to assume that they really would like to achieve those grade goals they've attributed to you. They already feel pressure and by setting expectations above where they are, but below where they'd like to be, there's a good chance for success.

If you notice an improved effort and continue to encourage their work, their grades will gradually increase. However, each time you overreact in disgust at their poor grades, they build evidence for your pressuring them. Be patient in awaiting the improvement and comment on their improvement in study. They probably have little study experience and poor study skills. It will take time for them to learn the process. You should gradually set your expectations of their effort higher. Eventually, when the positive results come fairly consistently, you'll be able to move into the background except for occasional encouragement for their successes. They want to achieve, and once they've discovered that they can, the defenses that they were accustomed to using will no longer be necessary.

In reversing underachievement patterns for dominant underachievers, you should plan formal daily meetings for elementary aged children and specific weekly meetings for students from approximately grades 5 through 12. Those meetings should include a review of the daily or weekly progress in each subject, discussion of behavior problems and improvements, and any rewards or punishments that you have built into your contractual agreement. The meetings should be set at specific times which should vary only for emergencies. Ideally, that weekly appointment should be with the same sexed parent or both parents. In either case, it must be very clear that neither parent will let the child escape from his or her commitment to making a strong effort. Those daily or weekly meetings should be kept as positive as possible, but if oppositional children use those meetings for a power struggle, be firm and don't let the children engage you in debate. Be sure contractual agreements are in writing so that rule bending can be avoided by referring to the contract. Rigidity when reasonable requests are made is not appropriate; however, caution is advised. Their claim of rigidity may only be a ploy to prove they can escape their responsibilities.

Communicating With Schools

School administrators, teachers or others will take the initiative to communicate with you if your children are dominant nonconforming underachievers. They will be causing teachers sufficient stress that you may already be accustomed to and fearful of teacher conference day. Teachers may blame you just as you find yourself blaming them for your children's problems. Neither of you will benefit by that process, but all of you are undoubtedly feeling helpless. An alliance between teacher and parents in support of these children is the goal.

Disagreements between parents and teachers are often part of the initiation of these children's oppositional pattern. If parents take their children's side against the teacher, it provides children with reinforcement for their oppositional behavior and they will not respect the teacher's authority. Certainly, not all teachers and schools are right in their approach to teaching your children, but neither are all parents. Since many children will exploit these oppositional positions by underachieving, it would be best to keep communications between teachers and parents private. Sometimes, when parents try not to involve their children in arguments with school staff, they make the mistake of conversing with their spouses or telephoning a friend within hearing of their children. This allies these children with their parents against their teachers, and although they delight in the support of their own parents, they are now engaged in a battle with their teachers which they feel they must win. Parents' disputes with the teacher support their "do it my way" position, whether or not it is a wise way they demand.

Despite the fact that I am recommending children not be involved in oppositional relationships between parents and teachers, it is vital that parents become advocates for appropriate education. Advocacy usually involves differences in opinions and recommendations for changes in the system. Every effort should be made to keep that role as positive and respectful as possible and to avoid confrontations with the school about issues in which you as parents are powerless to win. Inset 11.4 is an example of a parent oppositional situation and its recommendations for resolution.

For dominant nonconformers, any communication between parents and school contains a high risk of being reinterpreted or misinterpreted because the student feels more secure in an oppositional situation with a declared ally and enemy. They also may choose to change sides, and confuse parents and teachers alike, so it's very important that you do not conclude prematurely that teachers have wronged your children. Make efforts to clarify communications whenever in doubt.

In setting up a reporting system with the teacher, it will be very important that you also arrange for feedback to the teacher. That is, if teachers are making an effort to keep you aware of your children's daily or weekly progress and those forms do not reach you, they should be told about the problem.

Actually, since working with dominant nonconforming children is difficult and trying for all involved, you and the teacher will want all the support you can give each other. You will wonder how children can render intelligent adults so powerless.

Changing Peer Environments

By the upper elementary grades, peers begin to play a crucial part in children's educational environment. If peer relationships have been poor for dominant nonconforming children, becoming popular and a leader becomes an extremely important goal by

INSET 11.4 PARENT ADVOCACY CONVERSATION WITH SCHOOL

Scott Thornton, a third grade gifted achiever with an IQ score exceeding 145, was an applicant for a gifted specialty school. Although his ability and achievement ranked him at the very top of eligible applicants, the school had opted to use a random selection system based on a pool of eligible applicants. Scott was not selected despite his undisputed high priority need. Since the criteria for eligibility into the selection pool were fairly low, many students who were selected had considerably less need for a differentiated curriculum than did Scott. Initially, Scott's parents visited with school administration. This was followed by an official appeal process. Neither attempt was successful. Scott's parents turned to the legal process. Their consultation with me was based on my providing expert support for their position. Although I was willing to support their legal attempts, I indicated that I did not consider their efforts to be in Scott's best educational interests. In the six months since the beginning of their battle with the schools, Scott had begun underachieving dramatically. If they continued with the court suit, the time involved would not permit Scott to enter the gifted school during that school year, and perhaps not in the following school year. Furthermore, if the case were decided in their favor, it was not clear that it would affect the future selection procedure since there was a strong possibility of modification of that system.

I recommended that the Thornton's consider enrolling Scott in a nearby private school, perhaps not as excellent as the gifted school, but of a quality that would prove challenging to him and that would take him out of the oppositional position he was presently involved in. They could then separate him from the court case and perhaps pursue the case on its legal merits. My fear was that a year or two of opposing the system with the support of his parents would be sufficient to propel him into a downward cycle of underachievement that later would be difficult to reverse. If there had been a reasonable likelihood of Scott's rapid inclusion in the gifted school or if the court decision could have had the effect of insuring appropriate educational opportunities for other gifted children, there would have been value to the oppositional position. However, the chances of positive impact on Scott were small and the adverse effect on his attitude toward education and his efforts was dramatic. He was not a dominant nonconforming child initially, but in his new position as advocate for a different school, he was focusing a great deal of energy on directing his teacher regarding how he should learn and refusing to conform to that teacher's assigned requirements. To me, it seemed more important to be a child advocate than an issue advocate. The risk was too high. Scott did transfer to a private school with a much more positive attitude and renewed effort.

junior and senior high school. Since popularity is viewed as a dominant role, they want more than ever to take a leadership position among their friends. In order to lead they must conform to adolescent peer values, such as expressing opposition to adults. This is not difficult for them. It actually fits well with their developmental history of choosing allies who share similar enemies — the allies are their agemates, the enemies are all parents. The rebellious adolescent model fits well with their manipulative skill. Their self-confidence and peer popularity grows if they can display the greatest anger at the adult world.

That fit, of course, will depend on their finding a rebellious adolescent peer group. These exist in most secondary schools. They establish their group identity in opposition to schools, parents and achievement. Although the dominant nonconforming student gravitates toward such a group, and feels most accepted among rebellious friends, the group also reinforces the underachieving pattern which now feels "right." Underachievement helps to provide the sense of acceptance and popularity. High school peer groups that oppose school achievement and carry a "do the least you can" banner reinforce the adolescent underachievement pattern and make it extremely difficult to reverse.

If you are a parent of a younger child, hold on to your right to set limits to your children's friendship. They certainly need to select their own friends, but it is not "wrong" or "controlling" to impose value limitations on those friendships. They may be different for each family, but you should make the standards clear to your children. You can control those friendships while the children are in elementary school, although you probably won't be able to by high school. However, if they've internalized those values early, they will probably automatically consider them in selecting friends later. Be sure to include *achievement effort* as one of these values if you want your children to achieve.

There are many situations in which you cannot control friendships for adolescents, even though you realize these friends are having adverse effects on your child. The changing of peer groups is usually an expensive and not too popular alternative. Moving children to a private school is an effective approach if you are confident that the private school has a more positive peer population. Sometimes the reverse, moving from a private to a public school, is an equally good choice. Moving to another community can be effective, but I would not recommend moving only to change a peer group. Besides, your child may find an oppositional peer group in the next school district, in which case you've inconvenienced your family for naught. Special summer programs that involve highly motivated students who share your child's interests are excellent for promoting a pro learning attitude and can help children think anew about their anti-achievement attitude. Summer travel or wilderness experiences are excellent for encouraging personal self-discipline and confidence, and an achievement orientation.

If peers can get together, so can parents. Don't hesitate to contact some parents of your children's friends. If they share your concerns, you can support each other in providing guidelines and positive peer social experiences. In one large suburban high school, parents published a list of those parents who promised to provide drug and alcohol free parties. In fact, for many students it modified a negative social norm, although it certainly didn't erase the problem.

The peer impact on dominant nonconformers is both dramatic and extremely difficult to change. When you find that your children are with a positive peer group, be sure to be hospitable. The test of whether those peers are actually "positive" will be the effect they have on your child. Sometimes seemingly desirable peers are different than what you see.

Teacher Modifications

As with parents, dominant nonconforming children are also the most difficult group for teachers to change. If they've begun their nonconformity early they tend to be behavior problems. By junior and senior high school their nonconformity and opposition has extended far beyond underachievement and classroom misbehavior. They may be extending it to their social environment, and they may also be having problems with the law. They may be beyond teacher change. In some cases the greatest assistance that teachers can give is to refer these children for outside help and to be supportive of those professional efforts. The recommendations for classroom modifications will be those which can be made for younger children and for less extreme cases. For the latter two groups, there is much that teachers can do to help to avoid the problem and provide good school years for these children.

Forming A Teacher-Student Alliance

Oppositional children will form alliances with persons they perceive as strong enough to respect, provided these persons can communicate through the children's defenses that they value something within the children. Since these children were brought up in an early environment of extensive praise and admiration, and since they no longer earn that praise easily, if you are perceptive enough to see their inner quality they will value their relationship with you. However, your perceptions must be accurate and sincere. For some of these youth, their confidence in you is tied to your perception of their intelligence, for others their creativity, attractiveness, kindness, openness or street wisdom. If you honestly identify their valued strength, you accomplish the first step of your alliance.

The second step involves your power. They are accustomed to pushing limits. However, paradoxically, once they have outpowered a person they no longer respect him or her. They have not learned to appreciate the give and take of a parallel relationship. Instead, they tend to see persons as inferior or superior, outside or within their control. If you are perceived as within their control, they don't respect you. They will take advantage of your weakness by not doing their work and not taking responsibilities seriously. If you are in control, they may either respect or resent you. If it is positive control, coupled with the perception that you truly like them, they will respect you and they will perform at their best for you. If the control lacks that special positive relationship, you will be viewed as an enemy. They will manipulate confrontations and do all within their power — and their power is extensive — to avoid meeting their responsibilities and expectations. Teachers have very few controls they can use with these children. Failing grades, detentions, reprimands and punishments tend to be completely ineffective in motivating them toward effort. It is much safer to keep things as positive as possible. You will be much more effective using inspiration, persuasion and reward than using anger and hostility.

Brief personal and confidential meetings are the most effective way to convince children that you care. Working with them in setting short-term attainable goals and clearly agreeing on positive and negative consequences combines closeness with respect. Be sure to write down any mutual or contractual agreements to insure that both of you understand the obligations and consequences. This will avoid misunderstandings and 'memories of convenience." How can you take the time to give such individual attention? It is certainly more then required by your job. You can't do it for all children, but two or three amazing turn-arounds a year definitely would be an exciting accomplishment. That close positive and respectful relationship will encourage them to perform in your classroom, and you will be delightfully surprised by the evidence of hidden talent.

Behavior Problems

Children who begin their dominant nonconformity early are the behavior problems in elementary classrooms. They demand attention. They insist in pushing limits and disobeying rules. Boys may be physically belligerent; girls are more likely to be verbally aggressive. They frustrate the most tolerant teachers, and you are likely to find yourself scolding them often and inventing punishments to keep their misbehavior in control. They probably will cause you to lose your temper, although you repeatedly resolve that you won't.

Their main underlying motivation is class domination. They want to be noticed by teacher and students. They want to be in charge on the playground, they want to do only the assignments they enjoy and they want all these things and more instantly. They have not been taught the WAIT and WORK of effective learning and quality performance. Your scoldings, writing their name on the board and your noticeable impatience reinforces them with class attention, and they earn a reputation as the class 'troublemaker." They fulfill that reputation almost as if they have no choice, and indeed they often feel that they have no alternative. Their mischief maker stereotype moves ahead of them in school and teachers and peers alike anticipate the annoyance. Parents tell their children not to play with them, and as a matter of fact children avoid them because they fear they will be similarly labeled. Friendless or paired with other behavior problems, they aggressively search for ways to make friends. They don't see the relationship between their naughtiness and their peer problems.

Teachers will not be effective by using attention getting reprimands of any kind. Neither scolding nor placing this child's name on the board will improve the behavior. Quiet reprimands, personal signals, and brief "time-outs" are effective in modifying behavior. Small daily rewards or privileges may be effective. Withdrawal of privileges serve as an effective negative consequence. However, for elementary children both positive and negative outcomes must be short-term so that each day gives the child a new chance to establish that he can be good. Power and attention, unfortunately, are the most effective rewards for these children. Consequently, withdrawal of attention is the most effective punishment. Inset 11.5 suggests a token system which has been used effectively for encouraging on task behavior.

Daily notes home describing behavior to be reinforced at home are effective in improving behavior, if teacher and parent cooperate. The same form used for incomplete work in Chapter 9 can be used for behavior problems. Good days can be rewarded with special individual play or model airplane time with father or mother. Food treats (e.g., ice cream or candy) are effective but shouldn't be used if there are family weight problems. For children who are slightly older, good days can be counted up for a weekly activity with parents, for example, bowling, a movie or a pizza treat.

Unfortunately, positive consequences may not be sufficiently effective. *Unsatisfactory* days should be followed with consistently negative consequence, for example, no television, early bedtime, or time-out in their room. Parent/teacher consistency is the key. For a child who is a continuous behavior problem, there is little room for flexibility. Consistent positive and negative consequences which follow appropriate and inappropriate behaviors, respectively, will make it very clear that only appropriate behavior will be accepted. Five cardinal rules for behavior management of these children are:

INSET 11.5 TOKEN SYSTEM FOR SERIOUS BEHAVIOR PROBLEMS OF DOMINANT NONCONFORMING YOUNG CHILDREN

1. Select only one major behavior problem initially. For example, aggressive hitting is typically the first behavior chosen, to be followed by in-seat behavior, on task activity and finally good attention to teacher.

2. Plan private meetings with the child. The agenda for the first meeting should include the following:

   a. Menus of activities child would like to earn, e.g. computer time, game with friends, special time with teacher or parents, etc.

   b. Behavior to be changed.

   c. Positive consequences — one token every hour where no inappropriate behaviors have been shown.

   d. Negative consequences — time-out in enclosed attention free area, at the signal, for ten minutes of quiet time and voluntary return when child feels ready.

   e. Determination of price in tokens for menu items.

3. All contingencies should be decided together at the meeting. The teacher should indicate that he/she is trying to help the child improve behavior and be accepted by classmates. All tokens and signals should be prearranged and quiet.

4. Daily meetings should be held with the child to note improvement, show support and encourage continued improvement.

5. If parent cooperation is available daily or weekly communications should be sent home.

---

1. Focus attention mainly on positive behaviors; completely remove attention for negative behaviors.

2. Be consistent, firm and don't overreact.

3. Use short-term consequences or you will use up the few controls available to you.

4. Keep noting the positive qualities these children show, but don't overreact to these either.

5. Focus these children's high-energy constructively by finding positive active involvement for them.

These are difficult children. However, your patience and perseverance will be rewarded and it is possible to make a real difference for them in elementary school although, again, it will be much more difficult later.

Giving Them Power And An Audience

Dominant nonconforming adolescents who gain insight into their own behavior may admit to you that they often view their own actions as if they were on stage. They plan their behaviors with attention to how other people will react. It is truly as if they automatically and spontaneously manipulate people around them, without awareness. Some, who are especially sensitive and bright, realize they are manipulating others and even feel uncomfortable about the habit, but they do not know how to change. They were trained in showmanship as children and measure their self-worth by their impact on others.

Channeling their energies into an interest which gives them an intrinsic sense of accomplishment is the most effective way to help them build inner confidence and get them off the manipulation track. Their dependence on an audience can be used positively in selecting areas of strength from which they can build weak areas. It is a two step process. Step one includes finding an activity in which they are proficient and which provides an audience. Step two expands the activity to include developing a weaker area for the same audience. In step one they are focusing energy positively. This provides the vehicle which moves them to the second step, where they can challenge themselves with an experience which intrinsically rewards them for their involvement.

This method allows them to use their dependence on an audience to develop a level of confidence which they have rarely experienced. They will feel good about their accomplishment and realize that it is not an empty reward that comes from manipulation. As they build this new sense of confidence in one area, their performance in other school subjects and other behaviors should improve. Feelings of pressure and tension disappear as they finally realize that they are capable and that their ability is not merely a facade. It feels as if they are lifting a mask to find a real self below that is more effective and more satisfying than the mask they wore for show.

This approach of using an audience and a strength to remediate a weakness and build confidence is most effective for reversing underachievement with children and advocates who are manipulative, rebellious and creative. It is not as effective for the more aggressive and delinquent youngsters who typically require more help than the classroom teacher can provide. Inset 11.6 includes suggestions for some audience activating projects.

Changing Academic Grouping

Dominant nonconforming children search for sources of nonconforming power within their classroom and families. The last section suggested ways in which teachers could funnel this need by using their preference for an audience to assist in moving these children in more positive directions. Acceleration in reading or math groups also is a potent way to direct these children's power needs toward positive accomplishment. Underachieving children are typically placed in achievement groupings below their actual abilities and skills. Nevertheless, it is unfair to other children to move them to higher groups unless they have proven themselves able to learn the skills and able to pass the proficiency tests which will permit them to move forward. Be sure to caution them that they may remain in these higher groups only if they can maintain reasonable quality of performance.

Moving to a higher reading group is a highly visible indication of their improved competence and does help to channel their wish for dominance much more constructively. Even total grade acceleration can be appropriate for some highly gifted children, despite their behavior problems. If monitored carefully, it may provide the attention toward which the child's earlier behavior problems were targeted.

Providing A Sanctuary

Some dominant nonconforming children will benefit by a change in learning environment. That special or safe place can be within their existing school, outside the school but within the community, or within a different school. A sanctuary plan will be especially effective with Creative Chris, Manipulative Mary, Academic Alice and sometimes with Rebellious Rebecca,

INSET 11.6 SAMPLE AUDIENCE ACTIVITY PROJECTS WHICH HAVE BEEN SUCCESSFULLY USED WITH CHILDREN

Strength	Weak Area	Step 1 Strength Activity	Step 2 Weakness Activity
Reading	Writing	Reading to younger grade children	Write stories for these same children
Verbal ability, computers	Writing	Talking into tape recorder	Writing story with word processing program
Musical Talent	Perseverance, depression	Prepare for school musical	Take challenging vocal lessons
Creative Writing	Organization of time	Independent study course in Creative Writing	Part-time job contingent on successful organization of schooltime and assignments
Creative Art Design	Oppositional behavior at home	Redecoration of barn next to home for peer social activities	Respect of parent social limits
Computers	Math facts	Program math facts, design competitive game	Participation in math facts game individually or later in peer chosen competition
General academic excellence	Behavior problems	Partial acceleration in area of strength	Total acceleration based on behavioral improvement or improved skills in areas of weakness

depending on the form of her rebellion. Those who will benefit from a haven include children who wish to dominate based on intellectual, creative, artistic or political nonconformity. If their environment is labeled as special relative to intellectual challenge, creative or artistic talent or political stimulation, it reduces the pressure which they feel to dominate. Placement in such a group provides recognition of their status so that they no longer feel they must prove themselves superior. Within the group they find peer support for their personal nonconformity, while the pressure to be different and superior is reduced. For example, a Creative Chris within a group of children identified as highly creative can feel secure in the uniqueness of the group and can experience personal creative expression without the stress of having to be the most creative. An Academic Alice can reduce her personal pressure by telling herself that within the group all children are bright and "I don't have to prove my brilliance."

In order for a sanctuary group to be effective, it must emphasize noncompetitiveness and solidarity within group; it must be self-labeled or recognized as different than typical peer groups; and it must support positive productivity of all its members. Gifted classes in schools, special purpose church groups, private schools, community art or political groups can provide avenues for positive nonconformity in creative, intellectual and political areas. The main risk of such groups is that the leadership may redirect the peer nonconformity to nonproductive purposes. Since the group support provides the dominant nonconformer with a sense of power and elitism, it is extremely important that the group leadership maintains a positive direction which contributes to the participants' educational and maturational experience.

Sanctuaries that support uniqueness are a good way to use children's strengths to build their weaknesses. Their strength lies in their creativity, intellectual or artistic difference. Their weakness comes in their inability to conform long enough to learn skills which are important for societal productivity. If they are not included in a sanctuary group which provides positive direction, they are likely to be attracted to a nonproductive shelter or peer group. Teachers who hope to educate them can also guide them better if they can recognize and legitimize their nonconformity. Teachers who like them can ignite their enthusiasm toward productiveness. They will respond at their best within a sanctuary that values their nonconformity.

Maintaining Open Doors

A major parent and teacher concern relative to dominant nonconforming adolescents is helping these youth to avoid closing doors on future education and career opportunities because of their present rebellion. The careers in which they will eventually be happiest will involve challenge, creativity, leadership and typically, preparation beyond high school. Each time they push school and societal limits, they risk shutting off potentially bright futures. In their urgency to feel immediately unique and independent, they lose college scholarships, drop out of high school, or are placed in more restrictive learning and living environments. These failures limit the opportunities for the type of career and life experiences which would be most fulfilling to them. If you, as teachers, can assist them in jumping the necessary hurdles which will keep open those potential directions, you can make a real difference in their lives.

Unfortunately, there will be many times that adolescents return to you too late to finally acknowledge that they now understand your former message and wish they had heeded it. They realize that their preferred career opportunities are no longer available. Their creativity and their intelligence may go unchallenged for years because life or family circumstances now force their labor in an area far below their ability. Their choices have been narrowed to career underachievement, although they recognize how different it could have been if they had been able to postpone that pressing independence and dominance. In order for capable students to train themselves for careers that eventually offer challenge and creative outlets, they must often forego those immediate expressions of their independence. If you can help them to see that "bigger picture," your influence will be felt throughout their lives.

12

The Causes and the Cures

The Causes

Underachievement Syndrome is epidemic. The increasing number of children displaying symptoms of Underachievement Syndrome are not documented by statistics. Yet virtually all teachers will substantiate this conclusion based on their own classroom observations. There is certainly no one simplistic explanation for the educational dilemma which finds tens of thousands of children with good abilities who are not learning within the same classrooms where teachers successfully teach other youngsters. However, by focusing on both the main psychological causes for children's underachievement and on current social conditions, one readily recognizes that the interaction of these two variables is responsible for the increasing number of underachieving children. A parent or teacher alone is likely to have little effect on the overall societal conditions, but together or separately they can adjust their home and school environments to compensate for social impacts and can thus foster achievement within their children.

Essential Elements of Underachievement Syndrome

Five essential causes for Underachievement Syndrome have been described in this book. Although some of these elements also may be found in achieving children, their presence is less severe. The problem is increased or reduced in proportion to the degree or their presence, singly or in combination.

Initiating Situation. Most underachievement patterns are initiated in the first years of life. Attention addiction caused by a child being overwelcome, gifted, handicapped or ill may start the problem. Parents who are determined to do or give everything or who see their children as the center of their universe and their only purpose for being will foster the dilemma. Inadequate caretakers or particular sibling combinations also provide high risks for starting the syndrome. Although early home situations typically are the culprits, actual underachieving patterns may not show themselves until late elementary grades, middle school, senior high school or even college. In some circumstances actual conditions which initiate the pattern may happen later in childhood. Thus a poor teacher situation can start the pattern, and two consecutive "bad years" present a very high likelihood of beginning childrens' problems. Life circumstances such as a death of a parent, divorce, or a dramatic change in environment may also lead to underachievement in a formerly achieving child. There is almost always an identifiable point when the telltale symptoms of the syndrome begin, although the obvious underachievement characteristics may not show themselves until later.

Excessive Power. Excessive childhood power is characteristic of all underachievers. They have too much power, but typically feel as if they have too little. Their power is directed toward manipulating persons so as to avoid responsibility rather than move toward actual accomplishment. Of course, they don't intentionally control others to cause themselves, their parents or their teachers harm; they simply have learned a comfortable and, to them, successful human engineering style. Their maneuvering feels effective in the short run and they do not understand how they might otherwise interact. They affiliate with other persons in their environment in either dependent or dominant modes. The first style is covert manipulation and involves verbal and body language that requests sympathy and assistance. The second is more overtly manipulative; the children insist on pressuring parents, teachers and peers to conform to their wishes and preferences. Instead of parents and teachers guiding these children, they are in the powerless positions of allowing them to take their own path, regardless of the children's lack of wisdom or experience. Struggles for power are frequent and children trap their parents into arguments and debate. Children conclude these debates by domination or rebellion and adults lose their tempers and feel angry and frustrated. Both dependent and dominant children refuse to live within guiding frameworks set by their parents and their teachers, but instead push adult limits continuously either in passive aggressive or overtly aggressive styles.

Appropriate power for children comes when they are encouraged to be independent within limits set by adults. Their range of independent activities should grow with their demonstration of responsible choice.

Inconsistency and Opposition. Caretakers and parents are inconsistent and/or oppositional in the early lives of underachievers. Whether these caretakers are birth parents, grandparents, stepparents or foster parents, day-care teachers or babysitters, the stage is set early for conflicting sets of adult requirements. Inconsistency may take place within one adult or between many adults. For example, the parent who is living through a difficult period in her own life is likely to be inconsistent in disciplining and coping with her children. If there are numerous adults in the child's immediate environment, for example, grandparents, aunts, uncles and babysitters, all of whom have very different ideas about child rearing, not only is there a lack of consistency, but also likely opposition.

Opposure also may take place in the intact traditional two parent family, and almost always exists in or after a divorce. The characteristic antagonism is over how strict or how liberal to be with their children, with adults competing to be the 'better parent." The contraposition of a mean or strict parent with a kind or sheltering parent reinforces these children for avoiding effort. The children compete with and become antagonistic against the demanding adult. That parent feels frustration, anger and lack of control and becomes even more oppressive. The sheltering parent feels further pressure to protect the children from the "ogre" spouse. Although sheltering parents wish the children would apply more effort, they empathize with their feelings of inadequacy, poor self-concepts and their concerns with never being able to meet the difficult standards imposed by the ogre. Thus the children's escape behavior is actually fostered by the loving protecting parent. Although it is rarely possible to determine which adult is at fault, since together they give contradictory messages to their children, the pattern of avoidance and poor self-concept is set.

Oppositional caretakers also are responsible for the children's dominance or dependency. There is little reward for these children in achievement, since success does not create the close sheltering relationship caused by failure. Opposition robs the child of an achievement oriented model whom the child could identify with, rather than compete against.

Inappropriate Classroom Environment. Schools and teachers are important. They do make a difference. Classroom teachers who don't recognize the telltale symptoms of underachievement are likely to accidentally feed the dependent or dominant manipulations of these children. Particularly in elementary grades, these symptoms are easily misidentified as immaturity, parent pressure, learning disabilities or emotional disturbance. Instinctively, teachers are likely to respond to dependent children in ways that preserve their passivity, and to dominant younsters in ways that maintain their battle stance. The typical teaching approaches which are effective with achieving children may not work for underachievers. Achievers are much more receptive than underachievers to a large variety of effective teaching methods. Even the best teachers may fall into the unintentional traps set by Underachievement Syndrome children.

For gifted children, insufficient classroom challenge can pose special school problems. Unstimulating environments may actually initiate and maintain their underachievement even when there are no particular parenting problems. For example, the parent/parent opposure described earlier may be replaced by parent/school antagonism and may have a more detrimental effect. These children may accidentally receive the message from their parents that because school is not meeting their needs, they are not expected to complete boring assignments. Further, teachers may inform the children that their high abilities are imaginary, since their school performance is so poor. These children easily fall victim to Underachievement Syndrome.

Finally, although the majority of teachers in our classrooms are effective, some children fall prey to that minority of ineffective instructors. A few bad years, due to poor teaching, high teacher absenteeism, or a poor teacher/student match or outright antagonism between a teacher and a child, can be the cause and culprit of Underachievement Syndrome for some children. This is less likely to be the actual sole cause of the problem, but may have an exacerbating effect.

The most important quality of classrooms where children maintain an achieving mode is the presence of an appropriate relationship between the learning process and its outcomes. If assignments are either consistently too easy or too difficult, the setting which cultivates Underachievement Syndrome is present and the syndrome will worsen.

Competition. An environment which does not teach children to cope with competition fosters underachievement. If there is a competitive climate, but children find themselves consistently in the position of either losers or winners they are unlikely to learn a healthy competitive attitude. In the first case, they see no reason to make an effort since there appears to be no possibility of success. They withdraw from competition entirely. In the latter situations, winners who have not learned to cope with failure are disabled when they are not victorious and at least temporarily lose confidence and stop putting forth an effort. The winner role is less likely to result in permanent underachievement, since these children have built a firm history of confident acccomplishment. They are more likely to be sufficiently resilient to adjust their goals based on their foundation of past achievements. The continuous loser is less easily motivated toward effort, since previous sporadic attempts have resulted in failure. They are more likely to daydream about a magical deliverance than risk investing energy in tasks perceived as difficult.

Classrooms and families are inherently competitive since children automatically compare themselves with peers, teachers, siblings, cousins and parents. When they perceive they are falling short, because of either their own inadequacy or the superior achievements of their competitors, they assess the situation. They may set more realistic goals and continue to achieve, or else decide that their own inadequacy leaves them little reason to exert effort. That latter decision exhibits itself in the symptoms of Underachievement Syndrome. The source and degree of competition certainly feed into the syndrome, but children's appraisal of and response to that competition is much more important.

Social Changes

Social changes in our country have impacted dramatically on the psychological elements which cause Underachievement Syndrome. Although this book is not intended as a treatise on social or ethical directions in the United States, some important observations must be noted. While some may disagree with what this author suggests are significant societal directions, most conclusions presented here are sufficiently obvious that most readers are likely to concur. This listing is not intended to be all inclusive, but includes only a few of the main social changes that impact on Underachievement Syndrome.

Family. The structure and fabric of American family life has changed so dramatically that it leaves most persons over age 35 rather stunned: mother's with full-time careers, day-care centers, babysitters and relatives who take over child rearing, lack of clarity of roles for each parent, extramarital relationships, increasing divorce, living together without marriage arrangements, and disorienting visitation privileges and custody disputes. Young parents who look back to their own families and wish to use that model as a framework for guiding their children are likely to find themselves without a model or framework. The nostalgic image of a nuclear intact family with one set of loyal parents who are primarily responsible for child rearing still exists, but the actual number of children brought up in such secure structured environments is diminishing continuously.

Education. The size of schools and the tasks of educators expand regularly. Beyond the basics, and the familiar "beans, busses and basketball" are "breakfast, babysitting and bargaining." Educators who used to feel that too much school personnel time was devoted to discussing hot lunch programs, transportation and sports programs are now being asked to provide morning meals and after school care for children of working mothers. Union negotiations have also been added to teacher and administrator responsibilities. However, these six "b's" represent only a fraction of additional roles tagged on to teaching. The responsibilities of administrators and teachers have multiplied exponentially, and the first part of the old saw *"overworked* and underpaid" is sufficiently true to make many educators of long standing wonder about their own effectiveness as stimulators of children's learning and thinking. Certainly, there are many teachers who continue enthusiastically to excite children toward learning, but the fragmentation of their instruction into so many tasks and so many children detracts from their holistic pedagogic zeal.

Moral Standards. Some of you will lament the disintegrating standards; others may say that nothing has changed; and still a last group may agree that there has been change but prefer these more liberal standards of conduct. This book's task is not to provide commentary on changing moral standards but only to note that an environment which supports extensive alcohol consumption, drug abuse and permissive sexual behavior provides considerable temptation for adolescents. The ready availability of such distractions from the educational scene increases the difficulty of exciting adolescents toward learning.

Competitive Pressure. An increasing population, career demands for more extensive education, fragmentation in job responsibilities, complexity of business and government, and diminishing moral directives are only a few of the social changes which dramatically add to the competitive pressure in our society. Children don't escape from a secondary impact of adult competitive pressure because as parents struggle in their "dog eat dog" world they model to their children survival techniques as well as escape routes. Their children may copy any of those that they see or hear. The increased competition causes a communication of tension from parents to offspring, without parents ever purposefully putting pressure on their children. Adults, reflecting on their own career pressures, feel a legitimate concern for their nonachieving bright children. How will they make it if they can't even "win" in the small arena of school? In desperation at their children's poor competitive functioning they overreact to their victories and defeats, communicating a pressure far different from the problem solving approach the children should be learning.

Mass Media. Television and video films display in our living rooms the life-styles and financial rewards of the most successful. Commercials develop an unquenchable thirst for material possessions. Sports and music heroes are more reputed for the fantastic salaries they command than for their hard work or talent. Furthermore, the stories of their successes sound like magical fairy tales with little struggle and much luck. Hero's value systems appear free of ethical structure — alcohol, drugs, sex, violence and other illegal activities are associated with fame and success. The traditional "rags to riches" image which modeled for American children the path by which hard working, intelligent and creative people climb the ladder from poverty to wealth has been replaced by the media's magical system, with which any child would like to identify. Brilliant talent is miraculously discovered and a powerful fairy godmother transforms a poor unrecognized teenager to instant stardom.

Interaction Between The Elements And The Changes

Figure 12.1 illustrates the ramifications of social changes for the key elements that cause Underachievement Syndrome. Each of the social changes described have separate impact on each one of the key elements which cause the syndrome, and together the force is so great that it is unreasonable to expect schools alone to halt the epidemic. There is no immediate method of funneling taxpayer's money for a school cure, no specific message to give to your congress person, and no one particular bill or law that will lead to prevention or healing. The problem is too complex to remedy in so simplistic a fashion.

The social changes which have dramatic impact on underachieving children can be modified in your own homes and schools. Although each individual may feel helpless in terms of making major changes in our culture, the interpretation of social norms to your own children can be shaped and their effect tempered. For example, individual parents can do much to maintain a reasonably secure family structure. With reference to education, we can lend support to our school and help decrease the unreasonable demands which communities place on educators. We can teach our own children reasonable moral and ethical principles and can model these. We can show our children how to cope with competition and we can demonstrate valid temporary escapes. Finally we can limit their exposure to damaging mass media and interpret the rags to riches story without glorifying the magically produced heroes. By mitigating the impact of these social changes on our children's lives, we can counteract some of the negative effects and thus lessen the risk of our children falling victim to the underachievement disease.

Figure 12.1

RAMIFICATIONS OF SOCIAL CHANGE ON
UNDERACHIEVEMENT SYNDROME

Social Changes

Family
- Multiple Caretakers
- Dual Career Families
- Increasing Divorce
- Less Structured Adult Relationships

Education
- Increasing School Size
- Expansion of School's Tasks
- Fragmentation of Instruction

Moral Standards
- Alcohol and Drug Abuse
- Permissive Sex Behaviors

Competitive Pressures
- Increasing Population
- Extensive Educational Requirements
- Complexity of Business and Government
- Overreactions of Parents

Media
- Display of Opulence and Wealth
- Creation of Unquenchable Thirst for Material Possessions
- Hero Worship of Sports and Television Stars
- Magical Success Orientation

Essential Elements of
Underachievement
Syndrome

Initiating Situation

Excessive Child Power

Inconsistency and Opposition

Inappropriate Classroom Environments

Competition

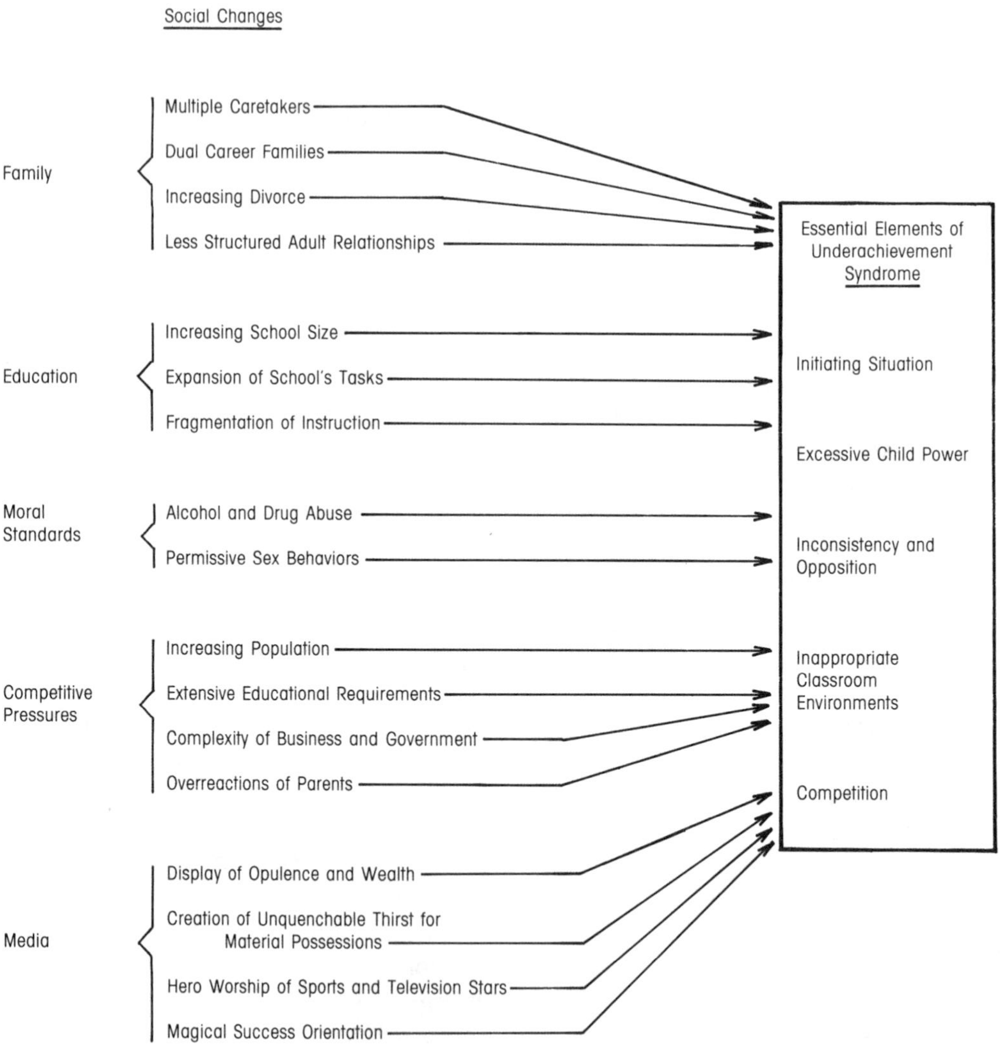

Recognition of the essential elements which cause Underachievement Syndrome will assist in preventing the problem in your own families and classrooms. You may or may not be able to prevent the initiating situation, but awareness will assist you in diminishing the deleterious effect on your children. You can have greatest impact by modifying the power, inconsistency and opposition variables in your family. If you are a teacher you can be instrumental in improving the school environment for many underachievers, although there may be many classroom issues beyond your control. As parents and teachers, instructing in and modeling functional competition can make a major contribution in your family and your classroom.

The potential for prevention of underachievement is not entirely within your control, but understanding the causes of the syndrome can assist you in your parenting and teaching ventures.

The Cures

A cure for Underachievement Syndrome *is* possible for your children in your homes and for students in your classrooms. It is not easy, nor is it likely that you can cure all youth who underachieve. Although most of this book has been directed at sharing methods that have been implemented effectively by parents and teachers through our Family Achievement Clinic, there are countless other alternatives for you to select or invent to use with your own children. The book has provided a trifocal model for you to follow. Within that framework there is space for your own innovation and adaptation.

Rimm's Laws of Achievement

Between the extremes of Murphy and Newton is a vast range of 'Laws' somewhere in which Rimm should be placed. Rimm's Laws have been written to summarize the main clinical, family and classroom observations presented in this book. As you create your own innovative approaches to helping children toward achievement, Rimm's Laws of Achievement will assist you in predicting the likelihood of their effectiveness.

RIMM'S LAW #1. *Children are more likely to be achievers if their parents join together to give the same* *clear and positive message about school effort and expectations.*

Meeting the expectations of parents is a high priority for most children, provided that the parents' goals are clear, consistent and within reach by reasonable effort. When one parent expects more of children than the other parent, or the second parent feels compelled to shelter children from the first, underachievement will surely follow. Compromise by all parents involved and a clear *single* message of reasonable goals must underlie all parent and teacher initiatives for dealing with underachieving children.

RIMM'S LAW #2. *Children can learn appropriate behaviors more easily if they have an effective model to imitate.*

Parents are the most available models. They should become aware of both the potential effectiveness and the problems of modeling attitudes and behaviors that children can copy. A parent also should describe his/her spouse to children in a manner which will encourage their identification. Nurturance, power and similarities are the three qualities which foster identification. If parents are not available or not appropriate as models, then school, community or other family relationships can be used to inspire children toward appropriate imitation. For males it is especially important to find a same sexed model; for females a same sexed model is not as critical, but does help the necessary alliance take place more easily.

RIMM'S LAW #3. *Communication about a child between adults (referential speaking) dramatically affects children's behaviors and self-perceptions.*

Parents and teachers should be sensitive to what they say to other adult's within their children's hearing. Talking about positive accomplishment will encourage children to take pride in their achievements, but expressing frustration with children's inadequate behaviors may damage their self-confidence. Discussing one's inability to control children's behavior will foster disrespect and belligerence. Referential speaking between adults sets a self-fulfilling expectation for children.

RIMM'S LAW #4. *Overreactions by parents to children's successes and failures leads them to feel either intense pressure to succeed or despair and discouragement in dealing with failure.*

A moderate problem solving approach to failure experiences helps children to deal with losing and see failure as a normal component of learning. It will help them learn to accept criticism and to patiently persevere. Pleasure, but not ecstacy, is an appropriate response to their success. Not only does the latter not seem genuine, but it encumbers them with the pressure to perform that way continuously. That may not be possible, initially. As they become more confident in their successes, you may increase your level of delight without fearing that they will be overwhelmed by pressure.

RIMM'S LAW #5. *Children feel more tension when they are worrying about their work than when they are doing that work.*

Children who exhibit tension symptoms usually do not need to have their workload reduced or simplified. For the most part they only need your assurance that they can accomplish their lessons and a clearly structured plan for producing their completed assignments. The ordering of their tasks and reinforcement will help them to successfully complete their tasks. Their tension will diminish as they build confidence in their work accomplishment.

RIMM'S LAW #6. *Children develop self-confidence through struggle.*

It is difficult for parents and teachers to calmly witness children's suffering. However, the children cannot develop self-confidence without struggle. To deny them the opportunity to push their own limits is to deny them the esteem and growth which comes from perseverance. Obviously, children who make sincere efforts without ever attaining success will not be encouraged to achieve. However, when persistence results in reasonably frequent successes children build the confidence and the character to cope with challenge and occasional disappointment.

RIMM'S LAW #7. *Deprivation and excess frequently exhibit the same symptoms.*

Our Freudian heritage has taught us familiar ways to evaluate children's psychological symptoms. However, these may be misleading. For example, we assume that attention-seeking children have not received enough affection, that angry youth have not been given enough freedom by their parents, and that children who exhibit tension have been pressured too much by adults. All of these may be true, but children exhibit identical symptoms if they are accustomed to recieving too much affection, if they have had too much power over their parents, or if adults have done so much for them they have not learned to cope with any pressure. Too much and too little are equally problematic, but it is essential to determine which is the culprit before prescribing appropriate treatment.

RIMM'S LAW #8. *Children develop confidence and an internal sense of control if power is given to them in gradually increasing increments as they show maturity and responsibility.*

If children are not given enough independence they do not develop a good self-concept. However, if power is given too early and then must be reduced as they reach adolescence, they feel controlled and angry, even though their limits are no different than those of their peers. Adults can better identify with this experience if they imagine how they would feel if their freedom to make choices were restricted by some outside force. The angry feelings of these adolescents are genuine, but they are not caused so much by too much structure as by a lack of earlier reasonable limitations.

RIMM'S LAW #9. *Children become oppositional if one adult allies with them against a parent or a teacher, making them more powerful than an adult.*

The feeling of power which they receive from dominating other powerful persons makes children feel both excitedly in control and frighteningly insecure. It creates an inertia within them to continue to maintain dominance over others as a measure of their self-confidence. When that feeling of control over others disappears they return to their frightening sense of inadequacy. The opposition which provides power without wisdom thrusts them into mood swings which vary with their control; they are very difficult to cope with through adolescence and adulthood. Appropriate independence and an internal locus of control can be fostered without oppositional alliances — but these alliances are reinforcing to adults as well as children, so beware. Children will not go through a rebellious and angry adolescence if parents follow Rimm's Laws 8 and 9.

RIMM'S LAW #10. *Adults should avoid confrontations with children unless they are sure they can control the outcomes.*

Confrontation without true control only results in further active or passive opposition. For many children, it will be less effective to command or demand than to persuade, inspire, model, share efforts, cooperate, encourage and create a positive alliance. Make a realistic appraisal of what will be effective with a child before plunging ahead with what instinctively feels right to you.

RIMM'S LAW #11. *Children will become achievers only if they learn to function in competition.*

Winning is not possible continuously. Children must learn to function appropriately when they "fail" or "lose." They should have balanced experiences of failures and successes and learn to use failure constructively to build success. Home, school and society are all competitive. It is not possible to withdraw and continue to feel confident. Parents and teachers can gradually teach children to learn to function competitively.

RIMM'S LAW #12. *Children will continue to achieve if they usually see the relationship between the learning process and its outcomes.*

Children acquire an internal sense of control by investing of themselves in an enterprise and finding they have performed well. This same sense of efficacy is reinforced by finding that lack of effort leads to a less successful outcome. Children usually are aware that there are differences in abilities, in teachers' perceptions and in levels of difficulty of assignments and tests that also can affect scholastic outcomes. However, when children make little effort and highly successful outcomes follow, or when they make a serious commitment to study with no success, or when the relationship between their work and their grades seems random, they lose that sense of internal locus of control. They begin to attribute their grades to luck or lack thereof. They blame teachers for their failures or they claim they are really not very smart. Frequently they may say they should study harder, but they rarely follow through because they don't truly believe studying will have an impact on their grades.

To establish an internal locus of control, a clear time and study structure combined with feedback that explains the performance grades, as well as the basis for earning them, are important. Although children are resilient enough to adjust to reasonable differences in criteria and teachers, they cannot establish that inner sense of control with unclear or random grades or academic material that is too easy or too difficult.

Cure For An Epidemic?

This is no wonder cure book. It will not cause Underachievement Syndrome to disappear from society. However, the book is not mere theory. It is based on real life experiences in homes and classrooms. Parents and teachers who take time to understand their underachievers, follow the steps of the trifocal model patiently, and apply the Rimm Achievement Laws to their own children will make an impact on their school performance. Symptoms of the syndrome will decrease and achievement motivation will improve in the same way that it is evidenced daily in the underachieving children who come to our clinic.

REFERENCES

Allen, M.S. *Morphological Creativity.* Englewood Cliffs, N.J.: Prentice-Hall, Inc., 1962.

Bloom, B.S. The limits of learning. Presented at the CEC-TAG National Topical Conference on the Gifted and Talented Child, Orlando, FL., December 1981.

Bloom, B.S. & Sosniak, L.A. Talent development vs. schooling. *Educational Leadership,* 1981, 39, 86-94.

Bossard, J.H.S. & Ball, E.S. Personality roles in the family. *Child Development,* 26; 71-78, 1955.

Covington, M.V., & Beery, R.G. *Self-worth and School Learning.* New York: Holt, 1976.

Crawford, R.P. The techniques of creative thinking. In G.A. Davis & J.A. Scott (eds.), *Training Creative Thinking.* Huntington, N.Y.: Krieger, 1978.

Davis, G.A. *Creativity if Forever.* Dubuque, Iowa: Kendall/Hunt, 1986.

Davis, G.A. & Rimm, S.B. GIFFI II: Group Inventory For Finding Interests. Watertown, WI.: Educational Assessment Service, Inc., 1979.

Davis, G.A. & Rimm, S.B. *Education of the Gifted & Talented.* Englewood Cliffs, N.J.: Prentice-Hall, Inc., 1985.

Guinness Book of World Records. Editor and Compiler: Norris McWhirter, New York, N.Y.: Sterling Publishing Company, Inc., 1985.

Harnick, S. *Free To Be You and Me.* Ms. Foundation, Inc., 1972.

Hetherington, E.M., & Frankie, G. Effects of parental dominance, warmth, and conflict on imitation in children. *Journal of Personality and Social Psychology,* 1967, 6, 119-125.

Meehan, T. Annie (from the book) *Little Orphan Annie.* The Chicago Tribune-New York News Syndicate, Inc., 1977.

Mussen, P.H., & Rutherford, E. Parent-child relations and parental personality in relation to young children's sex-role preferences. *Child Development,* 1963, 34, 589-607.

Osborn, A.F. *Applied Imagination* (3rd ed.). New York: Scribner's, 1963.

Rimm, S.B. GIFT: Group Inventory for Finding Creative Talent. Watertown, WI.: Educational Assessment Service, Inc., 1976, 1980.

Rimm, S.B. If God Had Meant Children to Run Our Homes, She Would Have Created Them Bigger. Reprint from *G/C/T,* Jan/Feb 1984, 26-29.

Rimm, S.B. Characteristics Approach: Identification and Beyond. *Gifted Child Quarterly,* Fall 1984, Vol. 28, No. 4, 181-187.

Rimm, S.B. AIM: Achievement Identification Measure. Watertown, WI.: Educational Assessment Service, Inc., 1985.

Rimm, S.B. GAIM: Group Achievement Identification Measure. Watertown, WI.: Educational Assessment Service, Inc., 1986.

Rimm, S.B. & Davis, G.A. GIFFI I: Group Inventory For Finding Interests. Watertown, WI.: Educational Assessment Service, Inc., 1979.

Rosenthal, R.J., & Jacobson, L. *Pygmalion in the Classroom.* New York: Holt, 1968.

Sheehy, G. *Pathfinders.* New York: Bantam Books, 1982.

Wechsler, D. Wechsler Scales of Intelligence (WISC-R). New York: Psychological Corporation, 1949, 1974.

SUBJECT INDEX

Complete this order form to order additional publications from:

APPLE PUBLISHING COMPANY*
W6050 Apple Road, Watertown, WI 53094
(800)475-1118   (414)261-1118   FAX (414)261-6622

_____	Underachievement Syndrome: Causes and Cures	$15.00
_____	Guidebook - Underachievement Syndrome: Causes and Cures	35.00
_____	How To Parent So Children Will Learn	15.00
_____	Gifted Kids Have Feelings Too	15.00
_____	Exploring Feelings (Discussion book for Gifted Kids Have Feelings Too)	15.00
_____	Group Inventory For Finding Creative Talent (GIFT) Specimen Set	12.00
_____	Group Inventory For Finding Interests (GIFFI) Specimen Set	12.00
_____	Preschool and Kindergarten Interest Descriptor (PRIDE) Specimen Set	12.00
_____	Achievement Identification Measure (AIM) Specimen Set	12.00
_____	Group Achievement Identification Measure (GAIM) Specimen Set	12.00
_____	Achievement Identification Measure - Teacher Observation (AIM-TO) Specimen Set	12.00

Total Amount _____

Name _____

Address _____

_____

Telephone Number _____

*A subsidiary of Educational Assessment Service, Inc. Send for free catalog.